REFORMED
SOCIAL
ETHICS

REFORMED SOCIAL ETHICS

PERSPECTIVES ON SOCIETY, CULTURE, STATE, CHURCH, AND THE KINGDOM OF GOD

HERMAN BAVINCK
EDITED BY JOHN BOLT

Baker Academic
a division of Baker Publishing Group
Grand Rapids, Michigan

© 2025 by John Bolt

Published by Baker Academic
a division of Baker Publishing Group
Grand Rapids, Michigan
BakerAcademic.com

Printed in the United States of America

Library of Congress Cataloging-in-Publication Data
Names: Bavinck, Herman, 1854–1921, author. | Bolt, John, 1947– editor.
Title: Reformed social ethics : perspectives on society, culture, state, church, and the kingdom of
    God / Herman Bavinck ; edited by John Bolt.
Description: Grand Rapids, Michigan : Baker Academic, a division of Baker Publishing Group,
    [2025] | Series: Reformed ethics | Includes bibliographical references and index.
Identifiers: LCCN 2024024333 | ISBN 9781540968128 (cloth) | ISBN 9781493449286 (ebook) | ISBN
    9781493449293 (pdf)
Subjects: LCSH: Christian sociology—Reformed Church. | Social ethics.
Classification: LCC BT738 .B3225 2025 | DDC 241/.0442—dc23/eng/20240628
LC record available at https://lccn.loc.gov/2024024333

Unless otherwise indicated, Scripture quotations are from The Holy Bible, English Standard Version® (ESV®), copyright © 2001 by Crossway, a publishing ministry of Good News Publishers. Used by permission. All rights reserved. ESV Text Edition: 2016

Scripture quotations labeled KJV are from the King James Version of the Bible.

Baker Publishing Group publications use paper produced from sustainable forestry practices and postconsumer waste whenever possible.

25   26   27   28   29   30   31   7   6   5   4   3   2   1

Contents

Preface

As my fellow editors and I indicated in the third volume of the *Reformed Ethics*,[1] the fourth section of Bavinck's manuscript, "The Life Spheres in Which the Moral Life Must Manifest Itself," remained unfinished, containing only Bavinck's lecture notes on marriage and family. Bavinck left an outline for five more chapters—on society; art, scholarship, and education; the state; the church; and humanity and the kingdom of God—but provided no material content. Our editorial team discussed providing content for each topic by incorporating excerpts from Bavinck's extensive bibliography of articles and books that fit the broad categories just indicated. Originally, this was to have been part of *Reformed Ethics*, volume 3. However, because the material would require far more editorial framing than we had done for the rest of the manuscript, we became uncomfortable in presenting these chapters as Bavinck's own work, similar to our treatment of Bavinck's own manuscript.[2] Consequently, in consultation with the publisher, we concluded that these five chapters needed to stand alone as a separate book with a clear indication of their distinct identity. This needs further explanation.

It is tempting to call this book Bavinck's *Reformed Ethics*, volume 4, and in a certain and very restricted sense that would be true. After all, its five chapters are the topics Bavinck himself indicated for the completion of his social ethics, part IV. In addition, Bavinck's own texts provide the main content of this volume; the fifth chapter is wholly Bavinck's, and the other chapters are primarily his own words and his own ideas. Nonetheless, this is *not* Bavinck's

1. See *RE*, 3, preface.
2. As indicated in the preface to vol. 1, in order to create a readable and easily usable text, we included in the published English translation considerable narrative connective tissue; see *RE*, 1:xiii.

Reformed Ethics, volume 4, and marketing it as such would have been false advertising. Not only was I, as editor, responsible for selecting the texts used in each chapter, but the narrative frame holding disparate material together is entirely mine. In other words, this volume, except for chapter 5, is my *constructed presentation* of four topics that Bavinck had chosen but never completed for his section on social ethics.[3]

That construction is most evident in chapter 1, "Society," which, ironically, is the only chapter for which Bavinck provided a detailed outline. As I indicate in the introduction to that chapter, I adjusted Bavinck's order of topics, amplified some, omitted others, and created three subsections that combined related topics. And in the third subsection, "Hospitality, Friendship, Sociability"—taking my cues from Bavinck's own notes pointing to a reliance on Hans Martensen's *Christian Ethics: Special Part*—I took large sections from Martensen and created a narrative in Bavinck's own style to cover the topics. I am confident that this section reflects Bavinck's authentic voice, but readers do need to be aware that I am acting here as a ventriloquist, speaking from my own perch, with Bavinck—I hardly dare say this!—as my dummy.[4] In addition, the entire chapter was introduced by a topic not on Bavinck's original list, the doctrine of creation, which I combined with the topic of vocation, Bavinck's second topic. The resultant opening subsection, "Creation, and Humanity's Twofold Vocation," I judged to be a necessary orientation to Bavinck's reflections on society because, among other reasons, it provides a hermeneutical key to Bavinck's reading of the New Testament and his understanding of Christian discipleship in society. Consequently, the doctrine of creation, particularly human creation, as Bavinck treats this in his *Reformed Dogmatics*, volume 2, serves as the introduction to Bavinck's view of Christian life in society.[5] My point in highlighting this here is simply that while the *content* here is definitely Bavinck's, the *presentation* of the content is mine.

Thus, to do this volume justice, one should read it as a work of *expository interpretation*. Each chapter is a heavily evidence-based *argument* for Bavinck's view of Christian discipleship in society, art and scholarship, education, the state, and the church, respectively. To make this clear, readers should note that in the chapters of this book, my editorial framing and Bavinck's

3. To be clear, the construction only uses building materials taken from Bavinck's own lumberyard.
4. With the complication (that spoils the metaphor) that the ventriloquist is putting some of the dummy's own words into his speaking.
5. A parallel section on creation, seen now as a work of divine art, also orients the material in chap. 2.

material are set in different typefaces. The only exception is that shorter quotations from Bavinck occasionally appear in the editorial framing material and footnotes and are set off with quotation marks.

There are three kinds of footnotes in this volume. All unmarked footnotes are those of the editor, produced specifically for this volume; Bavinck's original notes will be clearly marked "Bav. note"; in the case of excerpted material already published in English, Bavinck's own notes will also be marked "Bav. note," while editor's notes in such works will also be marked as "ed. note," as they were in the published works. All new translations of previously unpublished material are mine.

I also want to point out that the material in this volume is essential for anyone who desires a somewhat systematic summary view of Bavinck's social ethics. The Bavinck bibliography[6] contains hundreds of articles and books on the topics of society, education, state, and church. These are all ad hoc and targeted at specific problems or issues such as war and peace, new pedagogies, educational law, the secular state, and inequality and equality; or they consider specific figures such as Jean-Jacques Rousseau. This volume provides, for the first time in either Dutch or English, summary statements of Bavinck's main convictions and perspectives on these subjects in one convenient place. More can, and undoubtedly will, be said by Bavinck scholars on each topic, but this is the place from which they will need to begin. Further research into Bavinck's social ethics will also have to take his historical and sociopolitical *context* seriously; chapter 1 of this volume points the direction but itself makes only the smallest beginning.

I present this volume to the world as my adieu to thirty years of translating and editing Herman Bavinck. It has been a very rewarding journey and one in which I am deeply indebted to many people. First on the list are the men who established the Dutch Reformed Translation Society in 1994 to fund the translating and editing of Bavinck's *Reformed Dogmatics* into English. Baker Academic has been a wonderful partner, its leadership unfailingly supportive, its editorial staff doing consistently excellent work, and its production first-class. Editing the three volumes of Bavinck's *Reformed Ethics* was a team effort. My fellow editors—Jessica Joustra, Nelson Kloosterman, Antoine Theron, and Dirk van Keulen—combined their varied skills and knowledge, their unfailing grace, and their diligence and work ethic, through seven summer sessions of intensive labor, to produce quality manuscripts for publication. For this collaboration and their friendship I am profoundly grateful. On the

---

6. Available online (in English) from the Neo-Calvinism Research Institute, https://sources.neocalvinism.org/bavinck/.

basis of our experience we hold up this collaborative effort as a model for any translating and editing project involving the kind of archival manuscript that was entrusted to us. Many students have served as faculty assistants over the years that I was busy with Bavinck during my time as a professor at Calvin Theological Seminary, and I have indicated my gratitude elsewhere. Calvin's administration and Board of Trustees supported my work with sabbaticals, workload adjustments, and several grants from the seminary's Heritage Fund that made our summer editorial team sessions possible. Other individuals provided financial support and have been recognized elsewhere. This is my final "thank you" to all.

Serving as a midwife to the birth of Bavinck's major works into the English language has been for me an undeserved privilege and honor. God is good and all this is *ad maiorem dei gloriam*.

John Bolt

Acknowledgments

Thanks to the following parties:

To the editors of *Journal of Markets and Morality* for permission to use material from the following:

Herman Bavinck, "General Biblical Principles and the Relevance of Concrete Mosaic Law for the Social Question Today (1891)," *Journal of Markets and Morality* 13, no. 2 (Fall 2010): 437–45.

John Bolt, "Herman Bavinck's Contribution to Christian Social Consciousness," *Journal of Markets and Morality* 13, no. 2 (Fall 2010): 412–36.

To the editors of *The Banner of Truth* for permission to use quotations from Herman Bavinck, "The Problem of War," trans. Stephen Voorwinde, *The Banner of Truth*, July–August 1977, 46–53.

To Crossway, a publishing ministry of Good News Publishers, for permission to use material from Herman Bavinck, *Christian Worldview*, trans. and ed. Nathaniel Gray Sutanto, James Eglinton, and Cory C. Brock (Wheaton: Crossway, 2019). www.crossway.org

Abbreviations

ANF	*The Ante-Nicene Fathers*. Edited by Alexander Roberts and James Donaldson. 10 vols. New York: Christian Literature Co., 1885–96. Reprint, Grand Rapids: Eerdmans, 1950–51.
ca.	*circa*, about
CTJ	*Calvin Theological Journal*
d.	died
Denzinger	Denzinger, Henry. *The Sources of Catholic Dogma*. Translated by Roy J. Deferrari. Fitzwilliam, NH: Loreto, 2002.
DO	Dutch original
ed. note	editor's note
ERSS	Bavinck, Herman. *Essays on Religion, Science, and Society*. Edited by John Bolt. Translated by Harry Boonstra and Gerrit Sheeres. Grand Rapids: Baker Academic, 2008.
ESV	English Standard Version
ET	English translation
FC	Fathers of the Church
ff.	and following
FO	French original
Gk.	Greek
GO	German original
GrO	Greek original
HO	Hebrew original
Imitatio Christi	Bolt, John. *A Theological Analysis of Herman Bavinck's Two Essays on the* Imitatio Christi. Lewiston, NY: Mellen, 2013.
"Imitation I"	Bavinck, Herman. "The Imitation of Christ" (1885/1886); appendix A in *Imitatio Christi*.
"Imitation II"	Bavinck, Herman. "The Imitation of Christ and Life in the Modern World" (1918); appendix B in *Imitatio Christi*.
Institutes	John Calvin, *Institutes of the Christian Religion*
KJV	King James Version

LCL	Loeb Classical Library
lit.	literally
LO	Latin original
LXX	Septuagint
NIV	New International Version
no(s).	number(s)
NPNF¹	*A Select Library of Nicene and Post-Nicene Fathers of the Christian Church.* Edited by Philip Schaff. 1st series. 14 vols. New York: Christian Literature Co., 1887–1900. Reprint, Grand Rapids: Eerdmans, 1956.
NPNF²	*A Select Library of Nicene and Post-Nicene Fathers of the Christian Church.* Edited by Philip Schaff and Henry Wace. 2nd series. 14 vols. New York: Christian Literature Co., 1890–1900. Reprint, Grand Rapids: Eerdmans, 1952.
NRSV	New Revised Standard Version
p(p).	page(s)
par.	parallel
para(s).	paragraph(s)
PRE¹	*Realencyklopädie für protestantische Theologie und Kirche.* Edited by J. J. Herzog. 1st ed. 22 vols. Hamburg: R. Besser, 1854–68.
PRE²	*Realencyklopädie für protestantische Theologie und Kirche.* Edited by J. J. Herzog and G. L. Plitt. 2nd rev. ed. 18 vols. Leipzig: J. C. Hinrichs, 1877–88.
Q&A	question and answer
RD	Bavinck, Herman. *Reformed Dogmatics.* Edited by John Bolt. Translated by John Vriend. 4 vols. Grand Rapids: Baker Academic, 2003–8.
RE	Bavinck, Herman. *Reformed Ethics.* Edited by John Bolt with Jessica Joustra, Nelson D. Kloosterman, Antoine Theron, and Dirk van Keulen. 3 vols. Grand Rapids: Baker Academic, 2019–25.
ST	Thomas Aquinas, *Summa theologiae*
TBR	*The Bavinck Review*

1

Society

Although Bavinck added an outline indicating five more chapters after §58 in the full manuscript of his *Reformed Ethics*, this first chapter on society[1] is the only one in which Bavinck provided an additional outline of twelve topics to be included:[2]

Ownership, Possessions

Vocation

Interest, Usury

Money

Trade

Industry

The Social Question

Hospitality[3]

Friendship

Sociability[4]

1. DO: *maatschappij*.
2. DO: *eigendom, bezit*; *beroep*; *rente, woeker*; *geld*; *handel*; *sociale kwestie*; *nijverheid*; *gastvrijheid*; *vriendschap*; *gezelligheid*; *spel*; *ergernis*. Note: This list, like all the longer sections of material original to Bavinck, is presented in a different font. Smaller quotations from Bavinck in the editor's framing text are set off with quotation marks.
3. Bav. note: Rudolph von Jhering, *Der Zweck im Recht*, 2:329–51. Ed. note: This is a section on "social manners" (*Umgangsformen*).
4. The Dutch term *gezellig* is notoriously difficult to capture in a single English term, but here are a few favorites: enjoyable, pleasant, cozy, entertaining, sociable, companionable,

Games

Offense[5]

In this chapter, in consultation with the colleagues who partnered with me to edit the *Reformed Ethics*, I have adjusted Bavinck's order somewhat and combined some of his topics into single sections. When Bavinck writes about our human vocation before God, he always places our twofold calling in the context of humans created in God's image. I am, therefore, bringing Bavinck's second topic up front under the subheading "Creation, and Humanity's Two-fold Vocation" as the introduction to Bavinck's understanding of society. The topic of creation was not in Bavinck's original list, but, paired with the theme of vocation, it is a necessary orientation to Bavinck's reflections on society because, among other reasons, it provides the hermeneutical key to Bavinck's reading of the New Testament passages relevant to social questions.[6]

The topics of ownership and possessions, interest and usury, money, trade, and industry will be considered together under "Economic Life" and will be limited to considerations directly related to ownership and possessions, including private property. We lack adequate material to do justice to the remaining topics. I am retaining "The Social Question" as a distinct unit but reversing Bavinck's order, placing it before "Economic Life." This order helps us to understand the historical context of Bavinck's concerns and treatment of topics.

Similarly, the topics hospitality, friendship, and sociability will be considered together for reasons given above.[7] Bavinck's final two topics, games and offense, will also be treated in this section.[8] I am also adding two appendixes

---

convivial. Bav. note: [Regarding] sociability [*gezelligheid*] for society [*maatschappij*], see Adolf Wuttke, *Handbuch der christlichen Sittenlehre*, 3rd ed., 2:437–57 (§§287–91); for family, see H. Martensen, *Christian Ethics, Special Part*, 2/2:71–82 (§§36–38). Ed. note: The reference to Wuttke is to the second section, "The Christian Society" (*Die christliche Gesellschaft*), of a larger part, "The Christian Community" (*Die christliche Gemeinschaft*, pp. 397–538 [§§276–314]). Wuttke divides "The Christian Community" into four parts: "The Family" (§§276–86), "The Christian Society" (§§287–91), "The Christian State" (§§292–300), and "The Church" (§§301–14). Wuttke's final section is "The Kingdom of God and the History of the World" (§315). The parallel structure with Bavinck's own division of chapters in book IV of his *Reformed Ethics* is striking. Bavinck's reference to Martensen is to a section, "Hospitality— Friendship—Sociability" (*Gastfreiheit. Freundschaft. Gesellligkeit*), itself part of Martensen's discussion of the family. Bavinck's listing of these three topics, in the exact order Martensen discusses them, indicates his likely use of them in his lectures.

5. Jhering, *Der Zweck im Recht*, 2:392–93; Kuyper, "Indien het mijn broeder ergert."

6. In particular, whether or not—and if so, how—the redemption in Christ changes or eliminates important creational social institutions and structures.

7. See n. 4, above.

8. I am including these two topics under the category of sociability because that is where Martensen also treats them.

to this chapter: The first is a translation of a popular newspaper column published in 1902, "Masters and Servants."[9] This piece deserves to stand alone because it is a direct response to the hermeneutical challenge of interpreting the "master and servant/slave" passages in the New Testament epistles. The second is a brief statement by Bavinck on abortion, "The Right to Life of the Unborn." Bavinck delivered these remarks to a society of Christian natural scientists and medical practitioners on May 12, 1903, and they were published in the society's journal.[10] His words remain instructive and timely.

This leads to the following chapter outline:

Introduction: Creation, and Humanity's Twofold Vocation
1. The Social Question
2. Economic Life: Ownership, Property, Possessions
3. Hospitality, Friendship, Sociability
Appendix A: "Masters and Servants"
Appendix B: "The Right to Life of the Unborn"

I have thus reduced Bavinck's twelve topics to three major sections plus an enhanced introduction. Each section will be preceded by a brief editorial introduction, indicating, among other things, the reasons for my selection of material used. Details about the specific sources used for each of the sections will be provided in the footnotes.

FOR FURTHER READING[a]

All titles are by Herman Bavinck; original publication date in square brackets follows each item.

Articles/Essays

"Calvin and Common Grace." In *Calvin and the Reformation: Four Studies*, 99–130 [1909].
"Christian Principles and Social Relationships." In *ERSS*, 119–44 [1908].
"General Biblical Principles and the Relevance of Concrete Mosaic Law for the Social Question Today (1891)." *Journal of Markets and Morality* 13, no. 2 (Fall 2010): 437–45 [1891].

---

9. Bavinck, "Heeren en knechten."
10. Bavinck, "Het levensrecht der ongeboren vrucht."

"The Imitation of Christ and Life in the Modern World" [1918; referred to in this volume as "Imitation II"; in *Imitatio Christi*, 402–40].

"On Inequality." In *ERSS*, 145–63 [1913].

Books

The Christian Family [1908].

a. Chapters 1–4 are headed by a section of suggestions for further reading. These include references to full essays or articles excerpted in the chapter as well as additional material. Some bibliographic items are slightly abbreviated; see volume bibliography for full information.

INTRODUCTION: CREATION, AND HUMANITY'S TWOFOLD VOCATION

The biblical doctrine of creation is the starting point for Bavinck's understanding of society. Human beings, created in God's image and likeness, have a dual vocation: first, "a calling rightly to know their Creator, love him with all their heart and live with him in eternity";[11] and, second, an earthly vocation. The following paragraph clearly indicates how crucial the doctrine of creation was for Bavinck's view of society:

Because humans were image bearers of God, created with true knowledge, righteousness, and holiness, and inclined in heart and equipped to bring God's plan to fruition, they were given every necessary gift and power to fulfill this double calling. By creating humanity as male and female God equipped them to fill the earth and subdue it. This duality of sex, this institution of marriage, contains in nuce all subsequent social relationships: husband and wife, parents and children, brothers and sisters, servants and freemen, civil rulers and subjects. It is here also that we see, in principle, all the inequalities that would eventually come to pass among people: differences in body and soul, in character and temperament, in gifts of understanding and will, in heart and hand, and so forth. Inequality is a given of creation, grounded in the very will of God himself, and not first of all a consequence of sin. (*GBP*, 438; see proposition B1/C2, below)[12]

---

11. Bavinck, "General Biblical Principles and the Relevance of Concrete Mosaic Law for the Social Question Today (1891)," 437. For economy's sake, future references to this work will be indicated parenthetically within the text as *GBP*, followed by the page number. Bavinck prepared this address specifically for the First Christian Social Congress, held in Amsterdam on November 9–11, 1891.

12. Later in this chapter (in "1. The Social Question"), I will provide the resolutions of the First Christian Social Congress; see pp. 11–32.

What is true for creation is also true for re-creation (salvation). Jesus did not come—in the first place—to fix the social order (part of the second human task) but to save sinners from God's judgment and to make it possible for them to fulfill their first calling: "rightly to know their Creator, love him with all their heart and live with him in eternity."

The New Testament's primary concern is

restoring our proper relationship with God. The cross of Christ, therefore, is the heart and mid-point of the Christian religion. Jesus did not come, first of all, to renew families and reform society but to save sinners and to redeem the world from the coming wrath of God. This salvation of our souls must be our ultimate concern for which we are willing to sacrifice everything: father and mother, house and field, even our own lives, in order to inherit the kingdom of heaven (Matt. 6:33; 16:26; etc.). (*GBP*, 443)

Bavinck expresses this primacy using one of his favorite similes from our Lord's parables, the treasure of inestimable worth:

What he came to bring to earth is therefore something of inexpressible worth— the kingdom of God, not as a moral community that men would create, but as a heavenly, imperishable treasure (Matt. 6:20; Luke 12:33). The content of this kingdom is righteousness (Matt. 6:33), salvation from destruction (Matt. 7:13; Mark 8:35; 9:48), and eternal life (Matt. 5:3–9; 7:14; 13:43). The kingdom is thus of absolute world-transcending worth (Matt. 6:33; 13:44; Mark 8:36; Luke 10:42), and citizenship in it is only possible by way of regeneration (John 3:3), faith, and conversion (Mark 1:15).[13]

It would be a mistake to conclude from this that Bavinck considers Jesus so "spiritual" that he is indifferent to the natural, ordinary daily life of people. Was Jesus an ascetic? Bavinck categorically denies this; Jesus recalibrates the significance and meaning of daily life from the perspective of the treasure or pearl of great price that is the kingdom of God:

From this standpoint Jesus evaluates all natural things. He does not despise them, he is not an ascetic, he does not impose fasting (Matt. 9:14); he is hated as a glutton and a drunkard (Matt. 11:18); he celebrates a wedding (John 2), participates as a guest at many a meal (Luke 7:36), and considers food and

13. Bavinck, "Christian Principles and Social Relationships," in *ERSS*, 129. For economy's sake, future references to this work will be indicated parenthetically within the text as *ERSS*, followed by the page number.

drink, garment and clothing as good gifts of the heavenly Father (Matt. 6:25–33; Luke 11:3). He also honors marriage (Matt. 5:28; Mark 10:2–12), loves children (Matt. 18:2; 19:14), prizes a person's own home (Luke 9:58), and especially in his parables speaks openly about all of nature and the natural life, about all circumstances and relationships. The ascetic outlook on life is, in principle, foreign to Jesus. (*ERSS*, 129)

Jesus was not a social reformer, says Bavinck. Consequently, his summary of Jesus's relation to social conditions sounds—initially, at least—rather conservative:

Jesus is not a man of science or art, nor is he a politician or economist; he is no social reformer or demagogue, nor a party man or a class struggler. He accepts social conditions as he finds them and never tries to bring about a change or improvement in them. . . . He leaves all political and social circumstances and relationships for what they are; he never intervenes in any of this, either by word or actions. (*ERSS*, 130)

Bavinck continues his exposition of Jesus's relation to human society by noting that while Jesus was certainly aware of the wretched religious, moral, social, and political condition of the world into which he sent his disciples, he neither promised them a rosy earthly future nor commanded them to direct their efforts to social amelioration. In the Sermon on the Mount, Jesus said his followers should be prepared to suffer and called them to a higher righteousness. In fact, he calls "blessed"

not the people who by external observation of the commandments seek to establish their own righteousness, but those who are mentioned in the Psalms and the Prophets as the wretched, the needy, the poor, and so forth. These Jesus now calls the poor in spirit, the people hungering and thirsting for righteousness, the pure in heart, and so forth. When Jesus therefore pronounces these people blessed, he does not violate but endorses the Old Testament completely. He is not a new lawgiver who supplements or improves the Law and the Prophets, and thus actually dissolves them, but he fulfills them totally and therefore demands another and better righteousness than that of the Pharisees and scribes (Matt. 5:17–20). (*ERSS*, 132)

The gospel of the kingdom is not a program for a new sociopolitical order but a spiritual power that reorders the human heart. Continuing his explanation of the Sermon on the Mount, notably the series of "you have heard . . .

but I say" comparisons in Matthew 5:21–48, Bavinck insists that all literalism with respect to the Sermon (monks, Anabaptists, Quakers, Tolstoy, Charles Sheldon) violates the spirit of its message. Here is a summary of Bavinck's understanding of the *imitatio Christi* ideal:

> The true following of Christ therefore does not consist in copying him, in replicating him, in imitating his life and teaching but is found in the inner conversion of the heart, which gives us a true desire and choice to walk according to all, not just some, of God's commandments in spirit and truth. (*ERSS*, 133)[14]

Bavinck then draws the following conclusion:

> Therefore the words of Christ do not contain a political or social agenda; they cannot be imposed by means of the authority or force of a government and cannot be exacted with violence or under threat of punishment. At the moment someone does this, the words of Jesus are robbed of their spiritual essence and their core. They are religious-moral commandments that can be honored only in the way of liberty, spontaneously, from an inner compulsion of the regenerated heart. Only a good tree can produce good fruits. (*ERSS*, 133–34)

Bavinck goes on to discuss the abuse of Christian spiritual liberty as "an occasion for the flesh" in which Christians challenged the natural and social order—refusing all contact with pagans, refusing to obey civil authority, breaking up marriages with unbelievers, slaves refusing to submit to their masters. Bavinck describes the result as follows:

> The moral order that prevailed in the kingdom of heaven soon clashed with the rule of law in state and society. (*ERSS*, 134)

According to Bavinck, concerns about the misuse of Christian liberty help explain the "conservative" character of New Testament moral instruction:[15]

---

14. DO: *De waarachtige navolging van Christus bestaat daarom niet in het nadoen, in het nabootsen, in het naapen van zijn leven en leer, maar zij is gelegen in die innerlijke bekeering des harten, die ons een oprechten lust en keuze schenkt, om niet alleen naar sommige, maar naar alle Gods geboden in geest en waarheid te wandelen.* Ed. note: Though Bavinck does not provide a reference, the expression "according to all, not just some, of God's commandments" is a direct quote from Q&A 114 (Lord's Day 44) of the Heidelberg Catechism.

15. For more extensive discussion of Bavinck's understanding of the Sermon on the Mount in the context of the New Testament ethic as a whole, see *Imitatio Christi*, 294–307.

In reaction, all the apostles at that time began unanimously to oppose this abuse of Christian liberty by supporting the natural order, institutions, and relationships. Like Christ, they admonish fellow Christians to be long-suffering and patient, to be gentle and forbearing, to be humble and loving, to endure persecution and abuse quietly and obediently, so that evil may be conquered by the good. This becomes evident already in the first church in Jerusalem. (*ERSS*, 134)

The church did not challenge or seek to reform the institutions of society. This includes retaining the institution of private property.[16]

Just as with private property, so all natural ordinances and institutions are maintained by the church. The wealthy are nowhere called to divest themselves of their property, although they are urgently and often admonished not to put their trust in worldly goods, to guard themselves against miserliness, and to be compassionate and share (Rom. 15:26; Gal. 2:10; 1 Tim. 6:9, 17–19; James 1:10–11; 5:1–6). The poor are never encouraged to demand their share of earthly goods but rather to be satisfied and to work faithfully in their occupation (Eph. 4:28; 1 Thess. 4:11; 2 Thess. 3:7–12; 1 Tim. 6:6, 8; Heb. 13:5). Associating with unbelievers is permitted; believing spouses should stay with unbelieving spouses; governing authorities are to be obeyed; . . . each person should remain in the situation to which God has called him or her (1 Cor. 7:24). (*ERSS*, 135)

After a lengthy examination of the New Testament's treatment of slavery, including the implication of Paul's instruction to Philemon about the slave Onesimus, Bavinck contends that Paul's main message is that

external circumstances are not important to being a Christian; the important thing is to keep God's commandments, and that can be done in any situation. . . . External circumstances do not diminish being a Christian; one can be a Christian in any social position. Therefore, everyone is not to look at his position in life, whether slave or free, but at his calling, what he is in Christ. (*ERSS*, 137–38)

But does this then mean that the gospel has no renewing and transforming power in human relationships and social structures? On the contrary! The gospel plays a powerful transforming role in human society, but not as itself an actor in the political process. What is new about the gospel is not at all political, but it does turn the world of politics upside down.

16. See below, "2. Economic Life."

Although the gospel left everything unchanged in the natural relationships, it nevertheless preached a principle so deep and rich and extraordinarily powerful that it was bound to exert a reforming influence on all earthly circumstances. The gospel has to be understood clearly. It must be accepted the way it presents itself without turning it into a political or social system, and then it will reveal its permeating power. For what does this gospel proclaim? What was this new element that was unknown to all of antiquity and that made the ancient world shake to its foundations? It was this, that heavenly, spiritual matters, that the kingdom of God and his righteousness in Christ are a tangible, completely trustworthy reality and that their value infinitely exceeds all visible and temporal things. There is absolutely nothing that is considered great and glorious among men that can be compared with it. In order to be a Christian, a citizen of the kingdom of God and heir of eternal life, it matters not at all whether one is a Jew or a Greek, barbarian or Scythian, male or female, free or slave, rich or poor, socially important or unimportant. (*ERSS*, 140)

What Christ did is truly to level the social and political playing field.

The only way to enter the kingdom of heaven, which is available to all, is by way of regeneration, an inner change, faith, conversion. No nationality, no gender, no social standing, no class, no wealth or poverty, no freedom or slavery has any preference here. The old has passed; behold, all has been made new. The walls of division have fallen away, the palisades taken down; the gospel is intended for all and must be proclaimed to all. The despised and those without rights in antiquity—the barbarians, the uncivilized, the ignoble, women, slaves, publicans, sinners, whoremongers, idol worshipers—are all people of God's family, destined for his kingdom. Yes, if there is any preference then the poor, the ignoble, the unlearned, the oppressed are the ones who are considered first for the gospel. God chooses the poor, the despised, and the ignoble, so that no one should boast before him. (*ERSS*, 140)

Bavinck now turns passionately enthusiastic about the changes brought about by the gospel.

What a revolution this gospel brought about in the ancient world; it gave a reforming power to humanity! All people are equal before God. He rates no one inferior because of social standing or rank, because of simplicity or unimportance. God loves everyone who fears him from all peoples and generations and social classes. This is a raising in status, this is the birthday of a new humanity, the beginning of a new society. Christians, however different they were among themselves in origin and social status, were an elect family, a holy nation, a people made his own, a royal priesthood, one body with many members. (*ERSS*, 141)

The sentences that immediately follow are pivotal for grasping Bavinck's understanding of the gospel's importance, also for social transformation.

Even if Christianity had resulted in nothing more than this spiritual and holy community, even if it had not brought about any modification in earthly relationships, even if it, for instance, had done nothing for the abolition of slavery, it would still be and remain something of everlasting worth. The significance of the gospel does not depend on its influence on culture, its usefulness for life today; it is a treasure in itself, a pearl of great price, even if it might not be a leaven. (*ERSS*, 141)

But, of course, Bavinck continues,

it nevertheless is undeniable that Christianity indeed exerts such an influence. The kingdom of heaven is not only a pearl, it is a leaven as well. . . . In keeping God's commandments, there is great reward. In its long and rich history, Christianity has borne much valuable fruit for all of society in all its relationships, in spite of the unfaithfulness of its confessors. (*ERSS*, 141)

Before we move on to consider Bavinck's specific topics for this chapter, here is a brief summary of his main points about society:[17]

a. Scripture's point of departure is creation, because essentially all relationships are connected with it, and thus can only be known from it.

b. The intent of grace, which entered immediately after the fall, always and everywhere has been to maintain and restore these original relationships.

c. The gospel of Christ . . . presupposes creation, honors the work of the Father, and concurs with all natural relationships in human life that exist by virtue of God's will. In itself the gospel, the proclamation of the kingdom of heaven and his [God's] righteousness, is the good news of reconciliation and redemption from sin through the blood of the cross. This is the gospel that must remain, first in church and missions, but also beyond them, everywhere. It may not be robbed of its content or dissolved into a political or social program. Only in this way can the gospel be maintained in its everlasting, all-surpassing value.

---

17. What follows is directly from Bavinck's own summary, *ERSS*, 141–43.

d. Because the gospel is exclusively directed to the redemption from sin, it leaves all natural relationships alone. The gospel shuns every revolution that arises from unbelief, since by its overthrow of everything a revolution makes no distinction between nature and sin and eradicates the good with the bad. The gospel, on the other hand, always works reformationally. . . . by setting people free from guilt, renewing the heart. . . .[18]

e. From this center [of a new humanity] it influences all earthly relationships in a reforming and renewing way.

f. [The way of social reformation and renewal is opposed to any form of] conservativism that closes its eyes to changes in society and to radicalism or radical revolution.[19]

1. THE SOCIAL QUESTION

This section is based on two primary Bavinck sources: (1) "General Biblical Principles and the Relevance of Concrete Mosaic Law for the Social Question Today (1891)" and (2) "On Inequality." Since the first was a paper prepared specifically for the First Christian Social Congress held in Amsterdam on November 9–11, 1891,[20] a few observations about the historical context of the "social question" are in order.[21]

The term "social question" belongs to the nineteenth century and was a response to the dislocations of European life brought about by the Industrial Revolution. Working people left rural areas and flocked into the urban centers of Europe as cottage industries gave way to factory production. The social upheaval resulted in growing numbers of urbanized working-class poor who often struggled to meet basic necessities of life. English poet William Blake

---

18. Bavinck is explicit about the sociopolitical implications of this new reality: "[The gospel] is in principle opposed to all socialism, communism, anarchism, which after all never only oppose sin, but by their denial of the fall, identify sin with nature, unrighteousness with the very institution of the family and the state, and therefore creation with the fall" (*ERSS*, 142).

19. "While conservatism closes its eyes to changes in society, and radicalism fails to have a solid standpoint in the stream of events, a reformation that proceeds from a Christian principle combines both: being and becoming, the absolute and the relative, the unity of the divine will and the wonderful leading of his providence" (*ERSS*, 143).

20. Abraham Kuyper's opening address to this congress, "The Social Question and the Christian Religion" (translated into English by Dirk Jellema as *Christianity and the Class Struggle* [1950], and by James W. Skillen as *The Problem of Poverty* [1991]), is much better known than Bavinck's; both reflect the burning issue of the day as did Pope Leo XIII's famous encyclical *Rerum Novarum*, also from 1891.

21. For a longer introduction see Bolt, "Herman Bavinck's Contribution to Christian Social Consciousness"; most of what follows is taken from this introduction.

put an indelible stamp on our imagination's sense of this period of history with his famous reference to "these dark Satanic mills."[22]

The social upheaval was obvious, and social thinkers responded with a variety of "fixes," notably the secular socialist vision of Karl Marx and the Christian socialist visions of British Anglicans such as Charles Kingsley (1819–75) and Frederick Denison Maurice (1805–72), along with American Baptists Walter Rauschenbusch (1861–1918) and Francis Julius Bellamy (1855–1931). In continental Europe, a number of organized movements for social reform, called "Social Congresses," were organized, usually at national levels. The Evangelical Social Congress, for example, was a diverse social-reform movement founded by German pastors in 1890.[23]

The 1891 First Christian Social Congress was made possible by some thirty years of social group formation of workers in Europe more broadly and the Netherlands more particularly.[24] After the world's workers formed the International Working Men's Association (IWMA, later called the First International) in London on September 28, 1864, and the aborted revolutionary attempt by the Paris Commune to seize power in 1871, an increased anxiety about revolution and "socialism" grew in Europe. In the Netherlands, Guillaume Groen van Prinsterer (1801–76) and, later, Abraham Kuyper initiated an anti-revolutionary movement, eventually forming the Anti-Revolutionary Party in 1879.[25] In the decades leading up to the First Christian Social Congress, religiously neutral as well as expressly Christian—Protestant and Roman

22. In the poem "And Did Those Feet in Ancient Time," from the preface to his epic *Milton: A Poem in Two Books*.

23. See Maurenbrecher, "Evangelical Social Congress in Germany"; Liebersohn, *Religion and Industrial Society: The Protestant Social Congress in Wilhelmine Germany* (1986). The Evangelical Social Congress included in its leadership the social thinker Max Weber (1864–1920); the Christian socialist Friedrich Naumann (1860–1919); Adolf Stoeker (1835–1909), chaplain to the court of Kaiser Wilhelm II and founder of the Lutheran, anti-Semitic, Christian Social (Workers) Party (1878); and liberal, social gospel mainstays Wilhelm Herrmann (1846–1922) and Adolf von Harnack (1851–1930). See Pentz, "Meaning of Religion in the Politics of Friedrich Naumann"; Telman, "Adolf Stoecker"; Green, "Adolf Stoecker." The collection of essays edited by Adolf von Harnack and Wilhelm Herrmann, *Essays on the Social Gospel* (1907), reveals a great deal about the social gospel's understanding of the church's mission. It contains two addresses by Harnack, "The Evangelical Social Mission in the Light of the History of the Church," read on May 17, 1894, at the Evangelical Social Congress held at Frankfurt am Main, and published in *Prussian Annals* 76, no. 3 (1894), and "The Moral and Social Significance of Modern Education," read on May 22, 1902, at the Evangelical Social Congress held at Dortmund, as well as one by Wilhelm Herrmann, "The Moral Teachings of Jesus," read at the Evangelical Social Congress held at Darmstadt in 1903.

24. For details and chronology, see Peet, Altena, and Wiedijk, *Honderd Jaar Sociaal, 1891–1991*, 701–13.

25. Abraham Kuyper penned the party's first platform under the title *Ons Program (Our Program)*.

Catholic—worker groups and employer associations came into being. As the congress met in November 1891, the condition of workers and the "threat" of socialism were very much on participants' minds. And it is this issue that is crucial for understanding Bavinck's paper.

Bavinck acknowledges the reality of this social ferment and even highlights the economic disparities that gave rise to it. Elsewhere he speaks of

> the many highly deplorable disparities that exist in real life. What is the reason and why is it necessary that a few may live in luxury and that many may live a fairly carefree life but that the mass of humanity has to earn a living through hard labor? Who or what accounts for the differences between those whose homes are furnished lavishly or comfortably and the many who have to endure living in stuffy rooms, narrow alleys, and dreary slums that lack light and fresh air? (*ERSS*, 147)

Nonetheless, Bavinck does not make the reality of inequality his starting point, and he differs from the revolutionary and socialist understanding of the problem by refusing to accept inequality as prima facie proof of injustice. Instead, he considers inequality to be "only one instance of a worldwide problem of multiformity" (*ERSS*, 147). We will see how he develops this, first in the context of the social and economic questions that framed the First Christian Social Congress, and then from a more philosophical perspective in his essay "On Inequality."

a. Bavinck's "General Biblical Principles" (1891)[26]

As I noted in the previous section, Bavinck sees a twofold calling for humanity and insists that our first obligation is to set right our relationship with God:

> Thus, the first order of the day is restoring our proper relationship with God. The cross of Christ, therefore, is the heart and mid-point of the Christian religion.

26. Original title: "Welke algemeene beginselen beheerschen, volgens de H. Schrift, de oplossing der sociale quaestie, en welke vingerwijzing voor die oplossing ligt in de concrete toepassing, welke deze beginselen voor Israël in Mosaïsch recht gevonden hebben?" This work was published in *Proces-Verbaal van het Sociaal Congres gehouden te Amsterdam, den 9, 10, 11, 12 November 1891*, 149–57. The title of the published English translation was shortened; the full and more literal title would read: "According to Holy Scripture, what general principles govern the solution of the social question, and what signals [lit., "finger-pointing"] for this solution can be found in Israel's concrete application of these principles found in Mosaic law." The congress's discussion of the resolutions, in interaction with Bavinck, can be found in the published account of the congress, in *Proces-Verbaal*, 80–87. See https://www.google.com/books/edition/Proces_verbaal_van_het_sociaal_congres_g/vo9VAAAAcAAJ?hl=en&gbpv=1.

Jesus did not come, first of all, to renew families and reform society but to save sinners and to redeem the world from the coming wrath of God. This salvation of our souls must be our ultimate concern for which we are willing to sacrifice everything: father and mother, house and field, even our own lives, in order to inherit the kingdom of heaven (Matt. 6:33; 16:26). (*GBP*, 443)

We also saw that with respect to our earthly vocation Bavinck considers "inequalities" as a given of creation and not a consequence of the fall:

It is here [in creation] also that we see, in principle, all the inequalities that would eventually come to pass among people: differences in body and soul, in character and temperament, in gifts of understanding and will, in heart and hand, and so forth. Inequality is a given of creation, grounded in the very will of God himself, and not first of all a consequence of sin. (*GBP*, 438)

However, our world is one in which sin and its consequences are devastatingly real:

In the first place, the relation of fellowship with God was broken; sin brought unbelief, disobedience, and enmity against God. Sin leads us to forget the things that are above, to lose sight of our eternal, heavenly destination. Instead, sin throws us down to the earth and directs us to look for our salvation and happiness in its visible things.

Consequently, the right relation of humans to themselves was also disturbed. Proper balance was destroyed; soul and body, spirit and flesh are now at odds with each other. Head and heart, understanding and will, and desire and duty are in irreconcilable conflict as the various human gifts and powers engage in perpetual war with each other, are devalued or misused. Egoism replaces love in the human heart and as a result produces envy, deceit, hatred, murder, and so forth. Sin has thus become the basic given of human life, the motivating power of human conduct. (*ERSS*, 438)

"Irreconcilable conflict" and "perpetual war" not only describe the internal reality of our personal lives; that characterization also fits our relationships with fellow image bearers. We have become like ravenous beasts:

In this way the entire social existence of human beings becomes a war of all against all. Husbands and wives, parents and children, rich and poor, and so forth, come to be enemies of each other; differences become oppositions; inequalities are changed into clashing contrasts. Driven by egoism, everyone no longer thinks about that which they have but focuses on what belongs to someone else. Society becomes a stage-play about the struggle for existence, a world where one man acts as a wolf toward the others. (*GBP*, 439)

There are two additional consequences of our fallen, sinful condition:

(1) Our changed relationship to the natural world:

God remains the same and his command does not change: We are still given the responsibility to fill the earth and subdue it. However, the character of our labor now is changed: Women bear children in pain and sorrow, and men eat bread by the sweat of their brow because nature is no longer cooperative but antagonistic. Human dominion over creation has given way to a situation where nature is indifferent, even hostile, where "thorns and thistles," the animals of the field, and the forces of nature are our enemies. Our labor has become a struggle merely to survive. Paradise is closed behind us and we are sent out into the raw, wasted world without any weapons. (*GBP*, 439–40)

(2) Life under the judgment of God:

Furthermore, to top it off, in all this, humans feel the judgments of God that multiply above our heads. Rebellion against God's law never goes unpunished; sin is itself misery and is followed by an ocean of disasters. Shattered souls and broken bodies are the wrecks of justice; inner disturbance, a sense of guilt, an agonized conscience, and fear of punishment gnaw at the hidden life of every human being. Illness and troubles, tragedies and evils, mourning and death, all take away the joys of our earthly life. Dust celebrates its triumph in the grave; destruction sings its victory song. (*GBP*, 440)

The "nasty, brutish, and short" lives of humans are not the whole story, according to Bavinck. A world in sin and under divine wrath is still not a hellish existence:

This devastating path of sin's work over time is nonetheless restrained by God's grace. His thoughts after all are not directed to destruction but to the preservation and redemption of humanity. Already in his role as Creator and Sustainer God redirects sin, opposes it and reins it in so that sin does not annihilate creation and frustrate his decree.

God does this, in the first place, by the punishments and judgments that he links to sin. Restless souls, the trials of life, the struggle for existence, the toils of our daily labor, all of these are, at the same time, revelations of divine wrath and instruments of his common grace, by which he throws obstacles in the path of sin's progress and opposes the most horrific outbursts of sin.

In addition, with respect to human beings, God does this by allowing a few weak remnants of his image and likeness to remain [after the fall]. He grants them reason and conscience; preserves in them some knowledge of his existence and character, a seed of religion; a moral sense of good and evil; and a consciousness of our eternal destiny. In this way, God keeps before people a tie to another and higher world than the visible one limited by our senses. Even with all the corruption present among all people and every individual, there remains a natural knowledge of God [for everyone].

Finally, God does that by establishing the structures of family, society, and state among human beings. He awakens in the human heart a natural love between men and women, parents and children. He nurtures a variety of social virtues among people: a pull toward social relationships and a longing for affection and friendship. He also scatters humanity into different people groups and languages to protect them from total decline. Among those nations, he creates the national virtues of affection for and love of fatherland. He permits these different people groups to organize themselves into states to whom is given the calling to regulate the relationships among the many diverse spheres of society and maintain justice. (*GBP*, 440–41)

Bavinck cautions against placing too much confidence in this restraint and amelioration:

Nonetheless, this endowment of common grace and divine long-suffering is not enough; it restrains human beings but does not renew them. (*GBP*, 441)

With this observation Bavinck comes to the heart of his paper's message:

While the Lord permits the pagan nations to wander along their own path, he sets Israel apart and makes known to them his ways and his laws. God is Israel's King, Lawgiver, and Judge (Isa. 33:22). These laws regulated the totality of Israel's existence and life, not only externally but also internally, its religious and moral life and its statecraft and social relationships. (*GBP*, 441)

Bavinck then describes the institutions and structures that defined Israel's social life:

   a. Israel is the people of God, set apart from all the nations to be his holy
      people and called to walk in his ways (Exod. 19:5, 6, etc.). In the law-giving

at Mount Sinai, it is this religious destiny for Israel that stands in the foreground. However, it is not only the people but also the land that God owns as his possession. In the freedom of his decree, he took the land of Canaan from its previous inhabitants and gave it as an inheritance to Abraham and his seed. The land belongs to God and the Israelites are strangers and tenants (Lev. 25:23). Israel possesses the land in fiefdom to use as a renter. God manages it and determines how the land is to be divided among the tribes and clans (Josh. 13–19).

b. God maintains these tribes and clans and protects their inheritance. He promises fertility for Israel's families (Gen. 12:2; 13:16; Deut. 28:4) and kept alive among them the conviction that children are a blessing and inheritance from the Lord (Ps. 113:9; 127:3–5; 128:3). Inherited portions of land were passed on through sons; in families that had no sons, it was given to daughters but with the obligation that they marry men from their own tribal clan (Num. 27:8; 36:1–13). A childless widow was to be taken as wife by a brother or close relative of the deceased man in order that his name not be blotted out from the land and his inheritance given to another (Deut. 25:5–10).

c. In turn, the inherited portions of land were protected and preserved for the tribe and clan, especially by the principle of jubilee. In the Year of Jubilee, all Israelites whose poverty had led them into slavery were to be released (Lev. 25:39, 40 [also Deut. 15:12]); the right of redemption was to be available to them in perpetuity (Lev. 25:47)—their property could not be sold for good; it could only be used until the Year of Jubilee when it was to be returned freely, without payment of a purchase price, to the original owner. Even prior to this year, the owner or his redeemer retained the right to buy back the property (Lev. 25). However, this institution of redemption and return did not apply to houses in walled cities (Lev. 25:29–30) nor to land that was dedicated to the Lord (Lev. 27:16–21).

d. It was thanks to these stipulations that Israel avoided both pauperization and accumulation of land and capital. At the same time, this did not eliminate differences between rich and poor, freeman and serf. God willed that there should be poor (Deut. 15:11; Prov. 22:2), and bondage or serfdom was a lawful institution (Exod. 21:20ff.). Nonetheless, the basic necessities for a life of human dignity[27] were made possible for most Israelites. Contrasts [between rich and poor] were mitigated, in most beautiful manner on the Sabbath and the feast days. Poor and rich did not exist then; all lived, apart from their labor, freely from the hand of the

27. DO: *menschwaardig bestaan.*

Lord; all were free, throwing off their work clothes and donning festal garments. This was a time to rest from all labor and to rejoice in the presence of God.

e. In addition to this, we must not forget the ministry of mercy in Israel. Loans were to be given to the poor freely and willingly (Deut. 15:7); surety was not to be taken by force and even, in some cases, to be returned before sunset (Deut. 24:6, 10–12; Exod. 22:26). No interest was to be charged a brother Israelite (Deut. 25:19; Lev. 25:36), and debts were to be forgiven in the seventh year (Deut. 15); day-wages were to be paid in a timely fashion (Deut. 24:15). In addition, widows and orphans, the poor and the stranger were to be treated justly in the courts (Deut. 14:7; Exod. 22:21, 22); they had rights of gleaning after annual harvests (Lev. 19:9–10; Deut. 24:19–21) and to the entire harvest in the Sabbath year (Lev. 25:5); they also had rights to share in the meals from sacrifices and tithes (Deut. 14:28–29; 16:10–15; 26:12–13). Those with disabilities were not to be mocked (Lev. 19:14; Deut. 27:18), and the elderly were to be honored (Lev. 19:32). God's law even provided for the life and well-being of animals, including their rest (Exod. 20:10; Deut. 25:4; 22:6, 28). This entire ministry of mercy is repeatedly predicated on Israel's oppression and sojourning in Egypt (Exod. 22:20; 23:9; etc.). Israel's moral law is written from the vantage point of the oppressed. (*GBP*, 441–42)

According to Bavinck, it is to these Old Testament principles, and not to the moral teachings of the New Testament, that we must turn for guidance on a biblical understanding of society. He says that in the New Testament, "the law is not simply abrogated and set aside, but it is fulfilled in Christ and in this way reaches its own end." Therefore,

the New Testament does not give us laws that could as a matter of course be adopted by the state and enforced with its authority. Rather we must go to the Old Testament where the eternal principles are set forth by which alone the well-being of families, societies, and states can be guaranteed. These principles are not written on tablets of stone but penetrate the bodily tablets of human hearts and, through the church of Christ, the world. (*GBP*, 443)

We have seen that, according to Bavinck, the New Testament's primary concern is restoring our relationship with God.[28] Two consequences follow from this priority:

28. See above, pp. 13–14.

(a) All our social relationships are relativized:

> This new, reconciled relationship to God that is effected through faith in Christ
> is of such great significance and value that all our relationships and distinctions
> vanish because of it. In Christ, there is neither male nor female, Greek nor Jew,
> slave nor free (Col. 3:11). (*GBP*, 443)

(b) Soteriological equality does not eliminate other inequalities:

> However, this does not set aside all the differences and inequalities that exist
> among people in this earthly life. Property ownership does not disappear; the
> example of the Jerusalem church in Acts is all too often taken by itself and is
> too exceptional to provide a counter claim. The differences between rich and
> poor, slave and free, parents and children, civil authorities and subjects are as-
> sumed and honored fully by Jesus and his apostles in their words and deeds.
> Passages such as 1 Corinthians 7:17–24 make it clear that every person, even
> after their conversion, ought to remain in the calling to which they have been
> called. The differences that are present in creation by the will of God are not
> set aside by the Son in redemption. (*GBP*, 443)

Nonetheless, salvation in Christ does not leave the natural order unaffected:

> Redemption does change matters, however. From the principle of reconcilia-
> tion with God, all other human relationships are given a new ordering and led
> back to their original state. God is the owner of every human being and their
> possessions; we are simply tenants, renters, and must give an account of our
> stewardship (Luke 16:2; Matt. 25:14–30). Husbands and wives (Eph. 5:22; Titus
> 2:5; Col. 3:18), parents and children (Eph. 6:1–4; Col. 3:20–21), masters and
> slaves (1 Cor. 7:21–22; Eph. 6:5–9; Col. 3:22), civil authorities and subjects (Rom.
> 13:1–7; 1 Tim. 2:1–2; 1 Pet. 2:13–16; etc.), are all brought into proper relationship
> with each other. Distinctions in our social life remain, but they lose their sharp
> edge. The New Testament is overflowing with warnings against riches (Matt.
> 6:19; 19:23; 1 Tim. 6:17–19; etc.), but poverty is no virtue and the natural is not
> unclean in itself (Mark 7:15–23; Acts 14:17; Rom. 14:14; 1 Tim. 4:4). Work is com-
> mended and tied to food and wages (Matt. 10:10; 1 Tim. 5:18; Eph. 4:28; 2 Thess.
> 3:10). In Matthew 6:25–34, Jesus himself removes for his followers all anxious
> concern about this earthly life. Because the redemption in Christ renews but
> does not eliminate the various earthly relationships in which we find ourselves,
> there remains a large place for the ministry of mercy. Just like the poor (Matt.
> 26:11; John 12:8; Rev. 13:16), so, too, the many needy will always be with us.
> In the same way that Jesus the compassionate High Priest is always deeply

moved by those in need, so, too, he directs his followers especially to clothe
themselves with the Christlike virtue of compassion (Matt. 5:43–47; Luke 6:36).
Having received mercy from Christ, his followers are expected in turn to show
mercy to others (1 Pet. 2:10; Matt. 18:33). It is for this reason that the church has
a distinct office for the ministry of mercy. (*GBP*, 443–44)

I conclude my overview of Bavinck's presentation to the 1891 Christian
Social Congress with the seven resolutions he prepared for discussion and
debate. The congress turned these seven resolutions into eight, adding a new
one and also altering Bavinck's originals in some cases.[29]

Bavinck's Original Resolutions to 1891 Social Congress	Resolutions Adopted by 1891 Social Congress
	C1 (new): Holy Scripture teaches that human society must not be ordered according to our own preferences but is bound to those laws that God himself has firmly established in Creation and His Word.
B1: The inequalities that exist in every respect among people are grounded in the Creation, that is to say, in God's will itself, and serves precisely to make possible humanity's earthly task.	C2: **Even the existence of** inequalities among people is rooted in creation, that is to say, in God's will, and serves precisely to make possible humanity's earthly task.[30]

29. For ease of reference, I will number Bavinck's resolutions as "B1, B2, etc." and the
revised resolutions of the congress as "C1, C2, etc." They can be found in *GBP*, 445–46. The
changes from Bavinck's original will be highlighted in boldface. The discussion at the congress
about Bavinck's paper was also recorded, and I will include some of that discussion in my
footnotes; these notes are adapted from Bolt, "Herman Bavinck's Contribution to Christian
Social Consciousness," 425–36. The congress also added a new resolution (C1), which is an
important addition because it serves as a prologue and frame for the whole set. It also points
to the natural law of creation alongside Scripture as a source of human knowledge about
God's law.
30. C2: The concessive introductory phrase added by the congress likely signals concerns
among delegates that the resolution risked being charged with determinism. In his comments
in response to questions about this, Bavinck accented the threefold perspective required to view
humanity aright: in the state of original righteousness, in sin, and in grace. Note that this is the
same threefold perspective from which Bavinck views the entire moral life in his *Reformed Ethics*; book I, "Humanity before Conversion," deals with humanity as created (*RE*, 1, chap. 1) and
fallen (*RE*, 1, chaps. 2–6); book II (*RE*, 1, chaps. 7–12) considers "humanity after conversion"—
that is, in the state of grace; and books III (*RE* 2) and IV (*RE* 3), respectively, cover the "duties
of the Christian life" (the Decalogue) and "social ethics."

B2: Sin eliminated the unity of this diversity, turned differences into oppositions, and placed creatures in a relationship of enmity against God and to each other.	C3: **In general, the origin of all social ills and abuses comes from setting aside these ordinances and laws. Thanks to this, the differences that are present among creatures by virtue of creation** lost their unity, were changed into oppositions, and placed creatures in a relationship of enmity against God and to each other.[31]
B3: Redemption does not set aside the differences that exist thanks to God's will but renews all relationships to their original form by bringing all of them into a reconciled relationship with God.	C4: Redemption does not set aside the differences that exist thanks to God's will but renews all relationships to their original form by bringing all of them into a reconciled relationship with God.[32]
B4: According to Scripture the important general principle for a solution to the social question is that there be justice.[33] This means that each person be assigned to the place where, in accord with their nature, they are able to live according to God's ordinances with respect to God and other creatures.	C5: According to Scripture the important general principle for a solution to the social question is that there be justice. This means that each person be assigned to the place where, in accord with their nature, they are able to live according to God's ordinances with respect to God and other creatures.[34]

31. C3: Here the congress strengthened Bavinck's formulation by directing attention first to social ills instead of sin and highlighting human culpability for "social ills and abuses" as a consequence of "setting aside" God's ordinances and laws. While inequalities may be rooted in creation's diversity according to God's will, the fact that they are now a problem is a consequence of human action. This resolution also underscores the universality of sin and paves the way for a repudiation of all schemes such as socialism that place the blame for social ills on unjust structures and institutions. Sin is universal and points to a law-dimension that transcends our human constructions and structures; all utopian dreaming is rendered foolish, and all scapegoating rejected. The problem does not lie in certain people or specific structures; the cure does not depend on changing the structures and institutions. *Sin* is the problem and we are all guilty and culpable for it.

32. C4: This resolution was not altered. C4 is identical, word for word, with B3. Though the congress left this resolution unaltered, it does deserve a brief comment. Neither Bavinck nor the congress included a resolution about "common grace," the notion of God's providential favor whereby he bestows nonsaving gifts upon all people and restrains evil from developing full flower. Apparently, the delegates felt no need to make common cause with non-Christians— such as socialists, for example, who observed the same misery and showed similar concern and compassion for the growing numbers of working poor. Bavinck and the congress were trying to think through the social question *as Christians* who looked to scriptural revelation as their resource for uncovering the truth about human life, its meaning, and its destiny. Also noteworthy is that the appeal to Scripture is primarily to the Old Testament and the concrete life of Israel as a people, and not to the soteriological core of the New Testament. See note on B4/C5, below.

33. DO: *gerechtigheid*.

34. C5: This resolution was not altered. C5 is identical, word for word, with B4. In his comments during the discussion, Bavinck observed that "Jesus did not come to destroy the work of his Father [i.e., creation] but the works of the Devil. Grace does not set aside justice [*recht*] but restores it, first by justly restoring our relationship to God, and thereby making possible a just relationship to other people." The definition of justice that is provided is striking: "that

B5: Therefore, it is entirely in keeping with Holy Scripture to:

a. not only prepare people for their eternal destiny, but also to make it possible for them to fulfill their earthly calling;
b. in the political arena, uphold the institution of the Sabbath alongside the workweek so as to maintain the unity and distinction of our double calling;
c. guide all our life's relationships in a new way and restore them to their original shape by the same cross of Christ that proclaims our reconciliation with God. This has special relevance for the social arena, where [we should seek to]
   • prevent poverty and misery, especially pauperization;
   • oppose the accumulation of capital and landed property;
   • ensure, as much as possible, a "living wage" for every person.

C6: Therefore, it is entirely in keeping with Holy Scripture to:

a. not only prepare people for their eternal destiny, but also to make it possible for them to fulfill their earthly calling;
b. in the political arena, uphold the institution of the Sabbath alongside the workweek so as to maintain the unity and distinction of our double calling;
c. guide all our life's relationships in a new way and restore them to their original shape by the same cross of Christ that proclaims our reconciliation with God. This has special relevance for the social arena, where [we should seek to]
   • prevent poverty and misery, especially pauperization;
   • oppose the accumulation of capital and landed property;
   • ensure, as much as possible, a "living wage" for every person.[35]

B6: Civil authority, as God's servant called to maintain justice in society, has an obligation to test this justice and to base it on the eternal principles[36] laid down in Scripture for the various spheres of society.

C7: Civil authority, as God's servant called to maintain justice *also* in society, has an obligation to **base** this justice on **and deduce it from** the eternal **ordinances** [*ordinantiën*] laid down in Scripture for the various spheres of society.[37]

---

each person be assigned to the place where, in accord with their nature, they are able to live according to God's ordinances with respect to God and other creatures." It is the responsibility of civil authority to make this possible (*Proces-Verbaal*, 83). It should not be overlooked that this resolution underscores the forensic nature of our Lord's atoning death on the cross; our relationship to God is *justly* restored.

35. *C6:* This resolution was not altered. C6 is identical, word for word, with B5. I will reserve commentary on this resolution for the next section of this chapter, on economic life.

36. DO: *beginselen*.

37. C7: The change from Bavinck's term "principles" to the congress's "ordinances" may or may not be significant. The term *beginselen* (principles) was a Kuyperian code word, and the congress may have been signaling a subtle distancing from Kuyper (see Bolt, "Herman Bavinck's Contribution to Christian Social Consciousness," 429–30). However, the term *ordinantiën* was also a Kuyperian and neo-Calvinist favorite; see, e.g., W. Geesink's three-volume work on ethics, *Van 's Heeren Ordinantiën*. What is significant is the verb change from "civil authority . . . has an obligation *to test* [*toetsen*] this justice and *to base* it on the eternal principles laid down in Scripture" to "has an obligation *to base* this justice on and *deduce it from* [*af te leiden*] the eternal ordinances [*ordinantiën*] laid down in Scripture." Both formulations raise questions about whether the state has a task in exploring and investigating Scripture, but Bavinck's formulation seems more circumspect. It must be remembered that the "eternal principles" (or "ordinances") considered here are givens of *creation*. In his introductory remarks at the plenary session where this report was discussed, Bavinck clarifies his own position with this comment: "As God's servant, it is the state in particular that has been given the calling by God, first to

The final resolution is a reminder that "ye have the poor always with you" (Matt. 26:11 KJV).

B7: There remains, in addition to this, a very large role for the ministry of mercy since all kinds of miseries will always be with us and can never be removed by justice [alone].	C8: There remains, in addition to this, a very large role for the ministry of mercy since, **thanks to the working of sin and error,** all kinds of miseries will always be with us, and **in this earthly dwelling** can never be removed by justice [alone].[38]

b. Bavinck's "On Inequality" (1913)[39]

Two decades after his presentation to the Social Congress, Bavinck once again addressed the question of inequality, but now in a more philosophical manner. The triggering impulse for this essay is not so much the "social question," with its concern about the poverty and misery of the working class (though this is not absent), as it is the spiritual, moral, and social chaos of the modern world leading up to World War I. Here is how Bavinck describes it:

If in these busy, stressful times we look beyond ourselves at world events, we are constantly deluged by an overwhelming mass of incidents that are impossible to categorize or understand. And when we look inside ourselves, we see a restless sea of impressions, emotions, and moods, and we feel like a ship that is tossed to and fro. Sometimes in the vast restlessness of existing reality, we see things that weary us because of a certain monotony, but we also encounter things that move us and even bewilder us by their impenetrable mystery.

---

determine [deduce; *af te leiden*], from God's ordinances in nature and in Scripture, what justice [*recht*] is, and then to make it sovereign in every area that is its proper domain and to maintain it" (*Proces-Verbaal*, 83–84). It is fair to conclude, therefore, that Bavinck had in mind using Scripture as a testing rod in tandem with natural law and the traditions of human experience. If we think of Christian persons in offices of civil authority rather than of a hypostasized state as a single entity, it is not inappropriate to ask such persons to consider the scriptural understanding of human nature and human destiny when weighing a particular policy decision. That seems to follow from B5 and C6.

38. C8: Here the congress's insertions are helpful as a reminder that there is no metaphysical inevitability to the reality of poverty and misery. Sin, and especially the consequences of sin, *can* be ameliorated and overcome, never perfectly or completely but still in definite and measurable ways. The formulation carefully avoids locating the sin and error; by leaving it general (and universal) it implicitly repudiates efforts to pin blame on a specific group or class or to exonerate others. Sin is here and will remain here until the consummation—we are all sinners, we all need mercy, and we all must show mercy.

39. "On Inequality" (*ERSS*, 145–63) was originally published as "Over de Ongelijkheid" in *Stemmen des Tijds* 2 (1913): 17–43, and reprinted in Herman Bavinck, *Verzamelde Opstellen*, 151–71.

In both instances, questions arise: What accounts for such infinite variety and endless diversity in this one, vast universe? Might it be possible that this endless variety can be reduced to, or is derived from, one single source that might quiet our souls? (*ERSS*, 145)

This endless variety does evoke aesthetic delight since there is beauty in diversity. But seeing only beauty in diversity is superficial:

But this variety also hides a great many contradictions, for diversity is a pseudonym for a mysterious struggle between clashing powers. Just as nature has its days and nights, its summers and winters, so humanity faces good and evil, truth and falsehood, beauty and disgrace. (*ERSS*, 145)

Bavinck then proceeds to the biblical account of the fall and the divinely appointed enmity between the seed of the woman and the seed of the serpent. The evidence for the fallenness of the world is obvious to all:

We recognize this all around. There is no peace or harmony anywhere; instead, dissonance and struggle are everywhere. People, social classes, nations, political parties, and interests have clashed throughout the centuries, while inside each person the head and the heart, flesh and spirit, duty and desire, conscience and lust are constantly at war with each other. Is it perhaps possible that all these harrowing contrasts can be reconciled and brought together in a nobler synthesis that might satisfy us in our day and eventually conquer and destroy them? (*ERSS*, 146)

Speaking of this as "an all-encompassing problem," Bavinck reduces all the efforts to bring about reconciliation to two basic types that "especially have become prominent": *monism* and *pluralism*.

[There are,] on the one hand, the pantheistic or monistic systems that have tried to reduce variety to an appearance of reality with the slogan "variety is basically one reality." Thus they treat variety either as modification of a single reality, or they see it merely as man's imagination, which does not correspond to any objective reality. These are the views of the Greek Eleatic[40] and Stoic schools of thought that, overlooking gnosticism and Neoplatonism, have become part of the more recent philosophy of Spinoza, Hegel, and Spencer. They

40. Ed. note: The Greek pre-Socratic philosophical Eleatic school (at Elea, a Greek colony in Lucania, Italy) began with Parmenides (sixth to fifth century BC), the great philosopher of "being" who taught that everything is fundamentally "one."

may even have found a more consistent voice in the philosophy of Buddhism, which views the entire world as maya, the representation of the one, unknowable and unutterable It. (*ERSS*, 146)

By way of contrast, the pluralistic visions of ancient pagan polytheism and polydaemonism have also remarkably resurfaced in the modern era:

On the other hand, there are also the pluralistic systems that despair of ever finding one single reality and that do not go beyond accepting an original multitude of gods or spirits, of powers or matter. [This vision also] holds true for the dualism of the Persians and Manichaeans, for the theosophical distinction of the dark and bright aspects of God. And it is remarkable that they have reappeared more recently in this form as a reaction to monism. Not only is the pluralism of William James proof of this, but also the dualistic representation of a morally good God next to the mysterious power of nature and the even more prominent superstition and magic that increasingly spreads to our centers of culture. (*ERSS*, 146)

If these two answers are the basic options by which "religious and philosophic systems have approached the gripping problem of unity and multiformity," then, so Bavinck observes, "it is quite remarkable that in our day, more so than ever before, this idea of diversity has become a *practical* problem. The great diversity in our world is seen by many people today, especially in the social realm, as inequality" (*ERSS*, 146).

As in his 1891 paper for the First Christian Social Congress, Bavinck treats the social question of inequality as a subset of the larger metaphysical question of unity and diversity, "the one and the many." Taking his cue from the June 28, 1912, two-hundredth-anniversary birthday celebration of Jean-Jacques Rousseau, he gives the Genevan thinker the credit (or blame) for linking social misery to conditions of inequality. Bavinck traces the development of Rousseau's thought and his eventual adoption of the ideals of natural simplicity along with a profound critique of culture. Bavinck notes that although it may be too much to call this change in Rousseau "a religious conversion,"[41] nonetheless,

41. Ed. note: The following note is an enhanced and corrected version of Bavinck's original note (see *ERSS*, 148n7). Bav. note: Cf. John Viénot, cited by Gaston Riou, "Un sermon sur Jean-Jacques [Rousseau]," *Foi et Vie* 15, no. 13 (July 1, 1912): 399. But Paul Doumergue, who for the rest praises Rousseau's spirituality, observes correctly that the gospel was a law for him and that Rousseau, who considered sin only a human weakness, did not see the need for Christ as Savior and that therefore Rousseau's Christianity lacked precisely . . . a conversion (Doumergue, "Jean-Jacques Rousseau: Ce qu'était sa religion; ce que fut son christianisme," *Foi et Vie* 15,

it certainly was a remarkable and extremely important change. One could almost say that it inaugurated a new era. And it ran much deeper and was much more radical than one might have expected of a man like Rousseau. It started in his head, but then penetrated his heart and brought about a transformation of his entire life. From then on he abandoned the world, its praise, its pomp, and its honors and became even more than before a lover of solitude, a loner. He broke with society, with friends, and also with the philosophers of the day, those ardent missionaries of atheism. He cleansed his heart of greed and created for himself a different, moral world. Until then he had been a good person; now he became a virtuous person or at the least intoxicated by virtue. (*ERSS*, 148–49)

The great change that Rousseau experienced at that time, though in a way somewhat related to his former life, consisted in his sudden renunciation of the corrupt culture of his day and his return to the simplicity and truth of nature. (*ERSS*, 149)

Rousseau's return to nature was accompanied by his turn inward:

Until then he had lived at odds with himself and his surroundings. But now he rediscovered himself and nature at the same time, and he found the two to be in deep harmony. The language of his soul and of nature were one. Until that moment both had been buried in his thinking under the results of a rationalized reason and a corrupt culture. But now Rousseau had discovered both in their originality and truth and in their simplicity and beauty. And thus they became for him something different and much more meaningful: nature without and his soul within now set free from the unnatural trappings imposed on them by reason and culture, suddenly turned into revelations of one and the same God: a God who is pure goodness and from whose hands nothing evil can come. (*ERSS*, 150–51)

From this came the proposition that has guided revolutionary thought ever since:

The multitude of wrongs and all the misery in our world can only find their origin in society and the culture it has created. . . . The prime reason for evil is inequality and . . . it gradually produced wealth, luxury, idleness, and also the arts and sciences. (*ERSS*, 151)

---

no. 14 [July 16, 1912]: 419). Ed. note: To clarify, the article by Gaston Riou is the presentation of a sermon on Rousseau by John Viénot (1859–1933), a French Lutheran pastor and professor of church history at the Protestant Faculty of Theology in Paris. Doumergue's assessment is part of the longest section of his article, pp. 414–19.

Though Rousseau himself was not a revolutionary nor a communist or so-
cialist, "his teachings were thoroughly revolutionary." Rousseau's *The Social
Contract* and the 1789 French *Declaration of the Rights of Man and the
Citizen* were cut from the same cloth, although there were differences:

> Nevertheless, the basic thought in both is that man should abandon society as
> it has developed historically, with its differences and inequalities, and return to
> nature and its original rights. (*ERSS*, 151)

The influence of Rousseau's spirit has been lasting:

> Especially his idea of the injustice of social inequality has become deeply rooted
> in the hearts of men and has found wide acceptance. (*ERSS*, 154)

Bavinck then returns to the questions with which he began this essay:
"What accounts for such infinite variety and endless diversity in this one, vast
universe? Might it be possible that this endless variety can be reduced to, or is
derived from, one single source that might quiet our souls?" (*ERSS*, 145). This
time, however, he points to a different duality than the philosophical notions
of monism and pluralism he used earlier. Now he employs spatial imagery:
"from above" and "from below." This is a further refinement of the earlier
distinction because Bavinck judges that the opposition to social inequality
from above (he has in mind the world of ideas, theories and philosophies)
can be either pantheist (monist) or materialist (pluralist):

> This inequality is hard pressed in our day by opposition from two sides. On
> the one hand, it is attacked as though from above by the evolutionist mindset,
> which may be either pantheistically or materialistically colored. This mindset
> governs scientific thinking, either consciously or unconsciously, and tries hard
> to destroy all basic differences. The destruction concerns, first, the difference
> between God and the world but also the differences between man and ani-
> mal, soul and body, truth and lie, good and evil, Christianity and paganism,
> and so forth.

Bavinck uses the spatial imagery "from below," in contrast to the world of ideas
and philosophies, to describe revolutionary social and political movements:[42]

---

42. Ed. note: Of course, as Bavinck himself notes, this distinction is not a separation; it
does not deny the importance of thinkers like Rousseau and Marx in inspiring and shaping
revolutionary movements.

On the other hand, differences are attacked as though from below, by all those modern movements that seek to obliterate the difference between husband and wife, parents and children, the government and the governed, rich and poor, and so forth. Both movements are undoubtedly related, and it would not make much sense to fight against pantheism and materialism in the realm of thought while supporting socialistic or communistic emancipation in the realm of trade. (*ERSS*, 155)

Bavinck's critique of Rousseau's revolutionary ideas is indirect rather than straight-on. He appeals to that other "citizen of Geneva"—John Calvin— and his decidedly different vision. In so doing, Bavinck takes his cue from Rousseau himself:

Nevertheless, Rousseau, in spite of himself, acknowledges the greatness and superiority of Calvin. In the dedication of his *Discourse on Inequality*, which he offered to the "magnificent, much-honored rulers of Geneva," he states that he is happy he was born in Geneva, where equality and inequality are so well aligned. (*ERSS*, 159)[43]

If Rousseau is to be believed, notes Bavinck, then "the example of Geneva proves that Calvin's religious philosophy of life, when applied, also contains a promise for today's society" (*ERSS*, 161). Moreover, if one takes "Calvin's religious philosophy" seriously as an effective motivation of social reformation, then Rousseau's vision, which is the contradiction of Calvin's, will not effectively transform the social order for the better. Both were concerned with the problem of inequality, but what is the key difference between Calvin and Rousseau?

[For Calvin] it was not political and social inequality that struck him first of all, but religious inequality. When human nature in all men is equally polluted, how does one explain the profound and ever-continuing difference between those who accept the gospel and those who are lost? For Calvin and all the Reformers, this was the central and all-important difference that superseded all other differences because it was everlasting. And in answering this question, Calvin

43. Rousseau's most complimentary statement about Calvin is found in his *Social Contract* (book II, chapter 7, note), and it is a tribute to Calvin's social and political influence on Geneva: "Those who know Calvin only as a theologian much underestimate the extent of his genius. The codification of our wise edicts, in which he played a large part, does him no less honor than his *Institute*. Whatever revolution time may bring in our religion, so long as the spirit of patriotism and liberty still lives among us, the memory of this great man will be forever blessed" (Rousseau, *The Social Contract and Discourses*, 39n1).

saw behind all culture and nature the good pleasure of God, his sovereign and omnipotent free will as the ultimate and deepest cause. He did this in the company of Luther and Zwingli, while following the footsteps of Augustine and guided by Paul, disregarding culture and nature. . . . God's preordaining was the final, most profound cause of all differences among creatures, such as kind, gender, gifts, and in all that is [zijn] and is just so [zóó-zijn]. It is neither the free will of man, nor merit and worth, nor culture, nor even nature that is the source of all multiplicity in creation, but God's almighty and all-powerful will, which at the same time is wise and holy, though inscrutable and inexplicable. Culture, nurture, or free will is not the cause, for the fundamental differences precede these and are already present in nature. Nature is not the cause either, for it did not come into being and does not exist on its own but is carried by the word of God's power from its beginning and always. By his will all things are and have been created. (ERSS, 156)

Bavinck is acutely aware that such a conviction is demanding and not easy; it is, he says, a "confession which only a strong generation can accept." Through it, "Calvin taught his followers first of all acceptance, submission, and contentment in times of struggle and oppression." He wryly adds:

However, few people today will thank him for it. Sowing discontent and systematically goading people to be hostile toward all prevailing conditions and arrangements are held in much higher esteem by many. Rousseau is their great example, for he is the one who, blaming everything on society and culture, made people proud and rebellious, but he also caused them an endless series of disappointments, for revolution that runs counter to nature is a sword that always turns against the one brandishing it. "You can drive nature out with a pitchfork, but it always comes back."[44] (ERSS, 156)

Bavinck wants his readers to understand that this doctrine—"acceptance, submission, and contentment in times of struggle and oppression"—is not coldly fatalistic but a warm comfort:

Still, acquiescence is not nearly the only and most important thing that Calvin impressed on his faithful followers. The will of God, according to Calvin's

---

44. LO: *Naturam expellas furca, tamen usque recurret.* Ed. note: Bavinck cites no source for this saying, but it is from Horace, *Epistles* I.x.24 (LCL 194:316–17); the full quote is, *Naturam expellas furca, tamen usque recurret, et mala perrumpet furtim fastidia victrix* (You may drive out Nature with a pitchfork, yet she will ever hurry back, and ere you know it, will burst through your foolish contempt in triumph).

confession, may be absolutely sovereign, totally all-powerful, and inscrutable and therefore to be acknowledged with holy awe and deep reverence; yet it is for everyone who believes the will of a merciful and gracious Father, who loves all his children with an eternal love; his will may be hidden, but he always has wise and holy reasons for all the dark ways in which he often leads them. Such a will is not fate, in which a person acquiesces willy-nilly, but an object of childlike trust, an inexhaustible fountain of comfort, and the strong anchor of a firm and solid hope. (*ERSS*, 157)

Bavinck frames this in terms of God's fatherly love in Christ:

Remember that in spite of—no, in keeping with—the teaching of predestination, the abundant grace of God in Christ constitutes the heart and soul of Calvin's *Institutes*. For him this was the essence of Christianity, through which God tells us how much he loves us. He saw the will of God revealed in all things. Even in the iniquities of mankind. But basically and in essence this will is the saving grace that leads the world and mankind through the darkness to the light and through death to eternal life. . . . This comfort was unknown to Rousseau, but Calvin made it known to the Christians of his day for their comfort and assurance. Through the preaching of God's holy and gracious will, Calvin furnished faith, heroism, and inspiration to the least and simplest, to those persecuted for the sake of the gospel, to prisoners in their jails, to martyrs on scaffold and pyre, making them scorn all suffering and glory in oppression. (*ERSS*, 157)

This message remains relevant in the modern world's social and political upheavals:

And this comfort we need just as much in our day. For nothing is easier than to join Rousseau in sowing discontent in the hearts of men and to make them rebel against their own fate and society at large. (*ERSS*, 157)

Sowing revolutionary discontent is not an innocent pastime; Bavinck quotes Conrad Busken Huet about the dangers: "The danger is even great for us . . . that out of fear for the little man, we become flatterers of the people and courtiers of that which is common."[45] This results in terrible social and ecological damage:

But fundamentally such flattery is cruel, like offering a stone and a serpent to someone who prays for a loaf of bread or a fish. For when a person loses his

45. *ERSS*, 157; Bav. note: Conrad Busken Huet, *Het land van Rembrandt: Studiën over de Noordnederlandsche beschaving in de zeventiende eeuw*, 2:2, 139.

faith in a higher, better world, life here on earth begins to look more and more like a jail against whose walls he butts his head senselessly.[46] (*ERSS*, 157)

Bavinck also notes another major difference between Calvin and Rousseau: the latter "in the end . . . quietly withdrew into seclusion without moving a finger to reform society." The difference between that posture and Calvin's is enormous: "Calvin, on the other hand, derived from the same will of God which he had come to know in Christ as a will of grace, the motive for strong energetic and far-reaching actions." Acknowledging that there had been times in the history of Reformed churches when the doctrine of predestination was misunderstood and abused, Bavinck sums up the difference between Calvin and Rousseau:

If we steadfastly believe that the *will* of God is the cause of all things, then our reverence for that same will, which has been revealed in Scripture as the rule for our lives, must compel us to promote its dominion everywhere and as far as our influence reaches.

If you believe, with Rousseau, that society is the cause of all evil, then you have pronounced its death sentence: you have given man the right to execute people, and you have legitimized the Revolution. But if you believe with Calvin that the will of God, his will of good pleasure, is the cause of all things, then that will becomes his revealed will and the moving force and rule for our living. The words "Your will be done" encompass not only strength to acquiesce but also strength to act. (*ERSS*, 157)

From his comparison of Calvin and Rousseau, Bavinck draws a number of conclusions for his own day (and ours):

1. Christians have been given norms for their understanding of social life and do well to look to historical examples (such as Calvin) for guidance. Scripture and history teach us.
2. Christians should not confront the modern age only antithetically, "for it is governed by the same will of the heavenly Father who has assigned us a place to live and work." This means avoiding the simplistic and revolutionary condemnations of society found in Rousseau and his followers. There is much in the modern world for which we ought to be grateful; while

---

46. Bavinck's language reminds one of Max Weber's notion of "an iron cage," although Weber did not have revolutionary zeal in mind but the increasing rationalization and bureaucratization of modern life.

> we deplore the want and misery that people endure, when we consider the
> struggle of mankind against nature, and besides that the helplessness, weak-
> ness and depravity of so many individuals, we are amazed that there is not more
> suffering. . . . It is a greater miracle that the great majority of those huge masses
> of people receive their daily bread, rather than that many are not provided for
> regularly and suffer want. (*ERSS*, 162)

3. We must be grateful for the providential blessings that are ours, but the "social question" will not disappear, also because it is a spiritual problem that "is not susceptible to be solved by social legislation." Two things are required of Christians: informed action and sacrificial generosity:

   a. Informed action:

   > Serious study is required, both of the principles that are to serve us as a
   > guide and of the extremely complicated circumstances in which we live.

   b. Sacrificial generosity:

   > At any rate, we face a future in which the wealthy, in fact all the wealthy and
   > all who are endowed with many worldly goods and much property, will be
   > asked to demonstrate a much greater measure of self-denial and devotion
   > than in previous centuries. Riches, both spiritual and material, will become
   > much less a privilege to be enjoyed entirely for our own pleasure and only
   > for self. The apostle Paul's word calling all the members of the body to care
   > for each other with equal concern will assume more and more the character
   > of a duty.[47] (*ERSS*, 163)

That final point serves as a good segue to the next topic.

2. ECONOMIC LIFE: OWNERSHIP, PROPERTY, POSSESSIONS

As I briefly noted in the previous section, Bavinck's understanding that the gospel of the kingdom did not displace the natural and social relationships but left them intact was also applied to the institution of private property. Aware that this would be contested and that the practice of the early church described in Acts 2–4 would be a key argument against his position, he tackles it head-on:

> On the basis of Acts 2:44–45 and 4:32, 34, many have assumed that in this
> congregation people had all things in common. But a careful reading shows

---

47. Ed. note: The clauses in this sentence have been reversed from the original Dutch, and the English translation in *ERSS* has been slightly altered for the sake of greater clarity.

that this assumption is untenable. After all, the context in which these words appear clearly indicates that they intend to depict the harmony, the mutual love, and the willingness to sacrifice for one another in the first church. (*ERSS*, 134)

Bavinck contends that these passages do not furnish some kind of prescriptive model for abolishing private possessions but describe a disposition among members of the early church community, a sacrificial attitude in which one's possessions were held lightly and readily given to those in need.

In Acts 2:44 and 4:32, the words "They had all things in common" therefore do not imply that private ownership had been abolished and all possessions given to the church; they only intend to say that all members of the congregation considered their own property to belong to all; this is how ready they were to share and thus to help others. This is proved rather powerfully by the fact that some went further: they sold their property and gave the money to the apostles. (*ERSS*, 134)

Bavinck then puts these verses in context by noting three important qualifications to the gifts of those who "went further" in the early church:

First of all, this was a completely free, voluntary act (Acts 5:4); second, it was an exception through which Ananias and Sapphira sought to distinguish themselves; and, third, such an act is mentioned as something unusual (Acts 4:36–37), which definitely was not imitated by [many others]; according to Acts 12:12, Mary had a house of her own. The purpose of the generous sharing practice in the first church was therefore by no means intended to establish a community of goods, but only to take care of the poor. The money gathered by the sale of goods was not divided evenly among the members of the congregation, but it was used exclusively for the support of the needy. (*ERSS*, 135)

We now return to Resolution B5/C6 of the First Christian Social Congress.

B5/C6: Therefore, it is entirely in keeping with Holy Scripture to
   a. not only prepare people for their eternal destiny, but also to make it possible for them to fulfill their earthly calling;
   b. in the political arena, uphold the institution of the Sabbath alongside the workweek so as to maintain the unity and distinction of our double calling;
   c. guide all our life's relationships in a new way and restore them to their original shape by the same cross of Christ that proclaims our reconciliation with God. This has special relevance for the social arena, where [we should seek to]

- prevent poverty and misery, especially pauperization;
- oppose the accumulation of capital and landed property;
- ensure, as much as possible, a "living wage" for every person.[48]

This proposition, especially point *c* and its three bulleted points, was the defining and most debated one at the congress. Considering the built-up passion for the social question that was present everywhere in the second half of the nineteenth century and had given rise to the congress, this proposition is remarkable for its careful balance and nuance. An appeal to our dual calling—preparing for our eternal destiny and fulfilling our earthly duties—is never an excuse for indifference to such miseries as poverty; as redeemed imaged bearers of God, we are propelled by our eternal destiny to earthly love and obedience, to restructuring our life's relationships in accord with the cross, to self-denying, self-sacrificing love for our neighbor in need. Bavinck does not leave this as an abstract principle; three controversial imperatives follow from our cruciform life: preventing pauperization and accumulation of capital and landed property on the one side, and on the positive side, ensuring as much as possible a living wage for every person.

The article about a "living wage" generated a lively discussion at the congress. One delegate requested further elaboration on what constituted a living wage, especially because this was a favorite slogan of socialists.[49] In particular, the expression *menschwaardig bestaan* (lit., "existence worthy of one's humanity") is ambiguous; for one thing, it is not the same as a basic human need (e.g., food, drink, clothing, shelter); for another, "worthy" suggests a deserving that none of us enjoys as sinners.[50] In his response, Bavinck acknowledges that the origin of the notion is indeed from the socialist camp. "In spite of this, the expression is still *good*" (original emphasis). Bavinck indicates that he is not satisfied with merely the basics of survival:

The Fall did not turn the human person into an animal; he retains a measure of humanity and this gives him a right to an existence that is commensurate and worthy of his humanity.[51]

---

48. The exposition that follows is very dependent on Bolt, "Herman Bavinck's Contribution to Christian Social Consciousness," 432–36.

49. *Proces-Verbaal*, 364; the quotations that follow are from pp. 359–71. The question, it is worth noting, came from Willem Geesink (1854–1929), professor of ethics at the Free University of Amsterdam from 1890 to 1926.

50. *Proces-Verbaal*, 364; this objection was also raised by Prof. Geesink: "Holy Scripture never uses the words 'human' [*mensch*] and 'worthy' [*waardig*] in the same breath but teaches that human beings through sin have forfeited [*verbeurd*] everything."

51. *Proces-Verbaal*, 366.

Bavinck is unwilling, however, to get drawn into a debate about the details. The notion of "a worthy existence" includes a measure of relativity that is not unrelated to social class; different people have different needs:

A king on his throne who has only rye bread[52] available to him can be said to have a "less than worthy existence" no less than a poor laborer who gorges himself with steak and wine.[53]

Bavinck refuses to draw precise lines or establish formulas here but suggests that we are capable intuitively of sensing what is humanly unworthy. His own example is factory workers who never receive a day of rest (see B5/C6, *b*) but are treated as extensions of the machines they operate.

When we see people in our factories who have to work day and night and never get rest, who are treated worse than machines, then we sense immediately that this is no life for someone who is created in the image of God.[54]

He concludes:

All we can say is that every person, including the laborer, has a right to an existence before God, receiving sufficient food and drink to remain a full human being.[55]

It is interesting to note Bavinck's response during the discussion to three specific policy proposals: state-mandated just wages and salaries; progressive income tax; and nationalization of property, particularly land.

a. *State-mandated wages and salaries*. Under discussion was a specific proposal that the state mandate a just wage for all vocations according to their quality so that a workman's wages would be sufficient to meet the needs of a family with four to five children. Bavinck objects to the proposal on two grounds:

---

52. DO: *roggebrood*.

53. *Proces-Verbaal*, 366. In the charming fashion of proceedings during this era, an editorial insertion indicates that this comment was received with laughter and applause. Bavinck made a similar point in his discussion of the Eighth Commandment: "We are allowed to pray for wealth—that is, wealth taken in the sense of what is needed for one's sustenance, which is different for a king than for a subject" (*RE*, 2:391).

54. *Proces-Verbaal*, 366.

55. *Proces-Verbaal*, 366.

i. "It is impossible to establish a just wage on the basis of quality."[56]

ii. "Even if an objective standard for (i) was achieved, it could not be reconciled with the additional subjective condition of satisfying the needs of a family with four or five children."[57]

The proposal therefore is self-contradictory:

We have arrived at a double standard for a "just wage": an objective standard based on the value of the labor and a subjective standard based on the needs of the family. These two factors cancel each other out.[58]

b. *Progressive income tax.* Bavinck was asked the question whether a progressive income tax did not meet the concern of B5/C6, *c*, "to oppose the accumulation of capital and landed property." Bavinck's answer was a decisive "No!": "The movement to establish a progressive income tax as a way of preventing the accumulation of capital and letting the state—which can never be satisfied—gobble up all private wealth and property can never meet with our approval and must be opposed."[59]

c. *Nationalizing property and land.* Bavinck makes the same point in response to a specific question about the nationalization of property, particularly land. His answer is short: "I am opposed to nationalizing land because it precisely represents that greatest accumulation of property and capital by the state and conflicts directly with the right of ownership and private property."[60]

For more on property and possessions, see Bavinck's discussion of the Eighth Commandment (*RE*, 2:458–60 [§47]) and the Tenth Commandment (*RE*, 2:463–66 [§49]).

A Note on Riches, Capitalism, and Usury

Bavinck's most explicit (and critical) comments on riches, money, capitalism, and usury are found in the conclusion of his essay "The Imitation of

56. *Proces-Verbaal*, 367. Bavinck's example, which also led to laughter, was taken from the realm of science: "One person with the least effort produces the purest and clearest thought, while a dullard who labors for a week and produces barely a single thought—how does the state establish a proper scale for a just wage?"

57. *Proces-Verbaal*, 367.

58. *Proces-Verbaal*, 367.

59. *Proces-Verbaal*, 366.

60. *Proces-Verbaal*, 366–67.

Christ and Life in the Modern World,"[61] published in 1918, the same year that World War I came to an end. His fundamental principle: Christians must use and not abuse these gifts; the problem lies not in the material "stuff" but in the fallen human heart:

The teaching of Scripture that those who desire riches "fall into temptation, in a snare, into many senseless and hurtful desires, that plunge men into ruin and destruction" remains true. Our materialistic age confirms and seals the truth of this pronouncement. And yet, on the other hand, it is not the gold or silver, ownership or capital in itself that is sinful any more than science, art, the civil order, or even war, in itself is evil. Sin is rooted in the heart of man, and the struggle against sin is in the first place a struggle against self. What then do Christians hope to accomplish in their struggle against the world if they have not liberated themselves from the spiritual domination of all things?

This does not mean ascetic withdrawal; here the biblical principle "in the world, but not of the world" applies:

It is much easier to curse capital, to condemn war, and to reject all culture than it is to walk in all these areas as a child of God and a follower of Christ. And yet, it is precisely this that is required of us if we wish to remain standing in the struggle and to overcome the opponent as the early church did.

Then follows one of Bavinck's most explicit condemnations of economic sins in a statement that links orthodoxy with orthopraxis:

Even the most stringent orthodoxy cannot make good the sins of smuggling, usury, dishonesty and deception in business, or of social and political unrighteousness. Whoever confesses Christ must distance himself from all unrighteousness. Blessed are the pure in heart for they shall see God.

Bavinck is well aware that this understanding of Christian discipleship is demanding and difficult:

Even here it is difficult to distinguish the sin that must be hated from the sinner who must be loved, and it requires a costly act of self-denial and struggle to remain faithful in the small and great things and to keep oneself undefiled from the world. To mention but one example, think of modern capitalism, which

---

61. "Imitation II"; the passages that follow are from pp. 439–40.

is characterized, according to Sombart, by its total subjection of man to the corporation, a subjection that knows no standard, boundary or limit.

On the specific question of usury, Bavinck uses Calvin's position on usury to illustrate the universality and catholicity of his ethics. I cite the passage in full here because it also reveals important principles for how we should use Scripture in ethical reflection. Intentionally, Bavinck chooses to be on the same page as Calvin:

In order to prove this by one striking example attention may be called to the fact that medieval ethics consistently disapproved the principle of usury[62] on the ground of its being forbidden by Scripture and contrary to the unproductive nature of money. Accordingly, it looked with contempt upon trade and commerce. Luther, Melanchthon, Zwingli, and Erasmus adhered to this view, but Calvin, when this important problem had been submitted to him, formulated in a classic document the grounds on which it could be affirmed that a reasonable interest is neither in conflict with Scripture nor with the nature of money.[63]

A key principle for Calvin and Bavinck is their sense that ethical guidance for living in a God-honoring way should not be taken solely from Scripture and its laws without an accompanying consideration of the world in which God's laws are also to be found and applied.

He took into account the law of life under which commerce operates and declared that only the sins of commerce are to be frowned upon, whereas commerce itself is to be regarded as a calling well-pleasing to God and profitable to society.[64] And this merely illustrates the point of view from which Calvin habitually approached the problems of life. He found the will of God revealed not merely in Scripture, but also in the world, and he traced the connection and sought to restore the harmony between them.[65]

What Bavinck learned from Calvin was the important distinction between *nature as created* and *sinful nature*. Grace does not oppose nature but only sin.

Under the guidance of the divine Word he distinguished everywhere between the institution of God and human corruption, and then sought to establish and

---

62. Bav. note: "Usury" is here meant in the old sense of the taking of reasonable interest.
63. Bavinck, "Calvin and Common Grace," 128.
64. Bavinck provides the following as source for this reading of Calvin: *Commentary on Isaiah*, 23:13; *Commentary on Psalms*, 15:5; *Commentary on 1 Corinthians*, 7:20.
65. Bavinck, "Calvin and Common Grace," 128.

restore everything in harmony with the divine nature and law. Nothing is unclean in itself; every part of the world and every calling in life is a revelation of the divine perfections, so that even the humblest day-laborer fulfills a divine calling.[66]

3. HOSPITALITY, FRIENDSHIP, SOCIABILITY[67]

Hospitality, friendship, and sociability are familial virtues reaching out beyond the narrower confines of family life.[68] They are bridges from the family to society at large:

By the mutual relations both of families and individuals, wider circles of social intercourse are formed, among which may first be named that of *hospitality*. In its widest signification, hospitality is a form of sympathetic relation to other men, by which we open to them our house, our family circle, and let outsiders share the advantage of our own family life. Guests are not members of the family but are as visitors, admitted to the enjoyment of all the house affords. The proper and original meaning of the word hospitality (φιλοξενία) is the virtue thereby denoted as exercised towards strangers. (71, §36)

Holy Scripture encourages hospitality:

Hospitality is expressly inculcated in the New Testament. "Forget not to be hospitable, for thereby some have entertained angels unawares" (Heb. 13:2). The apostle is alluding to those patriarchal times, when angels visited Abraham under the oak at Mamre. . . . And the saying of the apostle still finds

---

66. Bavinck, "Calvin and Common Grace," 128–29.

67. As I noted above (see n. 4), Bavinck's topics in this section, including the order "Hospitality—Friendship—Sociability" (*Gastfreiheit. Freundschaft. Geselligkeit*), are taken directly from Martensen, *Christian Ethics, Special Part*, 2/2:71–82 (§§36–38). Since I include here material from *RE*, 2:44–48, where Bavinck directly engages Martensen's views on the ethical category of adiaphora (the permissible), and since Bavinck left no specific outline for this section beyond the three points of the subheading, I do more here than simply excerpt Bavinck's own writings: I construct an argument *in the style of Bavinck* using text from Martensen. This entire section is thus largely a construction by the editor; nonetheless, I am incorporating the Martensen material as if it were being used by Bavinck to make his case. Therefore, the same distinction between my narrative framing material in one typeface, and the Bavinck/Martensen material in the alternative typeface, is also used here. Specific references to Martensen's *Christian Ethics*, *Special Part* 2/2, will be given by page number and section (§) in the text.

68. This set of three together serves as the concluding section of "The Family," the opening chapter of Martensen's social ethics. Again, I note the parallel with Bavinck's own outline of *Reformed Ethics*, book IV; see n. 4, above.

its application. . . . In commending hospitality, we cannot fail to refer to that profound utterance of our Lord: "I was a stranger and ye took me in" (Matt. 25:35). (72, §36)

Friendship is a further extension of home and family life:

The exercise of hospitality is exclusively connected with the home, with the family. *Friendship*, however, considered in itself, is not necessarily connected therewith, but may also be independent of it. Friendship is a union between individuals for mutual help and strength, a union not founded on respect alone, but chiefly on sympathy. . . . A man may fitly have several friends. But genuine friendship is always a mutual personal appreciation and mutual relation of trust and faithfulness, in which one depends upon another, and is fully certain of his devotion and attachment of his interest and readiness to afford personal assistance. Hence, though it is possible to have more than one friend, one cannot, even though we have many acquaintances and are on friendly terms with them, have many friends. (72–73, §37)

There are varieties and different degrees of friendship:

We may feel attracted to a mutual giving and receiving with respect to a person, by one side of his nature, without such a feeling growing into a complete friendship. Genuine friendship, ruling the whole personality, is by no means an ordinary possession. It is always conditioned by a common view of life, a common conviction with respect to what is supreme, and most sacred, but not to the exclusion of differences in details, which may, on the contrary, contribute to promote both intellectual activity and development, as well as mutual interest. (73, §37)

The world of antiquity "offers us many touching examples of true friendship, and its thinkers (Aristotle, Cicero) have made it a subject of observation and investigation" (76, §37). By comparison, how does Holy Scripture fare on the question of friendship?

The Christian revelation has been reproached for giving no precepts concerning friendship. But if the New Testament contains no express precepts on the relation, this is something very different from saying that Christianity leaves no room for it. Nor are typical instances wanting in the New Testament. (76, §37)

Martensen appeals first to the admittedly unique relation between Christ and his disciples, appealing to Jesus's own words in John 15:14–15: "You are my friends if you do what I command you. No longer do I call you servants, for the servant does not know what his master is doing; but I have called you friends, for all that I have heard from my Father I have made known to you." He also refers to

> the disciples in their mutual relation, to Andrew, Peter, Philip and Nathanael, who in their early years were united to each other by their common love for an ideal, which they saw realized in Christ, concerning whom they joined in the confession: "We have found the Messiah" (John 1:41–49). (76, §37)

For the Old Testament, Martensen appeals to what he calls the "typical" friendship of David and Jonathan, adding a reference to Ecclesiasticus 6:16: "A faithful friend is the medicine of life; and they that fear the Lord shall find him" (KJV).

Martensen also points out that

> as a rule, friendships are formed in youth, in those years of transition, when common love for the ideal draws kindred souls together, and unites them in a faith in one and the same future, in common purposes and resolutions. . . . It is to be regarded as a special happiness, when the friendship formed in you is maintained and continued through after years. It more frequently happens that an altered view of life alienates friends from each other in the course of years,[69] that the hope of a lifelong friendship was an illusion, because natures were so different, a fact but gradually perceived, or because characters developed in an entirely opposite direction, and interests and duties were entirely changed. (73–74, §37)[70]

Bavinck would have concurred heartily with Martensen's comments about friendships among women:

> That which is true of male is equally true of female friendships. As a rule, a woman makes friends in her early years, before she becomes a wife and a mother. If she can still retain them after having been, by means of her husband,

---

69. The high mobility of our contemporary life is also a major contributor to loss of youthful friendships.

70. Clarifying the important difference between mere, even if friendly, *acquaintances* and *friends*, Martensen cites the poet Jens Baggesen (in his *Gjengangare*, or the *Revenant*), providing an English translation in the footnote: "For true friendship, it is not enough to have emptied a brotherly glass to each other, to have sat on the same form at school, to have met frequently at the same café, to have conversed courteously in the street, to have sung the same songs at the same club, to have worn the same colours as politicians, to have extolled one another in the press."

of her domestic affairs, transferred to other and quite different interests and views, she may regard her lot as a favoured one. A relation of heartfelt friendship, differing from love, which may be so beneficial in mature age, is in all cases objectionable between young men and women, because it is in their case so difficult to keep within the boundary line between friendship and love. (74, §37)

The reality of friendship points to a distinctive characteristic of good social intercourse or sociability.

Though friendship, as being a purely personal relation, may be developed independently of family life, it yet combines in an unrestrained and natural manner with hospitality: friends are accustomed to meet in social intercourse. What is sought in society is mental refreshment and recreation, by means of mutual communication and conversation. And just because refreshment and amusement are here the main point, social intercourse, so far as it pursues no aim external to itself, nor seeks or originates or effects anything special, must be regarded under an aesthetic point of view. Its yield is to be only the pleasure enjoyed during the hours of personal companionship. Hence it follows that this pleasure is an essential purpose of conversation, a purpose which will, however, assume a special character differing in different circles. (77–78, §38)

Two extremes are to be avoided in conversation:

On the one hand, conversation must not be empty and void of matter, which would render it tedious; still less must it involve what the apostle calls "foolish talking and jesting, which are not convenient," i.e., frivolous jokes; but neither, on the other hand, is it to be pedantic and didactic, as though the question were to work out the whole contents of our thoughts, or to exhaust a subject in a learned lecture, a proceeding which would involve labour and effort, when the intention is to rest from work, and even from mental exertion, not to confine the attention to one subject, but, on the contrary, to set it at liberty and ease. (78, §38)

It is here that Martensen introduces Bavinck's final topic, offense:

Hence conversation must be characterized by unconstrained ease, as well as by a certain generality, so that all may take part in it. Every member of the social circle should contribute to the animation and ennoblement of conversation. To remain silent is a neglect of social duty and may give offense; on the other hand, it is a transgression of social duty, and no less offensive, for any one to monopolize conversation, and transform other guests into mere auditors. When a family and its narrower circle of friends meet, conversation must assume that more kindly and intimate tone which it cannot take among strangers. (78, §38)

Games and Leisure/Amusement[71]

Martensen establishes the following criteria for determining the value of "social amusements":

We have first of all to inquire whether they have aesthetic value; and if this is not denied, they must then be found to be consistent with the rules of morality.

Taking dancing as an example, Martensen concludes:

That *dancing* has its aesthetic value cannot certainly be doubted, and occasionally it may be raised to an art. It proceeds from that lively pleasure which is expressed by easy and graceful movements of the body, in meetings of both sexes.

And what about the morality of dancing?

In an ethic[al] aspect, we remark that there are indeed dances and balls where virtue is danced away, but that, assuming purity and modesty to be maintained, dancing in itself must be considered morally allowable. (79, §38)

On card-playing:

Mere *games of chance*, in which all depends on accident, are in themselves insipid, but may become of very serious interest in a bad sense, and most powerfully excite the passions if money is played for, and comparatively large sums are staked; they are then absolutely immoral. As for ordinary games of cards, in which a mixture of chance and skill takes place, and only trifles are played for, just to give the game a certain appearance of earnestness, Schleiermacher thinks that the individual mental activity is in them so subordinate,

71. The heading "Games and Leisure/Amusement" is an interpretation of Bavinck's singular Dutch term *spel*, based on Martensen, whose concluding topic under "sociability" is an answer to the question "What value is to be attributed to social amusements, such as dancing, card-playing and other so-called social games?" (78, §38). For Martensen's own treatment of adiaphora, see his *Christian Ethics*, *General Part*, 415–23 (§§133–35: "The Obligatory and the Permissible. The Befitting. Ethical Forbearance [Accommodation]"). The reader is also referred to Bavinck's discussion of adiaphora in *RE*, 2:36–60 (§29).

that it must be better in social meetings to do something better, to impart to each other something more profitable, and that card-playing is always a sign of an imperfect and low grade of social life.[72]

Martensen says that he does "not feel called on to contradict this," adding: "But as card-playing cannot be regarded as in itself immoral, we adhere to the view that the question whether this or that person may seek or find amusement in it must be decided on purely individual grounds." He also suggests reasons for introducing card-playing at social gatherings: "In larger parties, cards must often be offered as an assistance, a resource, a kind of refuge for escaping from a conversation in which, for various reasons, we may not desire to join. The best use, perhaps, which can be made of this diversion may be the rest it gives from much talking, or from more serious mental labour" (79, §38).[73]

Unlike Kuyper in his explicit condemnation of the famous troika of "worldly amusements,"[74] Bavinck does not join the tradition that began with Gisbertus Voetius singling out theater, dancing, and card-playing. In his discussion of the ethical category of the so-called adiaphora or things "indifferent" or "permissible,"[75] Bavinck begins with the following claim:

The Old and New Testaments recognize no adiaphora.[76] The requirement is, "You shall love the Lord your God with all your heart," and so forth, and, "Be holy, for I am holy." That is absolute, comprehending our whole life, norming all our actions. Everything must be done to the glory of God, even eating and drinking (1 Cor. 10:31).

Bavinck roots this conviction in the doctrine of creation:

72. Martensen refers to Schleiermacher, *Die christliche Sitte*, 696; Schleiermacher prefers more intellectual games such as chess.

73. From this point on, to the end of this chapter, I will be using Bavinck's own text rather than Martensen's. However, this may include quotations from Martensen.

74. See Kuyper, *Lectures on Calvinism*, 73, where Kuyper argues that there is one exception to the broad Calvinist principle that Christian discipleship does not involve separation *from* the world: "For this very reason the Calvinist cannot shut himself up in his church and abandon the world to its fate. He feels, rather, his high calling to push the development of this world to an even higher stage, and to do this in constant accordance with God's ordinance, for the sake of God, upholding, in the midst of so much painful corruption, everything that is honorable, lovely, and of good report among men." But, Kuyper continues, there is one, and only one exception to this principle: "Not *every* intimate intercourse with the unconverted world is deemed lawful, by Calvinism, for it placed a barrier against the too unhallowed influence of this world by putting a distinct 'veto' upon three things, *card playing*, *theatres*, and *dancing*."

75. The following Bavinck excerpts are taken from *RE*, 2:44–45.

76. Bav. note: Paret, "Adiaphora," 124–25.

Everything created[77] by God is good if received with thanksgiving (1 Tim. 4:4–5). Greeting,[78] marrying—everything must be done "in the Lord." The whole of life is placed under the perspective of the kingdom of God—that is the truth to be found in pietism. Godliness has value for all things (1 Tim. 4:8).

Bavinck honored pietist sensibilities but also cautioned against potential spiritual dangers: "On the other hand, natural things are not to be viewed with fear, but everything created by God is good (1 Tim. 4:4);[79] the spiritual person discerns all things (1 Cor. 2:15)."[80] The key for Bavinck is Christian discernment and liberty:

Much is left to such a person's freedom. One must discern what is excellent (Phil. 1:10),[81] to test all things and hold fast to what is good (1 Thess. 5:21), always discerning what is the good and acceptable and perfect will of God (Rom. 12:2). Such persons must stand fast in their freedom (Gal. 5:1), and not allow themselves to be judged in relation to meat, drink, or Sabbath (Col. 2:16). Although Christians must flee the world, nevertheless Christianity is a life of freedom and delight. All things are yours (1 Cor. 3:22). The earth is the Lord's (1 Cor. 10:26). To the pure all things are pure (Titus 1:15).

Bavinck indicates his difficulty with the very idea of adiaphora in concrete ethical questions:

Protestants, Thomas Aquinas, Robert Bellarmine, and others hold that adiaphora, permissible things, exist only in the abstract. In their concrete form,

---

77. GrO: κτίσμα.

78. DO: *groeten*.

79. Bav. note: God gave Adam something permitted (Gen. 2:16): "You may surely eat of every tree of the garden." That was permitted to Adam, but not commanded.

80. In his *The Certainty of Faith*, Bavinck addresses with great care the need for followers of Jesus spiritually to navigate the biblical tension between affirming the goodness of God's creation and obeying the New Testament teaching to avoid "the world." After acknowledging that the tradition of pietism may have "overestimated and overemphasized the one thing needful, which on the other hand is often lacking in contemporary life," Bavinck sums up the difference in these words:

> While these nineteenth century Christians forgot the world for themselves, we run the danger of losing ourselves in the world. Nowadays we are out to convert the whole world, to conquer all areas of life for Christ. But we often neglect to ask whether we ourselves are truly converted and whether we belong to Christ in life and in death. For this is indeed what life boils down to. We may not banish this question from our personal or church life under the label of pietism or methodism. What does it profit a man if he gain the whole world, even for Christian principles, if he loses his own soul? (*Certainty of Faith*, 94)

81. GrO: τὰ διαφέροντα.

they are always subject to the moral law—though not in themselves, but by intention, goal, and circumstance—and thus cease to be indifferent, but are in fact commanded or forbidden.[82] In their concrete form, therefore, permissible things or indifferent things vanish altogether; the only thing remaining is the law, duty, and moral necessity. Consequently, while for many things it is not possible to determine in advance and in the abstract whether something is good or evil, nevertheless Protestants—for example, Flacius and his followers in opposition to Melanchthon, the Reformed against the Anglicans—still attempted to establish everything concretely and objectively according to the moral law, not leaving it to the individual. Against Rome, therefore, Protestants maintain the absolute validity of the moral law for all people and for all time. Rome argues that, except for what the law prescribes, the individual may choose to do more or less; it is the individual's choice. Protestantism argues that every individual is always directed in the concrete form of action by the moral law.[83]

This means that, to some degree, individuals must often make their own choices, guided by God's law and their conscience. Yet Bavinck takes issue with

Schleiermacher, Rothe, Martensen, and others [who] say that the permissible is definitely not arbitrary, indifferent, or contingent (they regard that as the Protestant position), but neither is it subject to the law, which, after all, cannot regulate everything. The permissible, therefore, can be morally determined only on an individual basis.[84] The more we observe an action in its concrete form, however, the more we are shaped and developed morally; and we will understand our actions all the more to be either commanded or forbidden by the moral law. The realm of the permissible is therefore always decreasing, and its sphere becomes ever narrower.[85]

He raises four objections:

First, this shortchanges the universal law; too much is assigned to subjective individual opinion. Dance, play,[86] theater, and so forth should also be able to be objectively determined as being either good or bad. Thus, here the permissible rests upon a defect in the law.[87]

---

82. LO: *in individuo; per intentionem, finem, circumstantias.*
83. *RE*, 2:51.
84. GO: *nur in individueller Weise sittlich Bestimmbare.*
85. *RE*, 2:52.
86. DO: *spel.*
87. Bav. note: Wuttke, *Christian Ethics*, 2:123 (§82).

Second, if in its individual and concrete form an action is not indifferent yet is presented by the subjective conscience on the basis of the moral law as being good or bad, then it is no longer permitted, but is either prescribed or proscribed.[88]

In the third place, how can it then also be claimed that with continuing moral development, the realm of permissible things decreases? The permissible is what is determined and stipulated by the conscience as being good or bad. Does the decrease in the realm of the permissible mean that the conscience henceforth no longer determines anything as being good or bad? Surely that cannot be. Does it mean, then, that the discipline of ethics will increasingly be able to say objectively about permissible things that they are good or that they are bad?

In the fourth place, to define the realm of the permissible as consisting of "what can be determined on an individual basis"[89] is completely wrong. For either we end up in a terrible subjectivism, or the definition says nothing. With the former, ethics can no longer talk about worship, images of the saints, and the like, about dance, play, theater, and the like, but everything must simply be left to the individual conscience. What is good for one is bad for another, which confuses the concept of Christian freedom. With the latter, the definition says nothing, because the individual always judges in a concrete case whether something is good or evil according to the universal moral law, subsuming that concrete case under that law and then drawing a conclusion.[90]

From the preceding, we must conclude that although Martensen's treatment of the famous threesome of theater, dancing, and card-playing, in which he distinguishes the legitimacy of the acts as such from contexts and uses that are immoral, has affinities with Bavinck's own theological affirmation of creation as good in itself, nonetheless we do find hints that Bavinck might raise objections to these particular forms of play and amusement. At the same time, he does not articulate and defend the traditional proscriptions as Kuyper does. Perhaps the best we can do is to repeat Bavinck's summary of Martensen's understanding of the permissible. Bavinck does not disagree with Martensen's definition but introduces the issue of giving and receiving offense, in a subtle and finally ambiguous way:

Martensen argues that the permissible does not fall outside the ethical but can be determined only on an individual basis. This occurs especially in the

88. DO: *ge- of verboden.*
89. GO: *Erlaubte* is the *nur individuell Bestimmbare.*
90. *RE*, 2:52–53.

aesthetic, "by the definition of the conception of the *Befitting* or *Seemly.*"[91] And then the question "May I go to the theater?" can only be answered by the individual. However, although all things are permitted, not all things are profitable (1 Cor. 6:12). The rule is, Whatever is not of faith is sin (Rom. 14:23). Now since such adiaphora exist, the question arises whether we ought not to abstain from them at times in order not to offend others and whether at other times we should do them in order to win over others.[92]

—————————— APPENDIX A ——————————

"Masters and Servants"[93]

The New Testament contains a number of sayings that indicate how the relationship between masters and their servants ought to be, such as Ephesians 6:5–8:

> Bondservants, obey your earthly masters with fear and trembling, with a sincere heart, as you would Christ, not by the way of eye-service, as people-pleasers, but

---

91. LO: *decorum*; see Martensen, *Christian Ethics*, 1:416 (§134); the quotation from Martensen was added by the editor.

92. *RE*, 2:48. Bav. note: Martensen, *Christian Ethics*, 1:418–20 (§135).

93. Bavinck, "Heeren en knechten," *De Bazuin* 50, no. 19 (May 9, 1902). I have translated the two words in the Dutch title as "masters" and "servants," which requires some explanation. The Dutch word *heer* is the conventional honorific for "man"—i.e., "mister"—but in formal or polite use it is also equivalent to the English "Sir," and in plural address, "gentlemen." The word can also be translated as "lord" and is the translation in Dutch Bibles for the Greek *kyrios* (Lord). In very formal, particularly upper-class British usage, "master" is the functional equivalent of American "mister." Contemporary English readers need to keep in mind the importance of class distinctions in Dutch society of the late nineteenth century. A *dienstknecht* (male servant) or *dienstbode* (girl-servant, maid) was a domestic servant and in a different category than a laborer, whether on a farm or in a factory. It is very well possible that Bavinck is using the word *heeren* in a mildly sarcastic manner, calling attention to the lordly manner of Dutch "lords of the manor" or "lords of industry." To capture this connotation in contemporary terms, readers might be helped by thinking of "Lords and Laborers" as a substitute title and, perhaps, even making the substitution in places within the article. Bavinck, interestingly, uses *knechten*—i.e., "servants"—in the title but *dienstknecht* consistently throughout the article. Since the ESV is the default translation in this volume and it translates the Greek word *doulos* as "bondservant" in the key passages Bavinck discusses, I have translated *dienstknecht* as "bondservant" in the contexts where the New Testament is clearly in view, and as "servant" when Bavinck has in view his own times. However, it is clear from the reference in the second paragraph to "the circles of our laborers," as well as his comment about the "freedom to strike," that he does have in view the larger picture of work, including the relations between employers and employees, factory managers and assembly-line workers, even though the language of "masters" and "servants" is taken from the arena of domestic service. Bavinck treats the subject of this article in much greater detail in his 1908 essay "Christian Principles and Social Relationships," in *ERSS*, 119–43, parts of which are excerpted in this chapter, above.

as bondservants of Christ, doing the will of God from the heart, rendering service with a good will as to the Lord and not to man, knowing that whatever good anyone does, this he will receive back from the Lord, whether he is a bondservant or is free.

Other texts such as Colossians 3:22, 1 Timothy 6:1–2, Titus 2:9, 1 Peter 2:18 speak in the same spirit. "With all fear and reverence, bondservants are to be subservient to their masters, not only those who are good and considerate, but also to those who are hard."[94]

In recent years, within the circles of our laborers,[95] the rumor has spread that all these admonitions directed by the apostles to bondservants are no longer in force. Our circumstances are completely different. Slavery was universal during the apostolic era. Servants then were not yet independent, free persons, but just like other possessions, were considered completely the property of their masters, subject to their arbitrary whims and without any rights over against them. The admonitions of the apostles were directed to such bondservants, as many as were "under a yoke" (1 Tim. 6:1).

But now, so it is said, we live in altogether different circumstances. Not only are laborers not slaves, they are also no longer serfs, bound to their masters;[96] they are completely free and independent and stand in relation to their masters as contractors who insist on a specific wage for a specific job. Furthermore, should they not receive this, they are permitted to go on strike and stop working on that job. Therefore, the admonitions of the apostles have lost their force for our times. They were valuable once upon a time—when slavery was universal—but are no longer valid.

It is not inappropriate to ask a counter-question to this new ethic.[97] The New Testament not only considers the relation of bondservants to their masters, but also that of masters to their bondservants. In Ephesians 6:9 we read: "Masters, do the same to them [that is to say, treat your bondservants with the same good will they must demonstrate toward you], and stop your threatening, knowing that he who is both their Master and yours is in heaven, and that there is no partiality with him."[98] In Colossians 4:1, Paul admonishes: "Masters, treat your bondservants justly and fairly, knowing that you also have a Master in heaven." And he writes to Philemon that he should receive his runaway slave "no longer as a bondservant but more than a bondservant, as a beloved brother" (v. 16).[99]

94. DO: *harden.*
95. DO: *de kringen onzer werklieden.*
96. DO: *lijfeigenen.*
97. DO: *zedeleer.*
98. I have provided the full text of Eph. 6:9; Bavinck only included the point that earthly masters have a Master in heaven, omitting the reference to the bondservants.
99. Textual reference added by editor.

Now here comes the counter-question: If the apostolic admonitions to bond-servants are no longer valid because of changed circumstances, do the admonitions to masters, for the same reason, no longer have any force? The one stands and falls with the other. If our servants are no longer bound to the word of the apostles that prescribes their subservience and benevolence, then their masters are also discharged from the same word that expects them to show benevolence and fairness to their servants. If the moral bond is broken on one side, it cannot be maintained on the other.

But there is still more. During the apostolic era, the relationship between masters and bondservants was not the only relationship that is regulated in a vastly different way from that of our day. Also completely different is the regulation of the relationship between husbands and wives, parents and children. Does this mean that the admonitions of the New Testament, directed to husbands and wives, to parents and children, therefore have no force nor value any longer? We read there: "Husbands, love your wives, and do not be harsh with them" (Col. 3:19). "Wives, submit to your husbands, as is fitting in the Lord" (Col. 3:18). "Fathers, do not provoke your children to anger, but bring them up in the discipline and instruction of the Lord" (Eph. 6:4). "Children, obey your parents in the Lord, for this is right" (Eph. 6:1).[100] Is it possible in our day to consider ourselves discharged from all these admonitions because the legal relationships[101] between husbands and wives, parents and children are regulated differently now than they were in the days of the apostles?

To pose these question is sufficient to answer them. However easily this happens now and then in some circles, we cannot and may not simply dismiss these admonitions of Scripture. If changed circumstances were sufficient for us to dismiss the words of Holy Scripture, then by this same rule, practically the entire Bible would be robbed of its validity. Because the Bible is a collection of books that did not fall from the sky but were written, under the leading of the Spirit, by different people in different times and circumstances, and therefore carry those identifying marks on every page. They are altogether historical books—that is, books that came into being in a particular group and time.

But the miracle of Holy Scripture is that history is made by God to be the bearer of an eternal, everlasting content. The human word has become an instrument to express God's thoughts. The Word, that was with God, became flesh and in this way dwelled among us. That also includes the admonitions with respect to husbands and wives, parents and children, masters and bondservants.

---

100. Textual references added by editor. It is striking that Bavinck inverts Paul's order and begins with the "superior" person.

101. DO: *rechtsverhouding*.

The legal relationships were completely different than are ours today. That is evident numerous times in the New Testament. But the remarkable thing is that Jesus and the apostles left those legal relationships untouched and directed themselves to the moral relationships. Jesus did not involve himself in politics and paid no attention to the social question. His advice: "Render to Caesar the things that are Caesar's, and to God the things that are God's" (Mark 12:17). And when two brothers were fighting with each other about an inheritance, he refused to serve as their arbitrator (Luke 12:13–14).[102] He did not come to establish a worldly kingdom, but to establish the kingdom of heaven on earth, a kingdom that was to work as a leaven on every terrain.

The apostles spoke and acted in the same vein. They did not abolish slavery and did not intervene in the existing legal relationships but regulated the moral relations that mutually exist between people. Paul did not only approve but recommended that slaves avail themselves of the opportunity to gain their freedom (1 Cor. 7:21). Nonetheless, the rule to which he holds is this: people should remain in the callings to which they are called. "For he who was called in the Lord as a bondservant is a freedman of the Lord. Likewise he who was free when called is a bondservant of Christ" (1 Cor. 7:22).[103] That is why Paul sent the runaway slave Onesimus back to his master, but now not as a bondservant, but as a brother in the Lord (Philem. 16).

The apostles were not revolutionaries but preachers of the gospel.[104] They did not overthrow the existing legal relationships, but brought into those legal relationships a different, new moral relation that would eventually, in the course of time, change and reshape them, not in a revolutionary but in a reformational way. That masters today no longer can or may treat their servants as slaves, and that servants now are free and independent persons, is for the most part thanks to the gospel proclaimed by the apostles. And then the source of this change is mainly the following admonitions: Masters, do what is right by your servants (Eph. 6:9); "Bondservants, obey in everything those who are your earthly masters, not by way of eye-service, as people-pleasers, but with sincerity of heart, fearing the Lord" (Col. 3:22).

One ought to think ten times over before rendering these admonitions null and void with an appeal to changed circumstances. Why? Because they hold out, not only to servants but also to their masters, a calling to do their Christian obligation. They don't alter the legal relationships but regulate the moral relation as such, the moral relation that can and must exist in all legal relationships.

---

102. Textual reference added by editor.
103. Textual reference added by editor.
104. DO: *Evangeliepredikers*.

They set forth a personal moral, spiritual bond that exists between husbands and wives, parents and children, masters and servants, a bond that far exceeds all created obligations in strength and durability.

--------------- APPENDIX B ---------------

"The Right to Life of the Unborn"[105]

Abortion[106] was justified in theory among the Greeks and Romans and the pagan world in general and was often practiced, especially during the imperial period.[107] A fetus was not yet thought of as a human being, as a person with rights. Parents could do with it as they pleased and had full disposition of their children's lives. Infanticide was a widespread custom.[108]

Holy Scripture has an altogether different position. Not only does it proceed from the conviction that God is the Creator and Determiner of life, but it expressly forbids killing a human being (Exod. 20:13) because everyone is created in God's image (Gen. 9:6). This commandment also extends to unborn children not only because God is the one who instituted and blesses marriage and children are an inheritance from the Lord (Gen. 12:2; Deut. 28:4; Pss. 113:9; 127:3; 128:3; Prov. 17:6) but also because it is clear from Genesis 38:9–10 (the deed of Onan) and Exod. 21:21, 23, respectively, that the sin of killing unborn fruit is a sin and therefore punishable.

The Christian church proceeded from this to oppose all manner of pagan sins that violated the Sixth Commandment: abortion, infanticide, abandoning children, suicide, gladiator sports, and the like. In particular, the Christian church acknowledged the human person, including the unborn child, as a citizen with rights[109] that must be respected in Christian nations. Church fathers, Scholastics, and Roman Catholic, Lutheran, and Reformed[110] theologians unanimously condemned abortion. Different views about the origin of the soul (traducianism or creationism) did not influence this position. Even though the Greek translation of Exodus 21:22–23[111] prompted the notion that the fetus, so long as it did not

105. Bav. note: From the gathering of May 12, 1903, in the "Excelsior" building, Amsterdam. Ed. note: The original (in PDF) is available from the Neo-Calvinism Research Institute, https://sources.neocalvinism.org/.full_pdfs/bavinck_1904_levensrecht.pdf.

106. DO: *vruchtafdrijving*.

107. DO: *Keizerstijd*.

108. DO: *zede*.

109. DO: *rechtssubject*.

110. Bavinck specifically mentions "Calvin, Voetius, e.a."

111. Exod. 21:22–25 reads: "When men strive together and hit a pregnant woman, so that her children come out, but there is no harm, the one who hit her shall surely be fined, as the

have a human form, was not to be considered a person, the idea is foreign to the Hebrew text. The same judgment was made by traducianists or others who believed that the human soul was placed in the fetus after a certain number of days. It is true that someone who killed the unborn before the soul entered was not, strictly speaking, a murderer; such a one was still guilty of the death of a being that was destined to become a human person.

There were a variety of reasons why some permitted abortion in the past and more recently, but we do not need to consider all of them now. It is well established in our circles that parental concern about the burdens of marriage, the desire to avoid shame among the unmarried, and fears about poverty or overpopulation do not count as grounds for abortion.

However, this is not the case when the question is posed about whether a doctor may procure an abortion when the mother's life is in danger.

In this instance we immediately and in the first place face the practical problem that doctors themselves among each other are not at all in agreement about the circumstances in which the pregnant mother is definitely in peril of life. In the case of excessive morning sickness, for example, one doctor says that the mother will surely die, while another denies this, and a third insists that even a procured abortion[112] cannot save her life.

Second, there are some considerations in favor of a procured abortion that certainly ought not to be considered convincing. These include the fact that a fetus is not yet fully formed as a human person; the conflict of duties[113] between the mother and the child; the advantage to the mother's life. The ends cannot sanctify the means, and evil may never be done in order that good may result. If the advantage to the mother's life became a decisive factor here, then it becomes difficult to resist and condemn infanticide and killing useless, worthless specimens of humanity.

Third, even if procured abortions were justifiable in some circumstance, there are surely objections to leaving such a decision up to each doctor. In every civilized country the law has a different basis and does not give this freedom to the doctor. Permitting such a freedom would ascribe to doctors a dangerous right and a dangerous power, open a door to misuse and arbitrariness, and create a precedent[114] that would make it difficult to resist granting it in other instances.

---

woman's husband shall impose on him, and he shall pay as the judges determine. But if there is harm, then you shall pay life for life, eye for eye, tooth for tooth." Whereas the Masoretic Text refers to harm to the child, the LXX uses the Greek verb ἐξεικονισμένον (= fully formed); verse 22 in the LXX reads: "not fully formed" (μὴ ἐξεικονισμένον); verse 23 reads: "fully formed," thus setting up the possibility to which Bavinck alludes.

112. Here and from this point on in the essay, Bavinck uses the Latin term *procuratio abortus*.

113. LO: *collisio jurium*.

114. Bavinck uses the term *antecedent*.

Of course, it is true that not all taking of a human life violates the Sixth Commandment. Killing another human being is permissible in self-defense, in war, and as legal punishment for murder. But none of these situations are comparable to those mentioned above and are validated by Scripture itself. A procured abortion presumes no guilt, neither on the part of the mother nor the child, and therefore cannot be included in those circumstances.

Of course, this does not forbid the application of all means that are directed to saving the life of the mother, even though the result—not necessarily and in all circumstances—is the death of the child. A distinction must also be made between a procured abortion and an artificially induced early birth.[115] And finally, circumstances may arise, both for doctors and for every person, in which there is a clear collision of duties[116] and in which active interference is necessary.

115. GO: *Frühgeburt.*
116. LO: *collisio officiorum.*

2

Art and Scholarship (School)

Bavinck left a single word, *geleerdenstand*, to indicate one of the topics in this chapter.[1] The literal translation of this term is "the class of scholars" and reflects the decidedly class-conscious society of Bavinck's time and place. For our purposes, it is best translated as "the world of scholarship." Since Bavinck

---

The original Dutch for this chapter's title is *Kunst en Wetenschap* (School). The Dutch word *wetenschap* (German: *Wissenschaft*) is usually translated into English as "science." Unfortunately, for English readers this connotes primarily, if not exclusively, the natural or physical sciences, whereas the Dutch and German denote the so-called human sciences as well. In distinction from the "arts," the term *wetenschap* refers to the world of scholarship that includes linguistics, aesthetics, philosophy, and the social sciences, not only mathematics, physics, chemistry, and biology, and is therefore best translated as "scholarship." See also n. 71 below.

1. Bav. note: Cf. Fichte; Kuyper, *Scolastica, of 't geheim van echte studie*; H. Druskowitz, *Eugen Dühring: Eine Studie zu seiner Würdiging*, 63–81; Schopenhauer; Friedrich Paulsen, *System der Ethik mit einem Umriss der Staats- und Gesellschaftslehre*. Ed. note: Kuyper's *Scolastica* was the publication of a convocation address he gave in his role as rector of the Vrije Universiteit, Amsterdam, in 1889. In 1900 he gave another rectorial address, which was published as *Scolastica, II. Om het zoeken of om het vinden? Of het doel van echte studie*. Both works have been translated by Harry Van Dyke into English under the title *Scholarship* with two parts: "Scholastica I, The Secret of Genuine Study," and "Scholastica II, The Goal of Genuine Study: To Seek or to Find?" These two lectures were published as a separate booklet, *Scholarship: Two Convocation Addresses on University Life* (2014), and then included in Kuyper, *On Education*, 98–132. The Druskowitz reference is to chap. 5: "Estimation of the Spiritual Greats—Critique of the Learned Caste" [GO: Schätzung von Geistesgrössen—Kritik der Gelehrtenkaste]. Eugen Karl Dühring (1833–1921) was a German philosopher and political economist who was influenced by Auguste Comte's positivism and taught an "ethical communism" from which he attacked the "Darwinian principle of struggle for existence." Source: *1911 Encyclopedia Britannica*, s.v. "Dühring, Eugen Karl," Wikisource, https://en.wikisource.org/wiki/1911_Encyclop%C3%A6dia_Britannica/D%C3%BChring,_Eugen_Karl. The reference to Paulsen is unclear; Bavinck fails to provide a specific edition or passage.

understands the world of culture to be no less rooted in creation than society is, I will again use the doctrine of creation as an orientation to the world of art and scholarship. This section will include a significant segment on the notion of "participation." After this introduction, we will consider the two topics in the title in the order Bavinck gave them. In the section on art, I will cover Bavinck's statements from his *Reformed Dogmatics* about God's own artistry and then his discussion of aesthetics in his essay "Of Beauty and Aesthetics."[2] In the section on scholarship/schools (education), I will first examine Bavinck's views on pedagogy for Christian day schools (elementary through high school), and then the life of scholarship in the university. The section on schools and pedagogy includes important material on Bavinck's views of a pluralistic society that complements the content of the preceding chapter. Again, Bavinck's words and transitional material from the editor are in different typefaces, with the exception that shorter quotations from Bavinck may be included in the editorial material. All notes are from the editor unless otherwise indicated.

FOR FURTHER READING[a]

Articles/Essays

"Classical Education." In *ERSS*, 209–43 [1918].
"Of Beauty and Aesthetics." In *ERSS*, 245–60 [1914].
"Trends in Pedagogy." In *ERSS*, 205–8 [1909].

Books

Brederveld, J. *Christian Education: A Summary and Critical Discussion of Bavinck's Pedagogical Principles.*
Christian Worldview [1904].
Jaarsma, Cornelius. *The Educational Philosophy of Herman Bavinck.*
The Philosophy of Revelation: A New Annotated Edition [1908].

a. Herman Bavinck is the author of all items in the For Further Reading list unless indicated otherwise; dates in square brackets are the original year of publication.

1. CREATION IS THE FOUNDATION

For Bavinck, the story of creation begins with God's decree, "the one, eternal counsel of God."[3] Creation is a work of divine art:

2. Bavinck, "Of Beauty and Aesthetics," in *ERSS*, 245–60.
3. *RD*, 2:342; references to this volume will be provided in parentheses in the text.

God is the supreme artist. Just as a human artist realizes his idea in a work of art, so God creates all things in accordance with the ideas he has formed. The world is God's work of art. He is the architect and builder of the entire universe. God does not work without thinking, but is guided in all his works by wisdom, by his ideas. (206)

But whereas God's artistry is "absolutely original," arising "from his own being" and therefore "one with his own being," earthly artistry is finite and derivative and "participates in God's being." What does Bavinck mean here by the notion of "participation"? Negatively,

the nature of this participation is not such that creatures are modifications of the divine being or that they have in some realistic sense received this divine being into themselves. But every creature has its own distinct being because in its existence it is an exemplification of the divine being. (206)

Creation as a divine work of art manifests its Creator.

Bavinck's doctrine of revelation is therefore the key to understanding his idea of participation. The name *Logos* is attributed to Christ because it

is the consistent teaching of Scripture that both in creation and re-creation God reveals himself by the word. By the word God creates, preserves, and governs all things, and by the word he also renews and re-creates the world. For that reason, too, the gospel is called "the word of God" (λογος του θεου). John calls Christ the Logos because it is he in whom and by whom God reveals himself both in the work of creation and that of re-creation (John 1:3, 14). (273)

Creation by the Word "rules out all emanation, every hint of an essential identity between God and the world" (419). When "the Scholastics," Bavinck adds,

wrote repeatedly about an emanation or procession of all existence from a universal cause and also occasionally of the creature's participation in the being and life of God, . . . they did not mean "*emanation*" in the strict sense, as if God's own being flowed out into his creatures and so unfolded in them, like the genus in its species. They only meant to say that God is a self-subsistent necessary being (*ens per essentiam*), but the creature is existent by participation (*ens per participationem*). Creatures indeed have a being of their own, but this being has its efficient and exemplary cause in the being of God. (419)

Bavinck's concluding summary:

According to the teaching of Scripture the world is not a part of, or emanation from, the being of God. It has a being and existence of its own, one that is different and distinct from the essence of God. And that is what is expressed by the term *ex nihilo*. (419)[4]

"Participation" is therefore an ontological term but one that points to the dependent difference between the Creator and the creature. The doctrine of creation in Christian theology gives it

a place between Gnosticism and Arianism, that is, between pantheism and Deism. Gnosticism knows no creation but only emanation and therefore makes the world into the Son, wisdom, the image of God in an antiquated sense. Arianism, on the other hand, knows nothing of emanation but only of creation and therefore makes the Son into a creature. In the former the world is deified; in the latter God is made mundane. (420)

By contrast,

Scripture, and therefore Christian theology, knows both emanation and creation, a twofold communication of God—one within and the other outside the divine being; one to the Son who was in the beginning with God and was himself God, and another to creatures who originated in time; one from the being and another by the will of God. The former is called generation; the latter, creation. By generation, from all eternity, the full image of God is communicated to the Son; by creation only a weak and pale image of God is communicated to the creature. Still, the two are connected. (420)

Remarkably, Bavinck speaks of a necessary connection between generation and creation: Without generation, creation would not be possible.

If, in an absolute sense, God could not communicate himself to the Son, he would be even less able, in a relative sense, to communicate himself to his creature. If God were not triune, creation would not be possible. (420)

Furthermore, creation is the "work of the whole Trinity," although in "Scripture it also stands in a peculiar relation to the Son." Both the Old Testament

---

4. On the creation as *ex nihilo* Bavinck immediately goes on to distance Christian thought from all philosophical attempts to give ontic status to this nihil or "nonbeing" (Plato, Hegel, Barth), referring to it as "conceptual confusion" (419). See also Bavinck's caustic comments about the Hegelian idealism in his *Philosophy of Revelation* (2018), 38–39.

(Gen. 1:3; Pss. 33:6; 104:24; 148:5; Isa. 48:13) and the New Testament (John 1:3; 1 Cor. 8:6; Col. 1:15–17) clearly teach "that God created all things by his Word."[5]

Christ is called "the firstborn of all creation" (*prōtotokos pasēs ktiseōs*, Col. 1:15), "the origin of God's creation" (*archē tēs ktiseōs tou Theou*, Rev. 3:14), the Alpha and Omega, the beginning and end of all things (Rev. 1:17; 21:6; 22:6), for whom all things have been created (Col. 1:16), in order to be again gathered up into him as the head (Eph. 1:10). (423)

In conclusion:

He is the First and the Last, the Alpha and the Omega (Isa. 44:6; 48:12; Rev. 1:8; 22:13). Of him, through him, and to him are all things (Rom. 11:36). (433)

From this, "Christian theology almost unanimously teaches that the glory of God is the final goal of all God's works" (433). Bavinck answers the two common objections against this conviction: (1) "On this view God is made self-centered, self-seeking, devaluing his creatures, specifically human beings, into means." Answer: "Inasmuch as he is the supreme and only good, perfection itself, it is the highest kind of justice that in all creatures he seek his own honor" (434). (2) It seems that "God does need his creature after all. Since the world serves as an instrument of his glorification, there is something lacking in his perfection and blessedness. Creation meets a need in God and contributes to his perfection." Bavinck's answer to this objection also provides deep theological insight into his theological aesthetics. He acknowledges the persuasiveness of this objection but answers it with an analogy from human labor:

At a lower level humans labor, because they have to; they are impelled to work by need or force. But the more refined the work becomes, the less room there is for need or coercion. An artist creates his work of art not out of need or coercion but impelled by the free impulses of his genius. "I pour out my heart like a little finch in the poplars; I sing and know no other goal" (*Bilderdijk*).[6] A

---

5. *RD*, 2:423.
6. Bavinck clearly loved this line and the larger poem from which it came; he used a lengthier version of it in "Contemporary Morality" (*RE*, 3:362):

I pour out my soul, like a finch in the trees,
And ask not whom my voice can please,
But permit my desire full ease.
I feel my poetic art.
And whether it flows from my own heart,

devout person serves God, not out of coercion or in hope of reward, but out of free-flowing love. (435)

God also delights in his creatures:

So there is also a delight in God that is infinitely superior to need or force, to poverty or riches, which embodies his artistic ideas in creation and finds intense pleasure in it. Indeed, what in the case of man is merely a weak analogy is present in God in absolute originality. A creature, like the creation of an artist, has no independence apart from, and in opposition to, God. God, therefore, never seeks out a creature as if that creature were able to give him something he lacks or could take from him something he possesses. He does not seek the creature [as an end in itself], but through the creature he seeks himself. He is and always remains his own end. His striving is always—also in and through his creatures—total self-enjoyment, perfect bliss. The world, accordingly, did not arise from a need in God, from his poverty and lack of bliss, for what he seeks in a creature is not that creature but himself. Nor is its origination due to an uncontrollable fullness (*plērōma*) in God, for God uses all creatures for his own glorification and makes them serviceable to the proclamation of his perfections. (435)

The doctrine of creation generates a worldview that honors the diversity of all things, each "created with a nature of its own and rest[ing] in ordinances established by God," and upheld by God "in a superlative kind of unity" (435). Great thinkers in the Christian church recognized this "unity, order, and harmony exhibited in the world [as] a powerful proof for the existence and unity of God" (437).[7] Bavinck goes on to quote a number of Christian thinkers who use aesthetic metaphors to describe this:

Thomas [Aquinas] compares the world to perfectly keyed stringed music, whose harmonies interpret for us the glory and blessedness of the divine life. "Its parts are found to have been arranged just like the parts of a whole animal, which serve each other reciprocally." (437)[8]

Or is poured into my bosom from somewhere apart,
    I sing and know no other goal.
From "Op een houwelicx-prent door Jacob Cats," in *De Dichtwerken van Mr. Willem Bilderdijk*, 2:4.

7. Bavinck refers here to Athanasius, *Against the Arians* II.28 (NPNF² 4:363); Athanasius, *Against the Heathen* XXXIX (NPNF² 4:25).

8. *ST* 1a q. 25 art. 6; *Commentary on the Sentences* II dist. 1 art. 1. Ed. note: There does not seem to be an English translation of this particular distinction and article; the Latin text is available at http://www.clerus.org/bibliaclerusonline/it/cgh.htm.

In Calvin's words, creation is "the theater of God's glory."[9] Bavinck cites at length the post-Reformation theologian Jerome Zanchi:

Nothing in the whole world is more excellent, more noble, more beautiful, more useful, and more divine than the diversity of its many elements, the distinction and that order in which one is more noble than another and one depends on another, one is subject to another, and one receives obedience from another. Hence comes the adornment, beauty, and excellence of the whole world. Thence arise its many uses, usefulness, and benefits for us. Hence, the very goodness, glory, wisdom, and power of God shines forth and is revealed more brilliantly. (437–38)[10]

2. Art (Aesthetics)[11]

The preceding is aptly summed up with a single poetic line: "The world is charged with the grandeur of God."[12] And God, who seeks his own glory, takes delight in the beauty of his works. No further justification is needed for his image bearers to delight in creating and enjoying beautiful art; they are imitating their Maker.

However, we humans do more than create and delight in beauty; we also think about what we are doing. Therefore, in addition to thinking about what is true and what is good, we also ask ourselves about the beautiful. This is the field of aesthetics. Bavinck observes that

even though the term "aesthetics" is of rather recent vintage, the idea indicated by it is much older and dates from the time of Greek philosophy. In the classical nation of poets and thinkers, the need soon arose to give an account of the essence and laws of beauty.

The honor of being the "father of aesthetics" goes to Plato, who

especially tried to give a metaphysical foundation to beauty and to derive it from the world of ideas. Even though we see many beautiful things on

---

9. Calvin uses this image frequently; see *Institutes*, I.v.8; I.vi.2; I.xiv.20; II.vi.1; III.ix.2; *Commentaries on the First Book of Moses, Called Genesis*, on Gen. 1:6; *Commentary on the Psalms*, on Ps. 138:1.

10. The passage is from Zanchi, *Omnium Operum Theologicorum*, 3:45.

11. The Bavinck material in this section is taken from Bavinck's "Of Beauty and Aesthetics" (see n. 2, above); page numbers are indicated in the text.

12. This is the first line of Gerard Manley Hopkins's poem "God's Grandeur," available online at www.hopkinspoetry.com.

earth, we do not behold beauty itself; this has a unique, perfect existence in the world of intelligible ideas. The ideas that belong there are more-or-less imprinted on the world by the demiurge and shine through the visible, and we therefore behold the beauty also in nature around us. And since art essentially exists in the imitation of nature, it also in turn displays beauty. But art is really an image of an image, an imprint of an imprint, and thus of secondary value; in the ideal world there is actually no place for works of art without a moral intent. (246)

This "metaphysical and normative aesthetics," which Bavinck also speaks of as "a more-or-less dogmatic aesthetics," influenced the church fathers, medieval theologians, and later Roman Catholic as well as Protestant theologians. In this view "beauty is originally supersensory, as spirit; it has objective existence and belongs to the worlds of invisible things as an independent reality or in God's consciousness as an idea." Its key components are "harmony, proportion, order, diversity in unity, and unity in diversity." In sum, "Beauty thus lies first in the content, in the idea, but harmony characterizes its appearance. Wherever in the world it in its various forms shows a finite expression of the infinite, beauty is absolute idea" (246).

The problem, of course, is that "the appearance in nature never fully corresponds to the idea." Consequently,

one can go in two directions in the consideration of art. If one is committed, with Plato, to the perspective that all art must be imitation of nature, and we see in art a weaker reflection of the beauty in nature, then art is naturally relegated to the third and last rank, and then has only subordinate value. (246)

One can, however, with the same fundamental metaphysical presupposition, go in the opposite direction and elevate art to the highest level:

If nature, because of the strength of its materialism, is only an inadequate reflection of the idea, then one can assign to art the purpose of overcoming this imperfection in the beauty of nature; it does so by corresponding to the idea and thus seeming to destroy the material completely through absolute perfection of the form. (247)

For an example, Bavinck points to the early work of the German philosopher and educator Friedrich Schelling (1775–1854), for whom art "assumes the highest position, even above religion and philosophy, because it is the complete revelation of the absolute, finally the perfect manifestation of the divine idea, the total reconciliation of the antithesis between the real and the ideal" (247).[13]

Before he turns to discuss more recent reactions against this "aesthetic dogmatism," Bavinck makes one more point. The "metaphysical aesthetics" just summarized underscores the uniqueness of art, according to Bavinck, because it understands

> that beauty affects human emotions in a special manner. Because beauty is related to the true and the good and is one with them in the absolute idea, it may not evoke any sensations that are opposed to them. . . . It has to be in service of moral purposes. (247)

Therefore,

> the true, the good, and the beautiful were often joined together in an unbreakable triad. However, beauty can still be distinguished from the good and the true. Beauty often evokes peculiar sensations and moods in human beings; it purifies our affections, reconciles the opposites in our life, brings harmony to the soul, and bestows peace and rest. (247)

In the nineteenth century, "after the disillusionment with idealistic philosophy," aesthetics stopped trying to "proceed from some kind of a priori dogma or . . . speculatively to understand the essence of beauty." Instead, aesthetics turned to the experience of beauty, to an "aesthetic from below" rather than an "aesthetic from above" (248). Bavinck approves of this move, though with some qualification. On the one hand, a more empirical aesthetics "will see boundless areas of investigation spread out before it; wherever its eyes turn, there are people who have enjoyed something beautiful or have made something beautiful." Aesthetics can also borrow a page or two from empirical psychology and

> try to find out which lines, figures, colors, shapes, changes in sound and tone, and so forth give the most pleasure to the most people. They can also try subjectively to penetrate these same people to discover what is going on in them when they see and enjoy something beautiful; what must be ascribed to the object and what to the subject; which aesthetic and non-aesthetic factors are at work; how the pleasure from beauty affects facial expression, bodily posture, increase in pulse rate; and so forth. (248–49)

13. In the twentieth century this line of thinking can also be found in the Schelling-influenced theology of Paul Tillich.

Among the "non-aesthetic factors" that "count just as much" even though
they "have little to do with aesthetics," Bavinck includes the following: "the
relationship to the artist, the fashion that frequently sets the tone also in art,
the high price that one pays for the art object, the thought about the adulation
of the people that one will receive as buyer and owner, and so forth" (249).

In addition, empirical aesthetics can explore three more questions:

1. Why and how do human beings have a sense for beauty? Scholars can
   investigate "the sense of beauty that is inherent in man. They can try
   to discern in what ways, from which factors, under what influences this
   sense came to be; how it developed through time in various peoples; and
   if there is unity among the motley, infinite diversity, what this unity is."
2. What makes an artist and why do they create? Scholars "can focus their
   attention on the artists who have created this beauty and determine what
   uniqueness separates them from other people, from what milieu they
   come, how they have developed themselves, what their special gift was,
   and in what direction they have cultivated this gift."
3. What art objects have human beings created? Scholars can "survey the
   art objects that have been created throughout the ages by various peoples
   and by all humanity and survey their origin, development, influence,
   similarity, diversity and so forth" (249).

Bavinck is positive about all this empirical scholarly activity.

Just as in philosophy in general, aesthetics may not neglect the objective data,
the facts, and phenomena in its domain. The philosopher may not close his
eyes to reality and may not construct the world from his own brain, and the
aesthetician must form and perfect his taste, his judgment, his knowledge from
the works of nature and art. Just as in all scholarship, so also in the theory of
beauty, observation and thought, inductive and deductive methods must go
together. (248)

In sum, "There is not a moment of doubt that empirical aesthetics has a
right to existence and that it has conclusively proved this right by its results"
(250). On the other hand, however, he also states that "empirical aesthetics is without doubt one-sided and cannot produce what it intends" (250).
This inadequacy "becomes immediately obvious when the beauty of nature
does not receive the attention it deserves, because here it is not possible to
conduct psychological, physical or cultural historical investigation." Noting
that when urban dwellers "feel fed up with disturbances and unrest, then the

desire for the beauty of nature returns, and one sees a return from the city to the country," Bavinck concludes:

> The beauty of nature may therefore not be put in second place behind the beauty of art. Both are revelations, each in its own way, of true beauty, which is not sensory but spiritual—according to Plato [it is] found in the ideal, and according to Holy Scripture [it is] found in God's splendor and displayed in all the works of his hands.

We must do justice, therefore, "to the truth that both natural and artistic beauty are independent revelations of beauty" (250).

Empirical aesthetics also cannot solve the mystery that is the human sense of beauty. Questions about the essence of art elude it. How does our sense of beauty differ from our religious, moral, and intellectual sensibilities, and how are these related to one another? "The more we think about this phenomenon, the more strange and mysterious it becomes. What is the nature of this aesthetic affection, and what is its origin?" (250). "Is this feeling, or whatever one may call it, innate, or has it developed slowly through selection or heredity in the struggle for existence?" (251). Is our sense of beauty only subjective—"an expression or symbol of our own inner life"? Noting that many different theories about art have arisen without any unanimity, "in spite of all the empirical and experimental investigations," Bavinck concludes:

> All the questions—just as in every investigation into the origin of religion, morality, culture, and so forth—finally lead to the conclusion that with the sense of beauty, we are dealing with a phenomenon that is part of human nature; a predisposition and susceptibility of the soul to find pleasure and to enjoy oneself in things that fulfill certain conditions. (250)

The same mystery attends investigations of the artist's creative gift. It is true that "knowledge about psychological, physical, historical, and social conditions can be of great service. If one studies the origin, disposition, development, and milieu of the artist, one can better understand and appreciate not only his person and character but also his art" (251). But here too we run into limits: "But even if we finally know everything about the artist's circumstances that has been brought to light by careful investigation, at the end we finally face a mystery, the secret of personality, the inscrutability of genius." Therefore, after extensive investigation of many factors, including heredity, we finally "cannot say else than what the ancients confessed. Art is a gift, the poet is not made but born, and an artist is an artist by the grace of God." In other words, we "are faced with an original power that is not explained by any law of nature, and it points back to a divine, creating Almighty" (252).

In the end, Bavinck says, all these empirical investigations "have not been able to lift the veil that hangs over the origin and essence of art and works of art" (252). He does believe, notwithstanding all the different theories about these foundational questions, there is growing acknowledgment "that with art, just as with religion, we must accept an original human impulse and an urge that we cannot explain from other inclinations or activities" (253). Art, in other words, is its own distinct sphere of human life, not reducible to other arenas.

To understand the role of art in human life Bavinck appeals to our experience of the world and to anthropology.[14] Our

> aesthetic relationship to our environment . . . is preceded by the intellectual, or rather, in general, the relationship of consciousness. We are so disposed from birth that we receive impressions not only from ourselves but also from the outside world and can transform these impressions into concepts. We have the wonderful capacity to absorb the world outside ourselves into our consciousness and thus to enrich our spirits. (254)

But we do more than receive the world through our senses and form ideas about it. "Besides, at the same time and in relation to it we have also received the power to penetrate into the world through our wills, to shape it according to our ideas, and to make it serviceable to our freely chosen purposes." In summary, "As conscious, thinking, knowing beings, we draw the world to ourselves and absorb it spiritually; and as striving, acting beings, we approach the world and influence it" (254). In other words, human beings are thinking and willing/acting creatures.

However, there is more: "In addition to these relationships, however, comes a third: the aesthetic" (254). Bavinck notes that some scholars have tried to reduce the aesthetic sense of beauty to one of the other two, either rationalistically as "a characteristic and operation of lower, sensory cognition" or as a practical "matter of desire and will" (254). Bavinck takes these reductions as an occasion to point to "the truth that in this world nothing exists by itself: everything is interrelated. In human beings themselves, there are not two or three capabilities that work apart from each other; the works that we produce

---

14. For a more complete statement of Bavinck's anthropology, especially his psychology, see Bavinck, *Foundations of Psychology*. A solid interpretation of Bavinck's anthropology and psychology can be found in Hoekema, *The Centrality of the Heart in Herman Bavinck's Anthropology*.

have this in common: they are the revelation of our activity and to that extent are all 'art'" (254–55). Nonetheless, this unity must not be allowed to obscure key differences "between science and art on the one hand, and between art and technology (and all practical labor) on the other" (255). Bavinck describes the contrast between art and scholarship thus: "The scholar wants to know, understand, and judge the world; the aesthetic person wants to enjoy it and revel in its beauty" (255). He acknowledges that there is a "close connection" between art and technology, "even more so in earlier times than today, now that the elevation of crafts can be called a pressing demand of our time." But a difference remains: "With technology and even with a craft, the purpose always lies outside the product, which for some reason must be practical and useful. But a real work of art contains the purpose in itself, apart from the service that it may prove to have" (255).

Bavinck goes on to underscore the unity between the true, the good, and the beautiful: "The connection and the differences among science, technology, and art can also, in a somewhat different way, be expressed with the idea that the true, the good, and the beautiful are one but also three." He points to Augustine, who "said, 'We are seized [caught up] by the love of searching out the truth [*rapimur amore indagandae veritas*],'[15] and he found this truth—this eternal absolute truth—in God alone, who was at the same time the highest good [*summum bonum*] and the highest beauty [*summum pulchrum*]." This carried over into Christian theology, where "God was often described as the highest truth, the highest good, and also the highest beauty. However, since this last designation had been touched by Neoplatonic influences, already in Augustine," Protestant theologians exchanged the term "beauty" "for the more Scriptural terms of majesty and glory. But all three existed originally in God, were one with his essence and thus actually were one" (255). Bavinck also underscores the unity of the true, the good, and the beautiful in his lecture on the kingdom of God: "The good, however, constitutes a unity. Freed from the destructive power of sin, it automatically organizes. The good is at the same time the beautiful; it consists in perfect harmony. The Kingdom of God in its perfection is the unity of all moral goods."[16]

Human beings are created with a variety of gifts and capabilities. "Among these gifts is the sense of beauty, the delight in appearance, the joy of observation" (257). The enjoyment of beauty differs among people; it is strong in some, weaker in others. But

15. Bavinck does not provide a reference for the Augustine quotation; it is found in Augustine, *On the Trinity* I.v.8 (*NPNF¹* 3:21).
16. Bavinck, "The Kingdom of God, the Highest Good," 140. The entire lecture comprises the content of chap. 5 in this volume.

beauty always awakens in us images, moods, and affections that otherwise would have remained dormant and not even known to us. Beauty thus discloses to us ourselves and also grants us another, new glimpse into nature and humanity. It deepens, broadens, enriches our inner life, and it lifts us for a moment above the dreary, sinful, sad reality; beauty also brings cleansing, liberation, revival to our burdened and dejected hearts. (259)

Beauty is the harmony that still shines through the chaos in the world; by God's grace, beauty is observed, felt, translated by artists; it is prophecy and guarantee that this world is not destined for ruin but for glory—a glory for which there is a longing deep in every human heart. (259)

He concludes: "Because beauty is such a rich divine gift, it also must be loved by us" (259). For this reason, Bavinck says,

We should be truly sympathetic (even though there are harmful exaggerations) if, as a reaction to intellectualism in education and nurture, "aesthetic culture" again has a modest place and if vocational training is again used for the renewal of artful crafts. The same holds true when aesthetic demands are made in home building and urban design as protection against the defacement of our landscape and when many attempts are made to educate our people aesthetically. (260)

Acknowledging that "our country is often characterized on the one hand by coarseness that mocks all dignity and on the other hand by a stiffness that is without charm," Bavinck does not offer an apology for his Dutch compatriots but insists that "such serious accusations must goad us to deny that with our deeds. Along with truth and goodness, beauty also needs to be honored" (260).

3. SCHOOLS AND PEDAGOGY

Bavinck devoted much time and energy to the cause of Christian education, especially to pedagogy and educational philosophy.[17] For Bavinck, pedagogy

---

17. This is reflected in the fact that all the major studies of Bavinck's thought in the first three decades after his death were devoted to his pedagogy and educational philosophy: Fr. S. Rombouts, *Prof. Dr. H. Bavinck, Gids Bij de Studie van Zijn Paedagogische Werken* (1922); J. Brederveld, *Hoofdlijnen der Paedagogiek van Dr. Herman Bavinck, met Critische Beschouwing* (1927); ET: *Christian Education: A Summary and Critical Discussion of Bavinck's Pedagogical Principles* (1928); L. van der Zweep, *De Paedagogiek van Bavinck* (1935); Cornelius Jaarsma, *The Educational Philosophy of Herman Bavinck* (1936); and L. van Klinken, *Bavincks Paedagogische*

was not just a sideline, a hobby only marginally connected to his "day job" as a university theology professor.[18] Rather, he considered it an integral part of his own vocation as a theologian interested in fundamental issues of worldview, including questions about God, the world, and humanity. This is apparent from his extended definition of pedagogy:

> Pedagogy is a philosophic subject and is closely related to theology or philosophy. It is true that recently there have been various attempts to loosen this bond and to make pedagogy a completely independent subject. These attempts, however, will not succeed because education always assumes an answer to questions about human origin, essence, and purpose; and this answer (if ever possible) cannot be supplied by any exact science, but only by religion or philosophy.[19]

This quotation is ample evidence that Bavinck had sufficient internal motivation to take up the issues of education and pedagogy. The subject was clearly in the wheelhouse of his own theological and philosophical passions. But before we go on to unpack the content of Bavinck's pedagogical reflections, there is also an external or situational motivation we need to note, one that presents interesting parallels to our own times.[20] During the second half of the nineteenth century, orthodox Dutch Calvinists, along with their Roman Catholic compatriots, were embroiled in a fierce struggle with Dutch authorities about the education of their children.[21] Both groups were marginalized minorities who sought freedom for parents to have their children educated according to their own respective religious convictions rather than by the broad, generally Christian, rationalistic deism regnant in the state public schools. They resisted having the state shape the religious consciousness of their children. In 1878, at the height of the struggle, Calvinists and Roman Catholics each presented their own petition to King William III pleading that

---

Beginselen (1937). Bavinck's significant involvement in various Christian school organizations is covered in R. H. Bremmer, *Herman Bavinck en zijn Tijdgenoten*, 243–47 (chap. 12, "Pedagog").

18. Bavinck published his major work on the subject, *Paedagogische Beginselen* (Foundations in pedagogy), in 1904, two years before vol. 1 of the second edition of his *Reformed Dogmatics* came into print.

19. Bavinck, "Trends in Pedagogy," in *ERSS*, 205.

20. See Glenn, "Look to the Dutch for True Educational Pluralism." Here is the parallel Glenn suggests: "Popular schooling is often a primary focal-point for attempts to make effective the hegemony of the sovereign state over every aspect of society, to achieve not only obedience to laws and policies but also an inner disposition immune to alternative or partial loyalties."

21. For a helpful overview of this conflict, see Wendy Naylor, "Editor's Introduction," in Kuyper, *On Education*, xi–xli. This volume contains the most important primary sources from the Calvinist side. For a book-length treatment, see Hooker, *Freedom of Education*.

he withhold royal assent to the new education bill that had been passed in parliament.[22] The petition failed to persuade the king, but the grassroots movement behind the petition also fueled Abraham Kuyper's successful entry into the center of Dutch political life. One year later Kuyper founded the Calvinist Anti-Revolutionary Party as the first modern Dutch political party and published its platform.[23]

The struggle for freedom and financial relief for Christian day schools was finally won in the "Pacification of 1917" when the Dutch parliament passed a constitutional amendment that granted a right to equal funding for religious schools.[24] Although it was still more than a decade away, Bavinck judged that the trajectory had been set already by 1906.[25] In remarks to a convention of the Alliance of Reformed Schools[26] on October 19, 1906, Bavinck joyfully celebrated the progress that had been achieved and spoke of the future with confidence.[27]

> The more we consider the history of primary education in our Fatherland and compare it with that in other countries, the more we feel ourselves disposed to gratitude for the direction that this history has taken and for the outcome to which it is being led. It is no exaggeration to claim that thanks to the many years of struggle we have achieved an existence for our schools that can be the envy of other nations. (3)

After this opening, Bavinck goes back into Dutch history to explain how the nineteenth-century struggle came to be:

> For centuries, both within and outside of Christendom, state and church had the same ideal of education and nurture. Here, in our country, after the Reformation, instruction in the schools was not the undertaking of the church but of the government.[28] The government set up schools or granted permission to do so; the government paid teachers from the public purse or prescribed them from benefices; the government supervised the instruction through its visiting

22. See Kuyper, *On Education*, 325–31.

23. The platform for the Anti-Revolutionary Party is available in English translation; see Kuyper, *Our Program*.

24. See Hooker, *Freedom of Education*, 26–27, 97, cited in "Pacification of 1917," Wikipedia, https://en.wikipedia.org/wiki/Pacification_of_1917.

25. This is one year after the defeat of Abraham Kuyper's government; Kuyper served as the Dutch prime minister from 1901 to 1905; more on this follows.

26. DO: *Gereformeerde Schoolverband*.

27. This speech was published as a separate booklet: Bavinck, *De Taak van het Gereformeerd Schoolverband*; page references that follow in the text are to this address.

28. DO: *overheid*.

inspectors,[29] and regulated the curriculum, the schedules, and the finances through its school statutes. Not only did the church acquiesce to this arrangement but also frequently urged the government to promote education and, for its part, emphasized the importance of religious instruction that all were convinced ought to be foremost among the school's subjects. In other words, state and church worked together in education; their unity was expressed in the unity of the national public school.[30]

This unity was already factually broken by the Reformation and could only be maintained with coercion exercised in unjust ways against many dissenters. It was completely shattered in the eighteenth century when rationalism arose with a new cultural ideal, an ideal that has taken on a variety of forms since then. Churches and religious movements gradually and partially gave up the ideal of unity. On the other side, during the nineteenth and twentieth centuries it was the state that held on firmly to the ideal of unity and sought to impose it coercively on the nation by way of the national public school. The state could not rid itself of the fear that pluriformity in education would endanger national unity and thereby threaten the legitimacy and very existence of the state itself. (3–4)

Bavinck acknowledges that the ideal of a universally accessible national public school is "powerfully attractive."[31] It is

the original, the oldest, the most universal ideal: one nation, one kingdom, and one religion, one education and nurture for all the nation's children—that was the idea that everyone regarded as self-evident with the civil authority leading the way through its laws regarding education. Even today, there are countless many who cannot divest themselves of such thinking and are reluctant to recognize the new circumstances into which the development of society has brought us. (4)

Bavinck then sketches two different directions in which the unitary ideal remains active. From the traditional "Right" a "not inconsiderable number nostalgically look back to the past and want to tie the education of primary schools to one or another church confession" (5). Bavinck acknowledges that this still is the case in countries where there is a Roman Catholic majority and even in Lutheran-majority nations such as Denmark, Sweden, and Norway. "There is," he says,

29. DO: *visitatoren.*
30. DO: *volksschool.*
31. DO: *machtige bekoring.*

also in our Fatherland a visible party that, in addition to strengthening specifically Christian education, also includes the Christianizing of public education.
These people have in view the thousands of children who are forced by various
circumstances to attend the public schools and receive there an education that
takes no account of the Christian religion. Indeed, this is a regrettable situation
and Christian action should not cease until these children can participate in the
blessings of a Christian education. (5)

However, Bavinck judges that this is a difficult task with a poor outcome likely.
Because the state must acknowledge the religious pluralism of its citizens—
"Christians and Jews, Roman Catholics and Protestants, traditionalists[32] and
modernists—religious education mandated by the state would have to undergo
a homeopathic dilution that would rob it of its power and satisfy no one" (5).

According to Bavinck, the party of the "Left" is "stronger" and consists
"of those who want to maintain the ideal of one national public school,
but one in which instruction is emancipated from Christianity, even from
all religion" (5). After many attempts to impose by law a "natural religion"
or a "Christianity that transcends divisions," Bavinck concludes that Dutch
national public schools became religiously "neutral." Furthermore, he contends, "this neutrality of public schools has for many years been a peculiarly
Dutch curiosity" (6). Judging this to be a "radical" (and "socialist") position,
Bavinck sketches potential consequences of this view by citing the French
senator Eugène Lintilhac (1854–1920), who insisted that "education should
be a monopoly of the state. . . . No citizen belongs to himself, all belong to
the state. Every citizen is required to offer his or her personal rights to the
state. The altar of the fatherland may not yield to the altar of the home. A
father does not have the right to set his child on a path that is at odds with
that chosen by humanity." Bavinck's conclusion: "At the end of the socialist path of salvation we find what Bebel calls the 'communist nurture of
children'" (7).[33]

Efforts to find a "middle way" between these two positions are doomed, in
Bavinck's judgment, in part because they fail the test of neutrality. Furthermore, history shows that "everywhere a pluralistic nation maintains religious
instruction in the public school, including, for example, in the United States
of America, it remains only a chimera[34] without substance, a form without
content. By the nature of the case, it prepares the way for neutrality and

32. DO: *rechtzinnige.*
33. GO: For the Lintilhac reference Bavinck supplies the following: *Handelsblad,* November
28, 1903; the Auguste Bebel reference comes from Tews, *Sozialdemokratische Pädagogik,* 11–12.
34. DO: *schijn.*

secularism[35] as the proponents of the 1857 law in our nation intended" (9). In addition, the nineteenth century also marked a shift in the understanding of religion itself. Bavinck describes the impact of this shift on the cause of religious instruction in public schools: "Proponents of religious instruction who have spoken out recently," he observes, "are all, more or less, under the influence of the newer religious studies and their discovery that religion is completely independent of all concepts and is essentially nothing more than an attitude of feelings, an emotion of the heart" (9–10).[36] Bavinck concludes that there is no possible resolution for religious instruction in public schools that would satisfy all. "The differentiation of religious thought and life is a fact that no one, especially not the state, can ignore except to its own peril."

Bavinck then offers a different plan that takes into account the new pluralism of Dutch society. "The resolution of the school conflict here and everywhere can only be found in accepting schools of all kinds in line with the religious condition of the nation." This means that "schools belong to the parents, and that a free school must be opened for the whole nation" (11–12). Should such a principle be generally accepted and applied, there "would be no more public schools, only particular ones. And in their midst, the Reformed take a distinct and honorable place." Not only were "Reformed schools, ever since the Reformation, the ordinary, public, and national schools[;] . . . once granted the freedom to do so by the government, without any coercion they established schools in ever greater numbers" (12).

This voluntary, associational life, both in religion and in society, is exactly what the process of differentiation requires. The Reformed community is, in Bavinck's judgment, in good shape to face the modern world. He speaks to the fears of those who believe that giving up on a "public school united in its direction" would mean that "the unity of the nation will be destroyed." This objection, he counters, has only "an apparent plausibility." Differentiated societies have ways of providing "their own corrective, setting association and cooperation over against fracturing and division." Bavinck points to the Anglo-Saxon world as proof: "Nowhere is the religious and ecclesiastical life as varied as in England and America; but also nowhere is the underlying appreciation greater and the longing stronger for association and cooperation in all circumstances and for all purposes." Bavinck attributes this to the social character of human beings that comes to the fore once they are liberated from the "artificial unity imposed by the state." He concludes: "Liberty achieves

35. DO: *ongodsdienstigheid*.
36. DO: *eene stemming des gevoels, eene aandoening des gemoeds*. It is also worth noting that by an act of parliament, the theology faculties of Dutch universities were turned into departments of religious studies in 1876.

what no coercive power of the state can; common needs bring together what the law cannot hold in unity" (13–14).[37]

What had been accomplished by 1906? Bavinck refers to the school law passed by the Kuyper government[38] that "brought about equal minimum salaries, paid by the government, for public and private schools alike; strengthened the equality of funding for school buildings; set forth identical conditions for the pensions of instructors, their widows and dependents." Consequently,

> both the material and spiritual situation has been changed. The pressure has been considerably eased: the heavy financial burden has been taken from the shoulders; fearful anxiety about old age, for the well-being of widows and dependents is gone; the future which had seemed so dark has become clear. Therefore, courage, inspiration, and enthusiasm have returned to the hearts of our teachers and schoolboard members. (14–15)

Bavinck frames this result in terms of the famous "social question" of the late nineteenth and early twentieth centuries.[39] "The social question," he contends,

> consists in large part in the quest for security of existence that people need in order to live and work in peace and quiet, a situation that in many ways is denied them because of changing circumstances. If they want to, people can say that thanks to the new school law of Kuyper (not definitively because there is nothing final in this fleeting world), the social question has been resolved. Insecurity has been replaced by security and safety. We can move ahead; the wagon is rolling again and the little ship of our schools has been brought into open water again. (15)

Bavinck continues with the sailing metaphor: "It is now up to us to sail forth with steady speed. The rest that has come about politically is least of all given to us for idleness and inactivity." Then follow these key sentences:

> The character of the struggle has changed, but it has not come to an end. Up to this point we fought to establish and maintain our schools, for the right and

---

37. Although Bavinck does not refer to Alexis de Tocqueville, his understanding of the link between liberty and a rich voluntary, associational life in America is similar to what the Frenchman observed in his *Democracy in America*. Tocqueville was known in Dutch neo-Calvinist circles; Abraham Kuyper references him seven times in his important 1874 publication *Het Calvinisme oorsprong en waarborg onzer Constitutioneele Vrijheden* (ET: "Calvinism: Source and Stronghold of Our Constitutional Liberties").

38. DO: *de school-wet-Kuyper*.

39. See the section "1. The Social Question," in chap. 1, pp. 11–32.

legal equality of the private school. Now, viewed externally, their existence is secured and their future ensured. The struggle continues therefore, not about the Christian school, but for the Christian school, for its inner confirmation and strengthening. We have moved out of the political period of the school struggle and into the pedagogical and methodological. (15)

That seems an appropriate point at which to move to our consideration of Bavinck's pedagogy.

That Bavinck considered the education of children a matter of importance for religious and theological considerations is evident in how he begins his *Paedagogische Beginselen* (Foundations of pedagogy).[40]

Among all the creatures on earth there are none born more helpless and in need of assistance than human beings. In general, animals can take care of themselves either immediately or shortly after birth. Children, however, are dependent on others for a long time and in everything. . . . They are born of communion[41] and tied to community, requiring the cooperation of community for them to grow and become mature. Unable to make claims of any right, they are forced to live from the unearned favor and gift of others. In other words, they live by grace. (9)

Bavinck goes on to say that this is also true more broadly for all of us. God willed

from the beginning to inculcate in human beings the feeling of dependence and humility, to imprint on us the awareness that we do not belong to ourselves, but are part of a greater whole, members of the organism of humanity. The helpless situation into which human beings are born has a great ethical significance, for humans themselves and for their environment. This obligates parents to care for their offspring, ties them closely to their family and calling, softens their morals, ennobles their inclinations, binds them closer together in love, and morally affects them in many ways. The power of a helpless child is great; it awakens helpfulness, love, and devotion, and gives rise to the most heroic deeds of self-denial. (9)

There is also a reciprocal moral lesson according to Bavinck. "The circumstance of dependency,[42] in which a child must live for a long time, is a mark

---

40. Bavinck, *Paedagogische Beginselen*; translations are from the 1904 first edition; original pages will be indicated in parentheses within the text.

41. DO: *gemeenschap*.

42. DO: *hulpbehoevenheid*.

of excellence[43] and an indication that he or she is called to develop higher" (9–10). This is a law of nature. In the same way that buildings "require more solid foundations, the greater they are," so too in the organic world: "That which ripens quickly also decays quickly.[44] A child requires long, tender care because he or she is human. This is rooted in a child's nature and is the condition of a child's existence and development" (10).

That this "parental care" is "natural," says Bavinck, "becomes even more clear when we consider that human beings at the time of their birth are not yet what they can become, and even less what they ought to become." This makes humans different from the angels and also distinct from animals. Unlike angels, animals do undergo a developmental process, but "with respect to animals, we do not speak of a goal, a destiny to which they must strive. They become what they will be by a natural process and not through free activity. If they fail to become what they could be, there may be a loss to their owner but the animal itself is indifferent to this because it is not a moral being" (10).

Therefore, the notion of "nurture"[45] is inappropriate with respect to the animal world. While some thinkers (Schopenhauer and Darwin) sought to minimize the difference between humans and animals and accentuate the similarities, especially at the physical level, Bavinck insists: "But the essential difference that exists, notwithstanding all the analogies between them, is also evident in bodily movements and activities. People bridle and refine their passions through higher motives." In addition to the contrast between the fleeting connection of animals to their offspring and the enduring love of a mother for her child, Bavinck points to language as a line of demarcation: "Human language does not take on an empty, arbitrary form but is the expression of thoughts and thus maintains the distinction between humans and animals because only among the former does it involve upbringing" (11).

Nurture differs essentially from human cultivation of plants and animals: "This essentially amounts to improving certain physical attributes by training some kinds of animals to specific bodily movements and acts. This training and improvement cannot be termed 'nurture.'"[46] The reverse is also true: "We should not use the language of training and improving for human beings. In

43. DO: *voortreffelijkheid*.
44. DO: *Wat vroeg rijp is, is ook vroeg bedorven*.
45. DO: *opvoeding*; another good translation for *opvoeding* is the more antiquated term "upbringing"; on its own, *opvoeden* can also mean "education."
46. DO: *opvoeding*. These two sentences have been reversed from the original to fit the narrative logic of my paragraph.

our day some want to go in the direction of improving humans into a higher type" (11).

Bavinck mentions here recent newspaper accounts of a

rich man in France who designated the returns of his capital to be directed to promoting marriage between the strongest men and women. But so long as physical strength remains distinct from greatness of soul and spiritual gifts from nerves and muscles, the difference will also remain between nurture and this kind of improvement. The human person exists between angels and animals, sharing with the former a spiritual, rational-moral nature. Humans are citizens in the kingdom of ideas and bound to the moral law. They need to be something and are not indifferent to what they will become. Humans share with animals the common reality that they can only become what they ought to be by way of development. They are born small, not big, young rather than old, as children rather than as mature. (11–12)

At the same time, a child is born with certain "capacities and aptitudes and is, therefore, not a '*tabula rasa*'; even a child is fully human. But a child is human in embryo, in potential, and needs nurture to come to where he or she needs to be. Nurture is both necessary and possible. Human beings need and are also suited for nurture" (11–12).

Human beings have bodies and souls, and both need care. Bodies need to be fed, and souls need to be nourished. "What feeding is to the physical life of humans, nurture is to the psychical existence of humans as rational-moral beings" (12).[47] The needs of body and soul must be distinguished but should never be separated. Bavinck even acknowledges some "truth"[48] in Feuerbach's famous aphorism that "human beings are what they eat."[49]

The unfed body starves to death physically; the unfed soul starves to death spiritually. Children who are not nurtured become wild like unpruned trees and become whatever accidental circumstances fashion them to be. Such children are like ships that are tossed about by the waves. People who are deprived of all nurture become a curse to themselves, are a shame to their families, a drag on society, and a dishonor to God. Nurture is essential, a vital condition for the spiritual, rational-moral well-being of humans. (12–13)

47. The contrast between "feeding" and "nurture" is expressed through a Dutch-language wordplay between *voeding* and *opvoeding*.

48. DO: *waarheid*.

49. GO: *Der Mensch ist, was er isst*. Bavinck provides no source; the aphorism can be found in Feuerbach, "Das Geheimniss des Opfers, oder Der Mensch ist, was er isst (1862)."

While the need to feed one's body is obvious, Bavinck insists that care for the soul is "even more necessary." The nurture of souls is a communal activity, "utilizing the goods given to and acquired by the human race."

In an unbroken line, one half of the human race is busy nurturing the other half. The preceding generation labors continuously to provide the physical and spiritual care to elevate the subsequent generation to achieve its own heights and to share its treasures. A fullness of abilities and powers comes into existence with every human child and every human generation, placing an obligation upon the mature half of humanity to cultivate them and bring them to development. (13)

Consequently, we need to acknowledge that there are "innumerable" influences on each person from the time of birth:

Nature and environment, family and society, vocation and class, church and state, conditions and circumstances, words and deeds. . . . We all live and grow up in a rich world of visible and invisible things, and consciously or unconsciously are formed and led by that world. While it is true that the idea of nurture usually (and correctly) has a narrower meaning, we may not overlook the great, formative power that, unconsciously and unintentionally, the entire environment and society presses upon each individual person.

In fact, Bavinck adds, "Rather, this power serves as the presupposition and foundation of nurture in its real and more narrow sense" (13–14). Bavinck concludes with a statement of faith about God's providence:

From a rational point of view, we could not even speak of nurturing human beings or humanity, if God did not stand behind all those factors that influence us either consciously or unconsciously; he is the Creator of heaven and earth, the real educator[50] of the whole human race and the one who holds all the threads of world-administration in his hands.

Notwithstanding the multitude of influences on the nurture of souls,

as a rule, nurture is regarded in a narrower sense. In some languages this is even included in the word itself. The Greek word *teknogonia* signifies the

---

50. DO: *eigenlijke opvoeder*; Bavinck provides the following footnote: "Otto Willmann, *Didaktik als Bildungslehre*, 1:18–19"; Willmann (1839–1920) was a German Roman Catholic philosopher and pedagogue who emphasized the social nature of education. Source: *Encyclopedia.com*, s.v. "Willmann, Otto." https://www.encyclopedia.com/religion/encyclopedias-almanacs-transcripts-and-maps/willmann-otto.

nurture of children as well as their birth. The Latin word *educare* means "to bring forth" and "to bring up."[51] The German *ziehen* [to pull, draw], *aufziehen* [to draw up, lift] is linked to *zeugen* [to engender, beget, procreate], and both meet each other again in *zucht* [breeding, rearing] and *züchten* [to breed, raise]. In the Dutch language *opvoeden* includes the idea that in upbringing a child is transported upward, led to heights, drawn higher."[52]

Nonetheless,

in all these languages, the word points us in the direction of the small circle of the family and not to the whole of society. Rearing children in a way that is directed by their life and well-being points us to the activity of the parents who gave them life. This activity initially is purely physical in nature and designed to sustain bodily life; gradually and to a greater degree, however, this activity takes on a moral and spiritual character. This is when we speak of nurture in its true sense, an activity that has the formation of the human being as a human person[53] and leads him or her from a state of immaturity and roughness to maturity, moral freedom, spiritual independence. (14)[54]

Because nurture "takes on such an ethical, spiritual character, it must increasingly become a conscious, intentional, systematic activity" (14–15). This means "that nurture increasingly becomes an art, a personal, conscious, intentional, ethical activity." Here Bavinck goes on to make a number of important distinctions between the nurture of the family and the education of the school. "Parental nurture is guided by instinct . . . and characterized by the bonds of love . . . because they gave life to the child." While truly caring parents do reflect on their activity and take advantage of broader insights, the tight bonds of love that characterize the inner circle of families

cannot be replaced by or improved upon by any profound pedagogical study. The heart often suggests to parents how they can provide the best for their children's bodily and spiritual needs. Deep affection often weighs against a lack of understanding; when no one knows what to do, a mother often is still able to find a way to the heart of her child. Experience teaches us that many

51. DO: *te voorschijn brengen en opvoeden.*
52. The original Dutch text involves a wordplay between *voeding* (food, nourishment) and *opvoeding* (nurture, upbringing). DO: *En in ons woord opvoeden ligt de gedachte, dat het kind door voeding omhoog gevoord, naar boven geleid, opgeleid wordt.*
53. DO: *den mensch als mensch.*
54. In parenthesis Bavinck adds: *erudire = e rudibus ducere* (to be led out of roughness—i.e., a state of being uncultivated or uncivilized).

parents who have never methodically reflected on child rearing and never studied pedagogy have nonetheless practically provided an excellent upbringing for their children and were able later to see rich rewards upon their labor. And conversely, there are learned and renowned pedagogues who in practice proved to be very clumsy and whose activity yielded no fruit. (15–16)

Bavinck draws one final distinction between "family and school, between nurture and education." The crucial distinction is that nurture is a broader category than education. It is true that they are closely bound together: "Education must always retain a nurturing character and have the whole person in view." Nonetheless,

education is not the whole of upbringing but only a part of it. Education specifically concerns itself with the intellectual faculties and tries to achieve this goal through acquiring material knowledge and formally by developing the entire intellectual faculty through practice of its capacity to observe, to understand, to reason, etc. (16)

Having considered the context and framework of Bavinck's work in pedagogy, particularly his understanding of the human person who is the object of all rearing, nurture, and education, we can move on to the content of Bavinck's Christian pedagogy.[55] "Christianity," Bavinck says, "brought about a great change in the theory and practice of education." It is important to be clear about the nature of this change; it is not direct, because "Christianity is not pedagogy as such, no more than it is a social or political system or some kind of special science." Bavinck points to regeneration and the new person in Christ, who is "a citizen of the kingdom of heaven," but Bavinck does not provide details as to how this new identity shapes pedagogy; he only states that it does. Christianity

had a most powerful influence on all of life in society and state, in science and art, and also on education and nurture. This influence is also shown in the fact that when Christianity through the ages split into various churches and confessions, each of these groups brought about special and unique changes in the common educational ideal. (205)

The essay from which I am quoting was published in 1909, and Bavinck indicates a general disillusion with the state of education everywhere.

---

55. My primary source will be Bavinck's essay "Trends in Pedagogy," in *ERSS*, 205–8; page references that follow in the text are to this work.

Enlightenment hopes in the triumph of reason and science were applied to education in the nineteenth century, and money was spent on education with "the promise that money given to schools would be provided through less cost for prisons." This promise

did not come true. The misery in the lower classes increased dramatically. With further research, science proved unable to solve the deepest problems. The better they became known, the soul and life and even nature proved to contain more mysteries. Russian and Norwegian novels brought to light unexpected depths of humanity and the world. (206)

Consequently,

the praise and jubilation about schools . . . gradually gave way to pessimistic complaints and unmerciful judgments. At times the criticism hardly left anything intact. Following Rousseau and Tolstoy, all of our culture was condemned and regarded as the cause of all our miseries. Our modern education was particularly considered to be an impenetrable thicket of foolishness, prejudices, and blunders. Education, it was said, destroyed all that was good in a child: desire for knowledge, capability of observation, independence and personality. Instead, education filled children with fear and fright, brought about anemia and nervous breakdown, and often caused suicide. It would be desirable if a flood would come and obliterate education from the earth. Even though the criticism was fortunately not always this shrill, nearly everyone became convinced that our system of schooling and education, which for years had been regarded as nearly perfect, was terribly deficient. Thus reformation had to come, not just here and there, on some issues, but completely and radically, in head and members. (205)

Bavinck divides the reform efforts into four groups. The specifics of these groups are not as important as Bavinck's summary in his conclusion, where he makes the following three points:

1. Negatively and formally, there is great agreement, because all these reformers consider the existing situation insufficient, and they press for transforming the whole school system, such as improvement in the training and position of teachers, better divisions and connections among the schools, sifting and selection of pupils, smaller classes, fewer subjects, and so forth.
2. As soon as principles enter the discussion, there are all kinds of differences and strife—about the relationship of Christianity and culture, family

and school, the individual and society, body and soul, mind and will, and so forth.

3. With a completely secular idea of the task of education, these differences are irreconcilable, because the purpose of the creature is never found in the creature itself, but from the nature of things, only in God, the Creator. (208)

Bavinck approaches the questions of his own day through a history lesson that goes back to the early church. In the midst of social upheaval and educational reform movements, what should a Christian education look like in content? In good measure it should have a classical tint.[56] From its beginnings the Christian church struggled with its distinct identity over against the "world" of its day.[57]

When Christianity gained entrance into the Greco-Roman world through the preaching of the apostles, it soon faced the serious question about its posture toward the existing richly developed culture. This question had to be faced practically even before it had been considered theoretically. The admonition of Christ and the apostles that one must not be conformed to the world, but must bear all persecution and violence patiently, resounded very seriously. In their teaching, critical and passive qualities were so obvious that there was virtually no room for active participation in the life of culture. (210)[58]

At the same time, Christians remained in the world:

They got married and were given in marriage, they had children and they had to educate them for some kind of occupation. They themselves were involved in various jobs and had to work for their daily bread. Thus they participated in manual labor and industry, in commerce and shipping, and even in the service of army and state. The same happened in relation to the ideal elements in the Greco-Roman culture, such as literature and art, science and philosophy. (211)

56. What follows is taken from Bavinck, "Classical Education," in *ERSS*, 209–43; the qualifier "in good measure" is important here; as we shall see, Bavinck's advocacy of a classical education is qualified. For a more comprehensive view of Bavinck's pedagogy, see especially Brederveld, *Christian Education*. For a more recent examination of Bavinck's pedagogy, concentrating on the classical accent, see Price, *Pedagogy as Theological Praxis*.

57. The New Testament is filled with warnings to Christians about the temptations offered by the "world" and its "enmity": John 17:14–18; Rom. 12:2; 1 John 4:1–4.

58. These last two sentences serve as an accurate summary of Bavinck's understanding of the imitation of Christ in the discipleship of the early church. See *RD*, 1:317–41; cf. *Imitatio Christi*, 317–19, 372–440.

This raised the practical question, "Where could one find such training apart from the pagan schools? After all, in the beginning the Christians themselves did not have their own institutions of education, except for the catechumenate, and for a long time in many places lacked such institutions" (211).

Bavinck then devotes several paragraphs to the early church debates between those who followed Tertullian's antipathy to Greco-Roman philosophy and culture and those who followed the Alexandrians, Clement and Origen, in warmly embracing it. He sees Augustine as the one who resolved the tension by affirming "marriage, family, occupations, science, art, and so forth as natural gifts that could be appreciated and enjoyed (as Augustine said, *magna haec et omnino humana* [this is great and wholly human])." But these created goods and gifts "were of a lower rank, inferior to and in service of the supernatural order, which had descended to earth in the church and in its hierarchy, mysteries, and sacraments." Christians were free to use all the treasures of pagan cultures: "They were like the people of Israel, who in their departure from Egypt had taken the gold and silver of their oppressors and decorated the tabernacle with it." Similarly, Christians also honored God

when they dedicated all human gifts and energies that had been revealed in ancient culture to its highest purpose. Thus the paintings in the catacombs already resembled the style of antiquity, the architecture of the churches was arranged according to the models of the basilica, and philosophy was used for the defense of the Christian faith. (212)

The history of Christian education as Bavinck views it is a history of repeated cycles of flourishing, decline, and renewal of the synthesis between the Christian faith and the cultural treasures of antiquity. Furthermore, the renewal and flourishing of Christian schooling is directly linked to the recovery and constructive use of the languages (Greek and Latin) and philosophy of the Greco-Roman civilization, reaching its apex in the trivium and quadrivium and curriculum of the medieval schools.[59] Bavinck was quite aware that this ideal of education was no longer fashionable in his day:

But above all, we live in a different time. Classical antiquity is so far removed from modern culture: because the latter rests in so many ways on different foundations and contains other elements, we hardly feel the relationship of our culture with the ancient. It lies so far in the past that we can no longer use it as

---

59. Also known as the seven liberal arts: trivium—rhetoric, grammar, and dialectic; quadrivium—mathematics, geometry, music, astronomy.

a model. It is not so much the Middle Ages, but rather the modern period which
began in the fifteenth century, that has created such a deep chasm between
antiquity and us. (228)

Bavinck identifies three "factors" that needed to be taken into account in
any educational reforms of his day:

1. "Awakening of the love of nature." From a medieval scorn of nature "as
something unholy, as the domain of the evil one, as the home and workshop
of demonic powers" that was to be avoided and suppressed, in the new understanding "the human subject experienced an awakening; it came to realize its
inner life; it regained its own soul and therewith the soul in nature" [229].[60]
This nature mysticism also led to a natural science

that tried to understand the world according to an analogy with man himself, as
a spiritual unity, as a living organism. The thinkers listed above[61] did not want
to explain the world mechanically and materialistically but dynamically, as a
continuing development of the life of nature, which at times was pantheistically
identified with divine life. (230)

2. Scholarship in a new mode. Following the lead of Roger Bacon (1219/20–
1292), people began to pursue knowledge via observation and experience
rather than primarily in books. But Bavinck also takes note of "the surprising
number of discoveries and inventions that occurred from the fifteenth century
onward." Bavinck points to the discoveries made by oceangoing explorers like
Columbus, Vasco da Gama, and Magellan along with the scientific discoveries
in astronomy by Copernicus, Kepler, and Galileo, and Newton's discovery
of the law of gravity.

And then followed the inventions of movable print, gunpowder, the compass,
optic glass, thermometer, barometer, burning mirror, air pump, and so forth.
Through all these things, man's horizon was broadened, his relationship to
the world changed, and learning was recognized as a force that could perform
great service to the struggle for existence. (231)

60. Bavinck identifies the following as key figures in this revived "nature mysticism": Francis
of Assisi; the Renaissance humanist Giovanni Pico della Mirandola (1463–94); the German
Catholic humanist and philologist Johann Reuchlin (1455–1522); the German Catholic humanist
theologian and cardinal Nicholas of Cusa (1401–64); the Italian polymath Gerolamo Cardano
(1501–76); the German polymath and occult writer Heinrich Cornelius Agrippa von Nettesheim
(1486–1535); and the Swiss philosopher, physician, and alchemist Paracelsus (1493–1541; full
name: Philippus Aureolus Theophrastus Bombastus von Hohenheim) [230].
    61. See previous footnote.

The philosopher Francis Bacon (1561–1626) turned the intellectual world toward empiricism and inductive reasoning. If learning was to be renewed and lifted up from its "lamentable state," past notions must be discarded: "Whoever wanted to achieve knowledge must first discard all preconceived notions" (231).

When a person has thus laid aside all prejudgments, then he himself must observe and experiment; in other words, he must apply the inductive method. He must not study things from books, nor let himself be led by theology or other speculations, because theology does not belong in scholarship and is purely a matter of faith. A person must look at things himself and ask them what they are. We will not derive any benefit from those who are in their element with words, who amuse themselves with dialectic subtleties, who derive all their wisdom from books. We can come to firm and certain knowledge only by way of pure experience,[62] by way of impartial observation and careful experiment. (231)

The end result was a revolution in European thought:

In this way Bacon called people from books to reality, from words to deeds, from verbalism to realism. He thus brought about a major revolution in the thinking and striving of the people of Europe. Until then people had looked backward. Christian Europe turned its eyes to the past, to apostles and prophets, to church fathers and Scholastics. Even the humanists, no matter how convinced they were of their own worth, looked up admiringly to the classics as their models. The sixteenth century was the era of the Reformation and the Renaissance.

However, with Bacon, and in a different way with Descartes, a change came about. They looked for paradise, the state of happiness of humankind, not in the past but in the future. The ancients might have been the pioneers of learning, but they were not the finishers; they must therefore not be followed but rather outpaced and surpassed. A new learning had to arise that would be practiced according to a strictly empirical and experimental method that would achieve power through knowledge and grant man dominion over nature. (232)

The flourishing of the natural sciences that followed this change led to a mechanistic and naturalist worldview: "In the beginning of this movement, Deism still accepted the working of a Creator and tried to maintain man's

---

62. LO: *mera experientia*.

independence and the immortality of the soul." This was an unstable situation
that could not and did not last: "However, materialism tried to understand
man himself as a machine and expanded its dominion over further, until a
reaction occurred toward the end of the previous [nineteenth] century and the
dynamic worldview once again found acceptance with many scholars" (232).

   3. Development and differentiation of society. Paralleling the separation
of academic subjects

> from theology and philosophy in the more recent era, in the same way society
> withdrew itself ever more from the custody of church and state. Society devel-
> oped its own existence and began to lead a life of its own. Through commerce,
> industry, worldwide contacts, machines, and factories, various occupations and
> companies increased continually, but the requirements for practicing these
> occupations became ever higher. The more society developed, the more it
> needed instruction and training. (232–33)

A new kind of learning was required:

> The old method of nurture and education had as its main purpose to have
> the student acquire a knowledge of the past and to induct him into one of the
> existing guilds for learning, art, or craft. This method worked well in its time
> but is not suitable today. It overloaded the memory, but critical thinking was
> underdeveloped; it created people learned but not wise, obedient but not
> independent. Today we need a different education, one that is derived from
> nature and that takes its position not in antiquity but in the present. Its purpose
> is to form a person to be an independent being, with his or her own thoughts
> and judgments, to be a useful, helpful member of society. (233)

Bavinck adds:

> This realistic idea in education firmly put itself in the present. It assumed that
> the material offered by the present was sufficient for education and nurture,
> and it took seriously the needs of modern society. These needs focused on
> the fact that there had to be schools that (in distinction from the humanistic
> institutions for the learned professions) would provide knowledge and skill for
> real life and would train young people for various occupations in society. (233)

   After providing examples of such changes in German schools, Bavinck
turns to his own country and points to the efforts to meet the needs of the
"so-called industrial-technical citizenry," not just for "vocational skills, which

at that time could still be obtained partially in the workshop [via apprentice-ship], but also for broader theoretical development," leading the government of Dutch prime minister Johan Thorbecke to create "higher burgerschools"[63] in 1863. These schools were situated "between the vocational schools and the gymnasiums" (233).[64]

Bavinck approves of these changes to broaden educational opportunities for students and acknowledges that "classical antiquity is no longer the ideal of education for us, and it will never again be that" (241). At the same time the benefits of knowing about the classical past must not be dismissed:

> But the great cultural and historical value of that antiquity has never been realized as well as today. The influence of Israel and also of Hellas and Latium on our culture is much more clear to us now than in previous centuries; these are and will remain our spiritual forebears. The study of antiquity is therefore not only of formal and practical value for the development of thinking, under-standing Greek and Latin terms in our scholarship, understanding citations and allusions in our literature, and so forth. Its lasting value also lies in the fact that the foundations of modern culture were laid in antiquity. The roots of all our arts and learning—and also, though in lesser degree, the sciences that study nature—are to be found in the soil of antiquity. It is amazing how the Greeks created all those forms of beauty in which our aesthetic feeling still finds expres-sion and satisfaction today; in their learning they realized and posited all the problems of the world and of life with which we still wrestle in our heads and hearts. They were able to achieve that, on the one hand, because they rose above folk religion and struggled for the independence of art and learning; but on the other hand, they did not loosen art and learning from those religious and ethical factors that belong to man's essence. In the midst of distressing reality, they kept the faith in a world of ideas and norms. And that idealism is also indispensable today; it cannot be replaced or compensated for by the history of civilization or new literature. (241–42)

---

63. DO: *hoogere burgerscholen*. The term *burger* can also be translated as "commoner" and used to contrast townspeople (*burgers*) with countryfolk (*boeren*) or with nobility (*edelen*). The term *hoogere burgerscholen* reflects the class structure of nineteenth-century Dutch society; these schools were intended to be a cut above the vocational/trade schools but still not intended to prepare students for university. A comparable distinction is made programmatically in North American high schools between the basic requirements for high school graduation and the preparatory set of courses for those who intend to go to college or university. Source: Van Dale Dictionary, s.v. "Burger," https://www.vandale.nl/.

64. The word "gymnasium" is used in various European countries, including the Nether-lands, for secondary schools designed to prepare students for higher education at a university. The education offered is academically rigorous and classical in its orientation.

Bavinck published this essay in 1918, just as World War I was drawing to a close. He expresses concern that the fierce nationalism that was estranging "nations from each other—nations that belong to each other according to history, religion, and culture"—would result in submerging "all unity and cooperation" under a sea of "enmity and hate for a long, long time, perhaps forever." He concludes:

> That is why it is an international concern to maintain and build on the foundations on which modern culture rests. If there is one thing that is essential in these grave times, it is that Christian nations be reconciled to each other, close ranks, and take to heart the call to conserve the treasure that has been entrusted to them in religion and culture. This is also true for religion, for the Christian religion. (242)

I conclude this section on Christian day-school education with Bavinck's own summary of the important principles of Christian pedagogy in a meditation on Proverbs 4:1–13, delivered as his opening presidential remarks to the General Assembly of the Association of Reformed Schools in the Netherlands, May 12, 1915.[65]

> The passage just read provides us with a complete program of upbringing;[66] all the principles of education are implied in it.[67] We are directed to the formation of the understanding as the *goal*[68] of education, not in the sense of capacity[69] but as the understanding acquired through instruction; this is synonymous with wisdom. Proverbs is not only concerned with the wisdom of the understanding but also with the wisdom of moral insight. Proverbs is both theoretical and practical in nature. It also provides wisdom for our acting.
>
> Second, the passage also proposes the *means* for obtaining wisdom: teaching, law, oral argument. The content is derived from all the law, first from the Law of God, but also from all his ordinances. Above all from his Word,

---

65. Bavinck, "Minutes of a short introduction inspired by Proverbs 4:1–13, delivered to the General Assembly of the 'Association of Reformed Schools in the Netherlands'" (see article "Verslag van een korte inleiding . . ." in bibliography). The account in this newsletter is not a verbatim transcription but an "approximate" (*ongeveer*) report; I translated the title as "minutes" following the actual term used in the published account—namely, *notulen*. Standard Bavinck bibliographies use the term "report" (DO: *verslag*).

66. After this initial translation of *opvoeding* as "upbringing," I will be translating it with the more familiar "education."

67. DO: *liggen er in opgesloten.*

68. DO: *doel*; the emphasis of Bavinck's five key terms—goal, means, method, significance, and fruit—is not original but added for greater clarity.

69. DO: *vermogen.*

but also insofar as they are known from history and nature and come to us through tradition. We must expand them and pass them on to succeeding generations.

Third, discipline is the way or *method* for achieving this. The Hebrew term for discipline has the broader meaning of instruction, admonition. The essence of discipline is not punishment, which is merely something incidental. Discipline is "instructing," in contrast with "instruction"[70]; it is exhortation and encouragement and therefore involves moral as well as intellectual guidance. Discipline and instructing come from the teacher-guide, but the son must also grab hold of them, preserve them. In other words, there must be activity from the side of the child. A child must be observant with heart and soul.

Fourth, the passage points to the high *significance* of wisdom. She is called a jewel, a crown, a pleasing addition. She is a "garland." Wisdom, therefore, has an aesthetic dimension; she civilizes and truly beautifies. Wisdom also controls form.

Finally, the *fruit* of wisdom is mentioned. Wisdom protects from error and gives life, a long life on earth. The Old Testament means here something more than life as mere existence; it has in view a life filled with joy. Wisdom makes one happy.

Thus, this portion of Proverbs provides for us a full program for education.

4. CHRISTIAN SCHOLARSHIP

Bavinck dedicated a book of 121 pages to the subject of Christian scholarship.[71] In what follows I shall outline the main points of his argument.

---

70. DO: *onderwijs*; *onderwijzing*; grammatically, Bavinck is distinguishing between a noun and a verb, between a "product" of education (content) and the activity of educating or teaching.

71. Bavinck, *Christelijke Wetenschap* (1904); page references that follow in parentheses in the text are to this work. The Dutch word *wetenschap* (German: *Wissenschaft*) is usually translated as "science." However, in English-speaking countries "science" is often used to refer only to the natural or physical sciences, while Bavinck's view incorporates the whole world of scholarship, including the so-called social sciences. In his dissertation on Bavinck's understanding of Christianity and culture, Bastian Kruithof puts it this way: "By a Christian science (*wetenschap*) Bavinck understands the whole realm of knowledge to which man is exposed and which he can investigate" (Kruithof, "The Relation of Christianity and Culture in the Teaching of Herman Bavinck," 14). Ordinarily, I will be translating *wetenschap* as "scholarship"; occasionally when it seems appropriate, especially as a reference to the natural sciences, I will translate it as "science," bearing in mind that the term extends beyond the natural sciences to include the so-called spiritual sciences (see n. 94, below). Scholarship on Bavinck's own scientific-scholarly work includes Kristensen, "Over den wetenschappelijken arbeid van Herman Bavinck" (ET: Kristensen, "W. B. Kristensen's 'On Herman Bavinck's Scientific Work'").

a. Context: The Neo-Calvinist Revival

Bavinck opens the work with a third-person account of the late nineteenth-century Dutch Calvinist renewal initiated by Abraham Kuyper and in which he himself played a significant role. It is best to look at this volume as Bavinck's mid-flight contribution to the very "scholarship" he is describing here.[72]

A serious and powerful impulse has been awakened in recent years once again also to construct Christian scholarship on the foundation of the Christian faith. People may disagree about the value of this fact, but that it exists cannot be denied. Gradually the circle is expanding of those who are dissatisfied with the direction of today's dominant scholarship, both in practice and in theory. Many long for something different, a different foundation and method for the practice of scholarship. Similarly, there can be no disagreement about the origin and character of this longing. For anyone willing to look, it is abundantly clear that it proceeds from and is led by religious motives. The foundation, method, and direction of contemporary scholarship stands under judgment in the name of religion, for the sake of Christian truth. The goal is to bridge the divide between school and life and come to the defense of the church's confession. Even those who sing the praises of contemporary scholarship cannot close their eyes to the religious character of this movement. Recently, Prof. Groenewegen of Leiden provided noteworthy testimony to this: "The religious reaction proceeded quietly; the public church-political reaction followed. And now, in conclusion, scholarship must crown that striving and, if it can, preserve and establish it. No one should fail to acknowledge the original religious motive in this undoubtedly powerful reactionary movement, a religious element that sometimes gives it a character worthy of respect." (5)[73]

Bavinck fully agrees with this judgment and observes that Christians in the eighteenth century had "sunk into a deep sleep" from which they were "suddenly awakened" in the early part of the nineteenth century as "the Christian, confessional, and ecclesiastical consciousness was shaken awake from its drowsiness" (5–6). He points to the spiritual-literary renewal movement known as the Réveil, along with the Secession of 1834, the political struggle for educational equity, the establishment of the Theological School in Kampen

---

72. Something of a parallel could be seen in Mark Noll's lament in his *The Scandal of the Evangelical Mind*, where his own work gave wonderful evidence of an evangelical mind fruitfully at work.

73. Bavinck cites H. I. Y. Groenewegen, "Wetenschap of Dogmatisme," 393; on the debate between Bavinck and Groenewegen, see Marinus de Jong, "The Heart of the Academy: Herman Bavinck in Debate with Modernity on the Academy, Theology, and the Church."

(1854), and the establishment of the Vrije Universiteit in Amsterdam (1880), as admittedly "weak" but nonetheless real evidence that a revival of Christian scholarship is taking place, one "that fills the heart with joyful hope for the future" (6).

This revival does not stand alone, according to Bavinck. He points to the revived interest in Thomas Aquinas among Roman Catholics after Pope Leo XIII's encyclical *Aeterni Patris: On the Restoration of Christian Philosophy*, on August 4, 1879.[74] In addition, all this is happening at the same time that it is also becoming evident that "the days of positivism are numbered" (7). For many, the philosophy of Kant

has lost its charm. The philosophy of Hume and Comte is increasingly set aside for that of Leibniz and Hegel. Everywhere we see a turn away from empiricism to idealism; after the overwhelming dominance of reason, feeling is asserting its rights. Theory yields to life and rationalism makes way for romanticism. Mysticism makes its entry into the world of art. In the natural sciences we observe a turnabout that would have been inconceivable a decade ago. Materialism was then held to be the highest wisdom, and the mechanical explanation of the world was judged to be the only scientific one. Today we now see that many of the best natural scientists turn from mechanism to dynamism, from materialism to energy, from causality back to teleology and from atheism back to theism. After the thirst for facts has been quenched, a hunger for knowledge rises to the top, a hunger to know about the origin and goal, the cause and essence of things. (7–8)[75]

"Naturally, this remarkable turnaround in scholarship also bodes well for religion" (8). Efforts by philosophers such as Ernst Haeckel using the natural sciences to sound the death knell for belief in "God, the soul, and immortality" failed to convince many.[76] "The metaphysical need lies too deep in human nature for any silencing of it to be enforced in the long run." Bavinck points to the "compensation"[77] for which people in his time are searching "in spiritism

---

74. Available at Papal Encyclicals Online, https://www.papalencyclicals.net/leo13/l13cph.htm.

75. Bavinck added footnote references here to Ludwig Stein, *Der Sinn des Daseins*, 84, and Prof. van der Vlugt in the Second Chamber (of the Dutch parliament), February 26, 1904 (*Handelingen*, p. 1391).

76. Ernst Haeckel (1834–1919) was a German zoologist and philosopher who popularized Darwin's theory of evolution in Germany. His most famous work is *The Riddle of the Universe* (German: *Die Welträtsel*), published in 1899. Bavinck frequently uses Haeckel as a foil; see Bavinck, *Christian Worldview*, 59–63, 69, 78; Bavinck, *Philosophy of Revelation* (2018), 16, 27, 36–39, 73–75, 81–85, 123–24.

77. DO: *vergoeding*.

and theosophy, in the worship of humanity and the divinization of culture," as a "clear proof of the necessity [to satisfy this metaphysical urge]." As people tired of "doubt and uncertainty," there arose "in broad circles a longing for a more or less positive Christian faith" (8). The "urge for a confession and dogmatics, for church organization and unity of liturgy," can even be found among the "modern theologians" (8).[78] Failure of the "exact sciences" to deliver what revisionists such as Ernst Renan "in their youthful enthusiasm expected" led people to "turn, not always in genuine sorrow but at least in despondent doubt, to the religion they first maligned." Bavinck considers this a valuable opportunity: "A time that displays such signs cannot be considered unfavorable for the practice of scholarship in a Christian spirit. It is therefore important that we give a clear accounting of what is involved in the practice of such scholarship, to ourselves and others, to friend and foe." A choice must be made: "Believing and unbelieving, Christian and positivist understandings of science and scholarship are diametrically opposed one to the other. Compromise is impossible here; a definite choice must be made" (9).

b. The Two Options: Christianity or Positivism

After stating the choice facing science and scholarship in these stark terms, Bavinck goes on to sketch a history of the two options, beginning with the idea of Christian scholarship. He tracks its origins to the early church, which faced a world of a "highly developed culture." It was also a tired culture, characterized by "eclecticism and syncretism and mysticism," along with a "doubting or mocking skepticism that asked, 'What is truth?'" (10). In such a world

of unbelief and superstition, the apostles of Jesus planted the banner of truth. The Christian religion is, after all, not only the religion of grace but also the religion of truth; it is the one because it is the other. That is why Holy Scripture speaks so frequently about truth; its essence and value is placed in the clearest light throughout the entirety of revelation. Because God himself is pure truth, the genuine and real God, in distinction from all creatures who have no existence

---

78. Bavinck added footnote references here to two articles in P. H. Hugenholtz Jr., ed., *Religion and Liberty: Addresses and Papers at the Second International Council of Unitarian and Other Liberal Religious Thinkers and Workers* (the gathering took place in Amsterdam in September 1903): A. Bruining, "Het aggressief karakter van het vrijzinnig godsdienstig geloof" (168–78); S. Cramer, "Does Liberal Christianity Want Organizing in Special Churches and Congregations?" (227–37). Cramer says: "I hold, that in our time with its dissolution of so many moral and social certainties, its relativism and its increasing clericalism and confessionalism, we liberals are perhaps more than ever in need of concentration and association; of churches and congregations, confederated and cooperating by conferences and by their press" (229).

in themselves; especially in contrast to human beings who are deceitful, and with idols who are nonentities and vanities. (10)

Furthermore, because Jesus is "the faithful witness, the firstborn of the dead,"[79]

his gospel is therefore also the word of truth. And so that we might believe this gospel he sent his Holy Spirit, who, as the Spirit of truth, leads us into all truth and testifies and seals it in our hearts. Those who accept this gospel in faith are in the truth; they are regenerated, sanctified, and set free by the truth.[80] They are in the truth and the truth is in them. They speak and do the truth and are willing to give up even their lives for their confession.[81] (11)

This conviction that the gospel provided all the treasures of knowledge led the early Christians to think of themselves as a people, a "third race," a restoration of the original people for whom God had created the world:[82]

They were the people of God, the oldest nation on earth for whom the world was created. In the New Testament all the divisions between Jew and pagan, between Greek and barbarian, were reconciled in a higher unity. This called them to a task that encompassed the whole world as those who with Christ were heirs of all things. (10)[83]

79. Taken from Rev. 1:5; not indicated by Bavinck.

80. In the original, Bavinck cites Adolf von Harnack, *The Mission and Expansion of Christianity in the First Three Centuries*, 1:219–782, at the conclusion of the lengthy paragraph from which I am pulling out key excerpts. I chose to move the reference to the beginning so that I can provide evidence (in footnotes) to show how Bavinck relies on Harnack for his summary reconstruction of early Christian history. Here is what Harnack says about the significance of wisdom, knowledge, and reason in the apostle Paul: "In Paul one feels the joy of the thinker who enters into the thoughts of God, and is convinced that in and with and through his faith he has passed from darkness into light, from confusion, cloudiness, and oppression, into lucidity and liberty" (*Mission and Expansion*, 1:224–25).

81. "It is with amazement that we sound the depths of all this missionary preaching; yet those who engaged in it were prepared at any moment to drop everything and rest their whole faith on the confession that 'There is one God of heaven and earth, and Jesus is the Lord'" (Harnack, *Mission and Expansion*, 1:239).

82. The language of "third race" is not used by Bavinck.

83. Harnack sets forth six convictions by which the early Christians defined themselves: "(1) Our people is older than the world; (2) the world was created for our sakes; (3) the world is carried on for our sakes; we retard the judgment of the world; (4) everything in the world is subject to us and must serve us; (5) everything in the world, the beginning and course and end of all history, is revealed to us and lies transparent to our eyes; (6) we shall take part in the judgment of the world and ourselves enjoy eternal bliss" (Harnack, *Mission and Expansion*, 1:302).

Working out this all-encompassing task in society and in scholarship did not take place overnight. Bavinck zeroes in on Augustine as the one who pointed the way in which "a Christian practice of scholarship" needed to go (15). He sums it up thus:

> We believe the truth of God precisely because we do not understand it; but, through faith we become equipped to understand it. Faith and science/scholarship are in relation to each other as conception and birth, as tree and fruit, and work and salary; knowledge is the fruit and wage of faith. (16)

"An edifice of Christian scholarship was erected" on the foundations of Augustine's work, an edifice that "stood for ages and still attracts the attentive observer to its greatness." Although it was practiced until roughly the middle of the eighteenth century, Bavinck notes that it "suffered from one-sidedness and inadequacies" (17). These inadequacies include (1) increasing separation of faith and reason; division of natural and supernatural truths; (2) too much focus on theology, particularly dogmatics; (3) devaluation of the empirical. All this led to a reaction and the critiques of thinkers like Immanuel Kant, followed by speculative philosophers like Fichte, Schelling, and Hegel. The idealism of the later three had its own reaction in the return of inductive empiricism in thinkers like Auguste Comte and John Stuart Mill. The goal was a complete "presuppositionless"[84] scholarship.

> According to this conception scholarship had earlier on taken place in a theological and metaphysical phase but now has left this phase and needs to go over to a positive period. Just as a sociological law that a human being is a theologian during childhood and a metaphysician in adolescence, in order to become a physicist in adulthood, so too the human race passes through these three periods. (23)

Consequently, the human race has

> come to awareness that the empirical and induction are the basis of all scholarship, that the human spirit does not ascend to unseen and eternal things, and even less is able to penetrate to the ground of phenomena. Not only God and divine matters, but also substance and attributes, causes and goals of things, are once and for all unknowable because of their metaphysical nature. (23)

---

84. GO: *Voraussetzungslösigkeit*.

Here is the contrast in a nutshell: "Previously science was described as an investigation in the essence and cause of things, as an effort to 'know the causes of things';[85] now it must be conceived of as striving to learn to know the 'connection of things'" (23).[86]

In his response to positivism, Bavinck points to the internal incoherence of the claim to have a "presuppositionless"[87] science. The very notion is itself

a fruit of positive philosophy. This philosophy is every bit as much a philosophy and in the same way as the philosophy of Plato and Aristotle, of Schelling and Hegel. And it is not the philosophy but the philosophical worldview of a specific thinker[88] and of a relatively small group of people who follow him. In fact, it first arose in the middle of the eighteenth century, flourished thereafter for a short time and now has already lost its credibility in scientific circles. (34)

Positivism is, in fact, "a specific philosophy that proceeds from certain metaphysical presuppositions every bit as much any other school of thought" (35).[89] Bavinck even appeals to the Dutch modernist Allard Pierson[90] for confirmation of the claim that "fundamental philosophical principles"[91] are essential for understanding the "origin, nature, and boundaries of our knowledge." The first basic philosophical principle for positivism is this:

Our knowledge can only come through sensory observation and experience. This is a decidedly foundational philosophical principle, and not one that is self-evident and clear as the day but one that incorporates an entire worldview and in fact is accepted as true by only a relatively small circle of people. The entirety of humanity, as its history proves, also in its scientific investigations, thought differently. It is superficially naïve to think that on this base one can stand on the sure foundation of visible and indubitable reality. (35)

Bavinck is willing to stipulate that

85. LO: *rerum cognoscere causas*.
86. LO: *rerum cognoscere nexum*.
87. GO: *voraussetzungslose*.
88. Auguste Comte.
89. DO: *richting*.
90. Allard Pierson (1831–96) was a Protestant theologian who resigned his position as a minister in the Walloon church in Rotterdam "because he could not reconcile being a minister with not believing in divine revelation." Wikipedia, s.v. "Allard Pierson," https://en.wikipedia.org/wiki/Allard_Pierson.
91. DO: *wijsgerige grondbeginselen*; Bavinck alternates this term with *wijsgerige grondstelling*; for the sake of variety I will also translate either term as "basic philosophical principles" or "fundamental philosophical principles" or "foundational philosophical principles."

all scientific investigation accepts beforehand and without proof the trustworthiness of our senses and the objectivity of the observed world. These things are not provable. Whoever doubts them cannot be persuaded by any arguments. Skepticism is more a matter of the heart than of the head. The reality of the world outside of us stands firm only through and before faith.[92] Accepting this is an act of trusting, in the most profound ground of trusting in the truthfulness of God. (35–36)[93]

Not only does positivism depend on fundamental philosophical presuppositions that cannot be demonstrated on the basis of its own methodology; it also fails in another sense. Positivism is unable by its methods to explain the internal, "psychical phenomena" that are as real as physical phenomena. We observe the phenomena of the physical world and make representations of them internally. But we do more; we also make representations of psychical phenomena that are investigated by those in the "spiritual sciences."[94] Psychical reality needs to be distinguished—but never separated!—from physical reality.

92. DO: *door en voor het geloof.* The two "truths" Bavinck has in view here with his play on *door* and *voor* are (1) trusting our senses and acknowledging the objectivity of the world outside of us is an act of faith; (2) the objective world is real and exists prior to our sensing and observing. The second point is directed at all forms of idealism. Taken together, these two claims set forth Bavinck's "realist" epistemology.

93. Bavinck provides two references: René Descartes, *Principles of Philosophy*, II.1; Land, *Inleiding tot de wijsbegeerte* bl. 97 v.; here are the full citations: René Descartes, *A Discourse on Method; Meditations on the First Philosophy; Principles of Philosophy*, trans. John Veitch (London: Dent, 1975), 199–200, available online at HathiTrust, https://babel.hathitrust.org/cgi/pt?id=iau.31858026462923&view=1up&seq=232; Jan Pieter Nicolaas Land, *Inleiding tot de Wijsbegeerte* (The Hague: Nijhoff, 1889), 97–102, https://www.google.com/books/edition/Inleiding_tot_de_wijsbegeerte/-hVWAAAAcAAJ?hl=en&gbpv=1.

Bavinck's appeal to Descartes here is noteworthy; he is using a "modern" thinker to undercut the modernist scientism of his own day. It is worth, therefore, reproducing Descartes's argument in *Principles*, II.1, also to clarify Bavinck's own epistemology and in anticipation of what I will say shortly about Bavinck's own Christian worldview:

God would, without question, deserve to be regarded as a deceiver, if he directly and of himself presented to our mind the idea of this extended matter, or merely caused it to be presented to us by some object which possessed neither extension, figure, nor motion. For we clearly conceive this matter as entirely distinct from God, and from ourselves, or our mind; and appear even clearly to discern that the idea of it is formed in us on occasion of objects existing out of our minds, to which it is in every respect similar. But since God cannot deceive us, for this is repugnant to his nature, as has been already remarked, we must unhesitatingly conclude that there exists a certain object extended in length, breadth, and thickness, and possessing all those properties which we clearly apprehend to belong to what is extended. And this extended substance is what we call body or matter.

94. This term (cf. German *Geisteswissenschaften*) must not be confused with the English term "social sciences" (psychology, sociology, economics, etc.), though they are included. In the nomenclature of European universities, the "sciences of the mind" also include philosophy, history, linguistics, philology, musicology, theology, and jurisprudence, disciplines that the English-speaking academy thinks of as "humanities."

We do not only simply know visible things; we also know invisible things; we are self-consciously aware of perceptions, representations, emotions, decisions of our will, that cannot be observed with our senses and nonetheless are undeniably real. We have to do with facts in our inner selves, facts that we perceive are as sure, in fact even more sure, than sensory phenomena. From within the life of our souls, powers invade our consciousness that are stronger than physical coercion. Emotions, passions, convictions, decisions, etc. are realities no less than matter and energy, even though we cannot see them with our eyes and handle them with our hands. If this is true, then the proposition that only that which is observable with our senses is real and that it alone can be the object and content of our scientific work is untenable. (38–39)

In summary, "We discover in our consciousness ideas, perceptions, representations, etc., that point back to the realm of the true, the good, and the beautiful" (40).

Bavinck points out that positivism attempts to answer challenges that arise from human psychical experiences by turning to psychology:

Of course, we can also investigate and study these ideas, etc. from a psychological perspective, but then we only obtain knowledge of an empirical reality that exists only in the subject. However, in the same way that the goal of study in the natural sciences as well as in historical studies is not, finally, to obtain knowledge of the development of human representations but knowledge of nature and history themselves, so too in the study of psychic representations we are not interested in knowing the process of those representations but in obtaining knowledge of the spiritual world, of which our perceptions are always an impure copy. All those who honor such an understanding of the spiritual sciences have left the foundation of empiricism and positivism and raised themselves to the world of ideas; they are treading the heights of ontology and metaphysics. (40–41)

That is an appropriate segue for us now to examine Bavinck's own ontology and metaphysics—that is, his worldview.

c. Bavinck's Christian Worldview[95]

As we saw in the beginning of this chapter, Bavinck's reflections on the world begin with the doctrine of creation. In the Reformed Dogmatics,

---

95. What follows is only an abridged summary; for a full statement, see Bavinck, *Christian Worldview*.

Bavinck intentionally juxtaposes the Christian worldview with two other worldviews: pantheism and materialism. Here is how he summarizes the failures of the latter two:

> Both fail to appreciate the richness and diversity of the world; erase the boundaries between heaven and earth, matter and spirit, soul and body, man and animal, intellect and will, time and eternity, Creator and creature, being and nonbeing; and dissolve all distinctions in a bath of deadly uniformity. Both deny the existence of a conscious purpose and cannot point to a cause or a destiny for the existence of the world and its history.[96]

The lengthy quote that now follows, summarizing a biblical worldview, directs us to (1) a clear distinction between Creator and creature, (2) a trinitarian foundation for all unity and diversity in creation, and (3) the importance of the notion of "organic" in Bavinck's thought.

> Scripture's worldview is radically different. From the beginning heaven and earth have been distinct. Everything was created with a nature of its own and rests in ordinances established by God. Sun, moon, and stars have their own unique task; plants, animals, and humans are distinct in nature. There is the most profuse diversity and yet, in that diversity, there is also a superlative kind of unity. The foundation of both diversity and unity is in God. It is he who created all things in accordance with his unsearchable wisdom, who continually upholds them in their distinctive natures, who guides and governs them in keeping with their own increated energies and laws, and who, as the supreme good and ultimate goal of all things, is pursued and desired by all things in their measure and manner. Here is a unity that does not destroy but rather maintains diversity, and a diversity that does not come at the expense of unity, but rather unfolds it in its riches. In virtue of this unity the world can, metaphorically, be called an organism, in which all the parts are connected with each other and influence each other reciprocally. Heaven and earth, man and animal, soul and body, truth and life, art and science, religion and morality, state and church, family and society, and so on, though they are all distinct, are not separated. There is a wide range of connections between them; an organic, or if you will, an ethical bond holds them all together.[97]

Bavinck is convinced that this trinitarian and organic worldview, and it alone, can give satisfactory answers to the three questions that must be faced

96. *RD*, 2:435.
97. *RD*, 2:435–36.

by every worldview, questions that date back to the Greek philosophers: "The problems that confront the human mind always return to these: What is the relation between thinking and being, between being and becoming, and between becoming and acting? What am I? What is the world, and what is my place and task within this world?"[98] Compared with the alternatives, only Christianity provides a sure foundation:

Autonomous thinking finds no satisfactory answers to these questions—it oscillates between materialism and spiritualism, between atomism and dynamism, between nomism and antinomianism. But Christianity preserves the harmony [between them] and reveals to us a wisdom that reconciles the human being with God and, through this, with itself, with the world, and with life. (29)

I will briefly summarize Bavinck's Christian worldview resolution of the three basic issues:

I. The Relation between Thinking and Being

Bavinck finds fault with empiricism and rationalism alike: "Empiricism trusts only sensible perceptions," while "rationalism judges that sensible perceptions provide us with no true knowledge" (32). Consequently,

in both cases and in both directions, the harmony between subject and object, and between knowing and being is broken. With the former [i.e., empiricism], the world is nominalistically divided into its parts; with the latter [i.e., rationalism], reality is hyper-realistically identified with the idea. . . . With both, the concept of truth, of "conformity of intellect and thing" [*conformitas intellectus et rei*], a correspondence between thinking and being, is lost.

Since "truth is the goal of all science," when truth is gone, so "is all knowledge and science. The Christian religion thus shows its wisdom primarily in this, that it knows and preserves truth as an objective reality, which exists independent of our consciousness and is displayed by God for us in his works of nature and grace" (33).

When one thinks this all through in its depth, Bavinck says, it becomes increasingly clearer that "all truth is understood in the Wisdom, in the Word, who was in the beginning with God and who himself was God." In sum,

98. Bavinck, *Christian Worldview*, 29; in what follows the page references in the text are to this work.

The human being is not the creator and former of the world; his understanding does not write its laws on nature, and in his scientific research he does not have to arrange things according to his categories. To the contrary, it is the human who has to conform his perception and thinking to God's revelation in nature and grace.

To buttress his point Bavinck provides a lengthy quotation from the German thinker Gustav Wilhelm Portig (1838–1911), a quotation that neatly captures his own conviction: "Reality does not have to make itself comply with our reason, but rather, on the basis of the whole experience of the whole age, our thinking must seek to lay bare the metaphysic that God has woven into reality" (47).[99]

Conclusion: All thinking must conform to the reality of being as created by God.

II. THE RELATION BETWEEN BEING AND BECOMING

According to Bavinck, "The second problem solved in our worldview is that of being and becoming, of unity and multiplicity, of God and world" (57). Bavinck says that from "antiquity, two philosophical directions stood in opposition to each other. According to one, there was only being and no becoming. Change and movement were a façade; time and space were but subjective 'ways of thinking.'"[100] And according to the other direction, being was nothing more than an 'object of thought';[101] only becoming was real" (58). In his day, Bavinck notes, the intellectual struggle is between advocates of an older, "materialistic-mechanistic worldview" and advocates of a newer, "dynamic or energetic" worldview.[102] The newer worldview is driven by the study of biology and the "problem of life." Pasteur's demonstration that "all life is from life"[103] and other scientific investigations "showed that the multiplication of cells happened only through reproduction and thus took place according to a rule: 'All cells come from cells.'"[104] Bavinck concludes: "Despite all the progress of science . . . the rift between the lifeless and the living nature of life, rather than being filled, only becomes broader and deeper. The machine theory of life seemed to be false. Powers other than the chemical and physical were at work in the world" (60–61). There is, in

99. Portig, *Das Weltgesetz,* 1:25.
100. LO: *modi cogitandi.*
101. GO: *Gedankendig.*
102. Bavinck several times refers to this as "neovitalism."
103. LO: *omne vivum ex vivo.*
104. LO: *omnis cellula e cellula.*

other words, an uncrossable metaphysical canyon between inert matter and living, organic matter.

To specify this further, Bavinck notes that of the "four fundamental concepts" that "the natural sciences always have to deal with: space, time, substance, and energy," the debate is not about space and time but about substance and energy.[105] "While materialism regards matter as an eternal substance and energy as pertaining to it, dynamism, to the contrary, sees energy as original and material as derivative" (61–62). Bavinck considers both the materialistic and dynamic worldviews to be too abstract and one-sided. Our experience of the world is much more concrete; we must be able to trust our sense perceptions. Though we are unable to penetrate to the essence of matter, "we nonetheless all have experience, through consciousness, of a series of properties that could only be caused by a material substance" (65).[106] While the dynamic worldview is an understandable reaction to mechanistic-monism, if

we find ourselves unable to affirm a material substance on the basis of these properties and have to regard matter as a mirage and an illusion, not only do these properties remain unexplained, but also the certainty of our knowledge is taken away. Things in themselves must then be something wholly other than whatever our capacities, in their most focused perception, make us think. Their occurrence to our perception is utterly different from what they really are. Our sensory organs lose their reliability, our sensory knowledge is done away with, and the conclusion that moves from appearance to essence is shipwrecked. We arrive at illusionism and subject all science to skepticism. (66)

This problem, however, is resolved in a biblical worldview:

The full truth is first presented to us in Scripture, when it teaches that things have come forth from God's "manifold wisdom" [πολυποικιλος σοφια], that they are mutually distinguished by a common character and name, that in their multiplicity they are one, and that in their unity they are distinct. (66–67)

If a dynamic worldview cannot explain our experience of a stable world of matter, the mechanistic worldview cannot explain development and teleology: "Nothing becomes, because there is nothing that needs to become, that must become. There is no goal and no starting point—and development is based precisely on both of these things" (81). Development "is found only in organic

105. Parenthetically, Bavinck adds four terms: quantity and causality; matter and energy.
106. In the next sentence, Bavinck names the following: impermeability, mass, inertia, expansion, and visibility.

beings, be they material or spiritual." Bavinck then goes on to use the term "organic" in the broadest sense of a cosmic worldview: "It is true that this world contains many inanimate, lifeless things, of which, in the strict sense, there can be no talk of development, but these are taken up as organic parts in the totality of the world, and that totality of the world is an organism that develops according to firm laws and strives toward a goal" (82–83). The world's multiplicity and underlying unity is finally to be found in the activity of the Creator God—the triune Creator God.

Therefore, to conclude this section on being and becoming, I need to go back to the opening section of this chapter, particularly Bavinck's statements on the Trinity, the generation of the Son, and the doctrine of creation. Here was the key statement:

> Without generation, creation would not be possible. If, in an absolute sense, God could not communicate himself to the Son, he would be even less able, in a relative sense, to communicate himself to his creature. If God were not triune, creation would not be possible.[107]

Here I only add Bavinck's specific appeal to the triunity of God as the foundation for the unity and multiplicity of creation:

> The dogma of the Trinity . . . tells us that God can reveal himself in an absolute sense to the Son and the Spirit, and hence, in a relative sense, also to the world. For, as Augustine teaches us, the self-communication that takes place within the divine being is archetypal for God's work in creation. Scripture repeatedly points to the close connection between the Son and Spirit, on the one hand, and the creation, on the other. The names Father, Son (Word, Wisdom), and Spirit most certainly denote immanent relationships, but they are also mirrored in the interpersonal relations present in the works of God *ad extra*. All things come from the Father; the "ideas" of all existent things are present in the Son; the first principles of all life are in the Spirit. Generation and procession in the divine being are the immanent acts of God, which make possible the outward works of creation and revelation. Finally, this also explains why all the works of God *ad extra* are only adequately known when their trinitarian existence is recognized.[108]

Therefore, this trinitarian pattern has its reflection and analogies in creation:

---

107. *RD*, 2:420.
108. *RD*, 2:333.

The doctrine of the Trinity provides true light here. Just as God is one in essence and distinct in persons, so also the work of creation is one and undivided, while ·in its unity it is still rich in diversity. It is one God who creates all things, and for that reason the world is a unity, just as the unity of the world demonstrates the unity of God. But in that one divine being there are three persons, each of whom performs a task of his own in that one work of creation.[109]

God's triunity is the foundation of Bavinck's "organic" worldview. "Just as God is one in essence and distinct in persons, so also the work of creation is one and undivided while in its unity it is still rich in diversity."[110] This "organic" perspective on unity and diversity is the foundation for a Christian theistic worldview. Over against all forms of monism, a theistic worldview recognizes

a multiplicity of substances, forces, materials, and laws. It does not strive to erase the distinctions between God and the world, between spirit (mind) and matter, between psychological and physical, ethical and religious phenomena. It seeks rather to discover the harmony that holds all things together and unites them and that is the consequence of the creative thought of God. Not identity or uniformity but unity in diversity is what it aims at.[111]

Bavinck concludes his chapter on being and becoming with another appeal to the creative artistry of God:

And viewed from the highest standpoint, the whole world is an organic unity, upheld by one thought, led by one will, directed to one goal—one "organon" [ὄργανον] that is also a "machine" [μηχανη] and a "machine" [μηχανη] that is also an "organon" [ὄργανον], a building that grows and a body that is built. It is a work of art from the Supreme Artist and from the Master Builder of the universe. (92)

III. The Relation between Becoming and Acting

Here is how Bavinck describes the "problem" in this third worldview issue: "Is there, in the stream of occurrences, still a place for personal, independent, and free acting? Can we on good grounds and in confidence continue to say, 'I think, I will, I act'?" (93). In other words, is there any room in the closed

---

109. *RD*, 2:420.
110. Bavinck, *Our Reasonable Faith*, 144.
111. *RD*, 1:368.

natural world for human freedom? Bavinck illumines the alternatives in the words of the German physicist and satirist Georg Christoph Lichtenberg (1742–99): "Should one say, 'It thinks,' just as one says, 'It is raining'? Is the impersonal, neutral 'it' of theosophy the only all-propelling power, or does the scheme of things allow space for personality and freedom? Is there only *physis* [nature], or is there also *ethos* [character]?" (93–94).

Bavinck seeks to resolve this dilemma with a phenomenological appeal to the paradoxical human experience of freedom, including the "remarkable and undeniable fact that where in reality we are free, we are in any case unable to find freedom to not be free. The reality, the possibility even, of freedom is contestable, but the right and duty toward freedom is indisputable" (94). In other words, we are never free to choose unfreedom. We experience lack of freedom, even coercion, in the laws of nature; these laws, including causality, are coercive because they do not involve human will and free choice. There is no act of human will that can successfully abrogate the law of gravity.[112] But now Bavinck appeals to the phenomenon of human consciousness, in which a world of freedom and choice is given to us. The word "given" is intentionally chosen here because, for Bavinck, the phenomenon of human consciousness is a gift of revelation. Self-awareness, for example, René Descartes to the contrary, is not the product of our thinking or willing:

In self-consciousness our own being is *revealed* to us directly, immediately, before all thinking, and independently of all willing. We do not approach it through any reasoning or exertion of our own; we do not demonstrate its existence, we do not understand its essence. But it is *given* to us in self-consciousness, *given*

---

112. Bavinck provides a helpful commentary on natural law in his "Contemporary Morality": Much misuse has been made of these natural laws, especially in the attack on miracles. They are often portrayed as forces that stand above the phenomena, controlling them with unlimited power. In point of fact, however, these laws are nothing but the particular ways in which the forces that are present in nature operate, ways formulated in what we call natural laws, which even today are known and described only very inadequately. Nonetheless, there is order and rhythm, number and regularity, in the world of visible things. The ordinances for heaven and earth have been established by the Creator; his covenant of day and night can be destroyed by no creature; seedtime and harvest, cold and heat, summer and winter, day and night do not stop but alternate, without people being able to do anything about that. All creatures have their own nature and their own law, which we must respect. Human beings are free only when they become acquainted with these laws and obey them. You cannot walk headlong through a stone wall. You cannot watch yourself through the window as you pass by on the street. You cannot bathe twice in the same stream. You cannot add one cubit to your stature. The English can make everything, but they cannot make a man out of a woman. And the practice of rote recitation in our current education system has not yet changed a dunce into a soaring genius. (*RE*, 3:332)

for nothing, and is received on our part spontaneously in unshaken confidence, with immediate assurance.[113]

The same is true of our awareness of the world, the reality external to us. It is also a gift; it just is there and is not the product of our thinking and acting. This reality exists before we become aware of it: "The world of perception is given to us in our consciousness, not as a dream or hallucination but as a phenomenon and representation, according to universal belief, the existence of an objective world."[114] However, our experience of the material and empirical world through sense perception does not represent the boundary or limits of our consciousness. At the core of our self-consciousness is "a feeling of dependence. In the act of becoming conscious of ourselves, we become conscious of ourselves as creatures."[115]

According to Bavinck, this happens in two ways:

a. We feel ourselves dependent on everything around us; we are not alone.
b. We feel ourselves, together with all creatures, wholly dependent on some absolute power which is the one infinite being.[116]

The experience of a reality beyond the physical and material that is also given to us and upon which we are dependent leads us to recognize norms and laws that are not merely outside of us but also "above us." And it is here that we as humans discover our freedom:

In these norms, another world—different and higher than is revealed to us in nature—makes itself known to us. It is a world not of obligation [*moeten*] but of belonging [*behoren*], of ethical freedom and choice. In these norms, a moral world order in the midst of and above empirical reality is maintained, a world of ideas, of truth, goodness, and beauty. (94)

This moral world does come with its own "obligations," but they are of a different sort:

Though it is the case that it despises all coercion, this world order in its moral character possesses a power surpassing that of nature. The question is not

113. Bavinck, *Philosophy of Revelation*, 53–54 (emphasis added).
114. Bavinck, *Philosophy of Revelation*, 58; Bavinck explicitly acknowledges the correctness of Schleiermacher on this point.
115. Bavinck, *Philosophy of Revelation*, 57.
116. Bavinck, *Philosophy of Revelation*, 57.

about whether humans can or want to obey its laws; it says categorically that it is appropriate to do so. You shall love the true, the good, and the beautiful with all your soul; and you shall love God above all and your neighbor as yourself. (94–95)

As we become conscious human beings, "we discover that there are laws and norms above us that direct us in order to elevate us above nature and force us to release from its coercion" (94).[117] The moral order impinges on all human beings with an imperial majesty that is superior to the laws that govern the natural world:

Everywhere in the world, strict causality prevails; nothing occurs by chance; everything has a cause. But in the moral order of the world, a power appears before us that seems to take no account of this causality. It accepts no appeals to our powerlessness and ignorance, has no appetite for excuses or facile explanations, and will not settle for good intentions or solemn promises; it does not negotiate with the conscience. But it demands that we all, without exception, always and everywhere, in all circumstances of life, conform ourselves to its command. Truth, goodness, and beauty lay claim to the whole person and never release us from its service. (95)

Bavinck is willing to speak of the moral order as a set of "ideal norms," but he insists that "ideal" here does not mean abstract or theoretical:

Ideal norms, therefore, do not exist only in theory. They are not abstract concepts that subsist outside life and have some value only in the academy. They are factors of reality itself. They are the compass of our lives. In practice, they apprehend us in every moment. All people naturally do the things that are in keeping with the law and by this they show that the work of the law is written on their hearts.[118] If we do not arbitrarily and superficially limit reality to what we see with our eyes and touch with our hands, these norms are then entitled to an equally objective and unquestionable existence, just as the sensible observations of nature are. With undeniable power, they establish in each consciousness, in head and heart, in reason and conscience, a witness to their existence. (105–6)

---

117. Bavinck cites here B. H. C. K. van der Wijck, "De wereldbeschouwing van een Nederlands wijsgeer." The article is an extended review of University of Groningen philosophy professor Gerard Heymans's book *Einfüring in die Metaphysik auf Grundlage der Erfarung.*
    118. A clear reference to Rom. 2:14–15.

The only reasonable explanation for the existence of such a moral order is the reality of the Creator God: "This objective reality of logical, ethical, and aesthetic norms points back to a world order that can have its origins and existence only in God almighty" (106).[119] But there is more to be said:

> And not only does the Christian worldview objectively restore the harmony between the natural and moral order, but through this it also brings about a wonderful unity subjectively between our thinking and doing, between our head and our heart. If the same divine wisdom grants things their reality, our consciousness its content, and our acting its rule, then it must be the case that a mutual harmony exists between these three. . . . The true, the good, and the beautiful are one with the true being. (110)

In sum, the God who created the world and established its laws and norms also created human beings in his image with the capacity to know what is real, what is true, good, and beautiful.

Bavinck does not overlook the reality of sin and its effects on our knowing, our willing, and our doing. Departures from the ideal norm do not detract from its authority; on the contrary, they confirm it:

> The divine authority and the absolute legitimacy of the ideal norms make us feel the deviations [from them]—which the human world shows us—all the more painfully. All people recognize that there is an awful distance between what ought to happen and what actually happens, between the demand and the fulfillment of the command. (110–11)

Attempts to explain sin as "a minor issue" arising "from matter, from the flesh, from the finitude and limitation of human nature" fail to do justice to "the majesty of the moral law." Whoever has beheld that majesty "can have no peace with these theories" (111). In response, Bavinck writes:

> There is but one view that allows sin to be what it really is and does not weaken its reality by reason, and that view is from Holy Scripture. Scripture does not flatter the human being, but tells him what he must be according to God's law and what he has actually become through sin. . . . Among all religions, it is Christianity alone that views sin as strictly religious-ethical, detached from all substance and distinguished from all physical evil. (111)

---

119. Bavinck cites here E. W. Mayer, "Über den gegenwärtigen Stand der Religionsphiloso-phie und deren Bedeutung für die Theologie."

Sin places us before an antinomy: If people "are unbiased, recognizing sin for what it truly is, there remains no possibility of salvation for them. If they, on the other hand, hold fast to the possibility of salvation, then they are forced to deprive sin of the serious character that they had first assigned to it" (113). The solution?

Once again, it is the Christian religion alone that reconciles that antinomy, that fully recognizes the moral decay and inability of human nature and yet opens to us a way of salvation. The salvation known by it, though, is not a human act but is only the work of God. The continued existence of the world, the history of the human race, the character of sin as something that should not be, the necessity of the idea that the good must triumph because of its absolute validity can lead us all to the supposition that there is a salvation. For why would creation continue to exist if it were not destined to be established through re-creation from out of its ruin? But if it is understood that salvation is nothing other than the work of God, it is evident that it can be known by us only through revelation, and then salvation must itself supervene in the world as such a work of God and be an ineradicable component in the history of our [human] race. The Scriptures teach us to understand salvation as such. (113)

Christian scholarship built on the foundation of a biblical, Christian worldview leads quite naturally to the idea of institutional location for such work; it leads to the idea of a Christian university.

5. A CHRISTIAN UNIVERSITY

We return here to the conclusion of Bavinck's book on Christian scholarship.[120]

These principles concerning the relation between Christianity and scholarship ultimately have an inherent pressure to be embodied in a Christian university. This is not a new idea. Until the beginning of the nineteenth century, all schools, not only primary schools but also higher education, proceeded from a definitely Christian, even a confessional-churchly point of view. The new is what Prime Minister Kuyper called the "indifferent" system, the apparently neutral notion of the idea of scholarship. And while the older view has earned its spurs, the new view has yet to prove not only that it is sound but also that it is possible and sustainable. (108)

120. Bavinck, *Christelijke Wetenschap*; Bavinck's discussion of a "Christian university" can be found on pp. 108–21; page references that follow in the text are to this work.

The ideal of an "indifferent" or "neutral" scholarship is not consistent in its application. On the one hand, the purportedly "neutral" and "presuppositionless" standpoint "never seems to conflict with scholarship that proceeds from the philosophical principles of Spinoza, Kant, Marx, Comte [and others]." Why not? The "principles of Spinoza, Kant, Marx, and Comte" clearly proceed from philosophical presuppositions; their philosophical systems are not "neutral." Bavinck points out that so-called neutral scholarship does run into conflict with scholarship "that proceeds from the foundation of a confession in the Christ of the Scriptures" (109). Thus, it turns out that the call for "neutral" scholarship is often only a way of masking opposition to specifically Christian scholarship. Furthermore, the ideal also runs shipwreck on the shoals of lived experience: "Universities are not castles built in the sky; they are institutions with established histories and bound to all sorts of traditions. They are influenced by their total environments and have lost their independence and freedom as they became organs of the state" (110). Bavinck brings up Immanuel Kant's *Conflict of the Faculties*[121] and the Königsberg philosopher's defense of a limited academic freedom. According to Bavinck,

Although theoretically a proponent of academic freedom, [Kant] nonetheless subordinated it to the highest good of humanity and the ethical community, and regularly urged great caution in its practical application. He contended that although we are to pay attention so that all we say is true, we are not obligated to speak all truth publicly. One must proceed very cautiously with a people's faith. The Bible and the dominant religious ideas of a particular age must be used as means to promote the moral dispositions and moral community. It is foolish to express thoughts against the Bible in schools, churches, and popular writings. That would only lead to a nation losing its faith and surrendering itself to total unbelief. Rather, one should use the people's love of its old church faith as a means by which eventually to introduce the new rational faith. It is prudent for everyone to speak with caution to avoid the shame of being forced later to recant. (110)

Bavinck concludes that "the notion of absolute academic freedom, considered from the perspective of principle, is advocated by no one and nowhere praised in practice" (111). It is important carefully to define academic freedom:

---

121. Immanuel Kant, *The Conflict of the Faculties* (*Der Streit der Facultäten*).

But academic freedom must be carefully distinguished from freedom of conscience, freedom of religion, and freedom of the press. In a narrow sense, academic freedom is the right of professors in institutions of education to openly express their opinions and to cultivate disciples. This right is in fact limited everywhere and can be nothing other than limited. The concern of the state, public order, older tradition, good morals, to a greater or lesser degree, all tie down academic freedom. (111)

To illustrate those limits Bavinck uses the example of a "professor at a state university [who] proclaims nihilism, anarchy, and the right of revolution and regicide, defends suicide, perjury, usury, theft, and polygamy, etc." He acknowledges that there is a difference between verbally defending such ideas and spurring on the deed. Nonetheless,

> if the disciples draw out the consequences of their teacher's words and take the words of their teacher and turn them into action, then act consequently, then the complaint is fully justified that cutting off the branches is of little benefit as long as the axe is not laid to the root of the tree.

Bavinck deems that it is not necessary to judge someone as "narrow minded" when they question the state's response as only "passively observing" such speech (111).

At the same time, Bavinck does not give up on the principle of academic freedom. Not only is the modern state neutral with respect to confessional claims, but

> just as in the totality of life, and especially in the arena of scholarship, it is of greatest difficulty to maintain an even balance between authority and freedom, preservation and progress. Freedom has its own rights alongside authority. When something new is proclaimed, it evokes strangeness and opposition but nonetheless can later prove to be the truth.

From this, and

> especially because the current state lacks the competence and capability[122] to guard the principles and must allow all kinds of teaching in its universities, [the state] should rejoice in the fact that its citizens at various levels of education,

---

122. DO: *bevoegdheid en bekwamheid*.

on their own, have longed for and erected schools that are established on Christian foundations. (111–12)

Christian schools at all levels have been a blessing for the nation, and Bavinck adds this jab: "The state should not be ashamed nor sorrowful that it has finally adopted a more friendly attitude toward these schools" (112).

All scholarship—and that includes Christian scholarship—must be open to the wider world of scholarly work. "It cannot be restricted within the boundaries of a single university, not even all universities together. Nor is it restricted to one office or vocation, one group or class of people called to do so" (113). Nonetheless, the task of developing "scientific" thinking—that is, "developing skills for independent observation and thinking"—belongs to "institutions of higher learning."[123] "Scientific research is the chief means by which the university cultivates people of clear insight and independent judgment" (113).

Does this require, as many argue, that university students should "have opportunity to listen to professors with differing and extremely divergent viewpoints"? In that case, says Bavinck, "one would expect that every faculty and every university at home and abroad would produce a directory of professorial principles and propositions" (114). In fact, the Dutch universities of his day are not like that at all. Appointments to faculty positions in each university are based on ideological compatibility; it is rare that an appointment is offered to someone "with different convictions." Bavinck does not find fault with this but considers it a "natural" development: "This lies also in the nature of the case. Professors have the right to lecture and therefore in the first place look for colleagues among their kindred spirits, people with whom they can be friends and scientifically compatible." Bavinck notes the irony of this reality; it represents a real conflict between what is professed by "tolerant" modernists and what they practice: "According to the doctrine there is room for everyone; in practice there is room only for our friends" (114).

But Bavinck also considers the ideal of offering a full range of viewpoints and opinions to university students to be

psychologically and pedagogically untenable. It rests on the false premise that young people, fresh out of high school,[124] already have the desire and ability to see with their own eyes and independently choose among various ideas and theories. Secretly, the thought is enclosed that intellect is the highest and

123. DO: *Hoogescholen.*
124. DO: *gymnasium of hoogere burgerschool*; see n. 64 above.

well-nigh only human faculty and that everything must be judged by the standard of reason. Thus, authority and faith, heart and conscience add nothing to
the scale of judgment. In fact, our universities as a rule pay no attention to them;
it is as if one ought to be ashamed of them. Professors pay scarce attention
to religious and moral questions; and if they dò, they treat them most often as
ideas of the mind and not as realities of life. (114–15)

Consequently, "school and life stand apart. In the universities this means that
learning is the students' own responsibility; they must determine themselves
what will become of them." Would it be a surprise, Bavinck asks,

if young people, roughly twenty years old, whose unique social environment
placed them completely outside ordinary life, and who therefore viewed everything from a decidedly one-sided viewpoint, were impressed with the thought
that they did not need to be bothered by any authority or tradition needed
to form their own world-and-life view? Three possible results flow from this
situation:[125]

a. One group of students "inwardly opposes the teaching of the professor,
   rejects his mentoring, and with great prejudice repudiates everything he
   says." In this instance, "the instruction is as good as utterly useless."
b. "Another group goes along and takes what the professor says on authority, just as always."
c. "A third group becomes dispirited and skeptical and has no concern for
   principles but throws itself into practice." (115)

Bavinck is concerned that "students become acquainted with other viewpoints and insights in a fair-minded way. But this can happen just as well in
schools that proceed from specific Christian principles as in those that purportedly take a neutral stance" (115). In fact, Bavinck argues, such Christian
schools may even be superior in presenting a diversity of viewpoints. Christian
universities, it is safe to say,

in our day generally take different viewpoints more seriously than universities
that are completely captive to the modern worldview and consider themselves
in tune with the spirit of the age. It is precisely because they take their position
in the arena of scholarship from within their Christian confession that Christian

---

125. Bavinck refers here to a speech given by Vrije Universiteit classics professor Jan Woltjer
in the Senate (First Chamber) of the Dutch parliament; the speech was published in *De Standaard*, February 19, 1903.

universities are regularly compelled painstakingly to conduct their scholarly work at the highest level. (116)

Christian professors are obligated, in other words, to state the views of their opponents fairly and sympathetically.[126]

But then, "after an objective rendering of someone's alternative view," a professor at a Christian university will follow with a "critique that proceeds from the truth of the Christian world-and-life view." This is not extraordinary, according to Bavinck:

The professor at a neutral university does the same and cannot do otherwise. If he is not satisfied with a simple "I don't teach, I just tell,"[127] then he will subject the views of others to a judgment, that will involve his own conviction and belief, no matter how factually and objectively they are stated. Everyone who lives and works from a serious foundation is a propagandist. Even a skeptic is still a propagandist for the dogma of doubt. (116)

From the side of the university student Bavinck also challenges the posture of scientific neutrality.

In the same way that universities and their faculties, in conflict with their own theory, are generally staffed by people of one mind, parents in general also send their children to universities whose foundation and direction is in keeping with their own convictions. The only difference is this: modernists and liberals, radicals and socialists are perfectly satisfied with the status quo and precisely get the schools they want for their children. Confessionally committed Christians, on the other hand, for the same reasons that the universities so wonderfully satisfy the kinds of people just mentioned, are not and cannot be satisfied with these schools and must provide for themselves what is withheld from them by the state. (116–17)

Then, in a clever turnaround, Bavinck observes, "Without a doubt, if all the public schools in the Netherlands were explicitly Roman Catholic or Reformed, in the same way as is now the case for their opponents, the aforementioned parties would protest to the authorities and plead for freedom and equal rights" (117).

---

126. Here, as in perhaps no other way, Bavinck the scholar practiced what he preached. As beginning readers of Bavinck's *Reformed Dogmatics* have frequently found, they sometimes need to read passages several times to know whether they are reading Bavinck's own thoughts or his summary of an opponent. He is that fair!

127. FO: *je n'enseigne pas, je raconte.*

What is at stake here, according to Bavinck, is the unity of life and thought. He even contends: "A Christian university has an important advantage over a neutral university in that it restores the tie with life" (117). With an unstated assumption that most Dutch citizens are still Christian, Bavinck contends that the situation in the Netherlands, where Dutch public universities are committed to a neutral stance that in practice is hostile to the Christian faith, is "unhealthy":[128]

It cannot be good that school and life, scholarship and practice, theology and church stand so far apart as is the case today. This is most obvious in our religious life, where preachers trained in the public university then honestly and with integrity proclaim what they have heard and learned in school. But it is also true that lawyers, doctors, teachers, and so on now generally have religious and moral convictions that are opposed to those of the populace. This cannot remain the true and normal situation. If there is no reconciliation between these two positions, we are in the danger once faced by the ancient world, that this dualism will destroy the development of our civilization as well as the religion of the people. In fact, everyone is convinced of this. There can be no esoteric scholarship alongside exoteric scholarship; there is no double truth. (117)

How can this dangerous situation be rectified and the dualism overcome? One could accommodate the Christian faith to modern thought:

One side argues that our people need radically to revise their religious and moral ideas and adopt the viewpoint of contemporary scholarship. In particular, this demand is placed before theology and church,[129] but in principle we hear this longing expressed everywhere. Representatives of the modern worldview— evolutionists, ethicists, criminologists, and so forth—dedicate themselves to this and seek to persuade the authorities that the people need to be freed from their old traditions and that already in the elementary schools the conclusions of modern scholarship need to be made known. That is why we have had such a fierce struggle about education, both at the lower and higher levels. It is all about what will lead the people and the future: the Christian or the modern worldview. (117–18)

For many modernists, the Christian religion stood in the way of progress. Bavinck cites German socialist politician Eduard David (1863–1930) to the

---

128. DO: *ongezond*.
129. Bav. note: Friedrich Delitzsch, *Babel and Bible: A Lecture on the Significance of Assyriological Research for Religion* (Chicago: Open Court, 1906), xxii–xxiii.

internal missions along with that of diaconal mercy also should be designated as evangelization.

3. "EVANGELIZATION"[9]

This thirty-two-page brochure was published in a series under the broader rubric of "Christianity and society."[10] On a formal level, this seems fitting in a chapter titled "The Church" in a volume of social ethics. The material that follows is different from Bavinck's theological treatment of the church in his *Reformed Dogmatics*, although we can see similar methodological moves here. Bavinck begins, as he usually does, with a brief linguistic or lexical observation about the word "gospel" in the Greek world outside its specific use in the New Testament. He demonstrates his knowledge of the archaeological scholarship of his day by referring to the Calendar Inscription of Priene celebrating the birth of Caesar Augustus as the beginning of a new messianic age; that is, the inscription proclaims a "gospel" of good news.[11] That the experiences of human beings, as reflected in the world's various religions, are an essential component in Christian theological reflection is one of the hallmarks of Bavinck's method. The subheadings are not original; they were added by the editor.

THE "GOSPEL" OF CAESAR AUGUSTUS

The term "gospel" (or "evangel"), so familiar to us, was derived from the Greek language and existed long before the first century of our era, when the writers

---

9. Bavinck, *Evangelisatie*.

10. DO: *Christendom en maatschappij*. The series *Christendom en Maatschappij* was edited by P. A. Diepenhorst; *Evangelisatie* was published as no. 9 in the fifth series. Another title in this series, from the same year, is P. A. Diepenhorst, *De Vrije Schol in de Grondwet* (Utrecht: Ruys, 1913).

11. A letter from Paul Fabius Maximus, proconsul of the province of Asia (dating from around 8 BC), called for "the birthday of our God [τοῦ θεοῦ]" to be celebrated on September 23 because it "signaled the beginning of Good News for the world because of him [ἦρξεν δὲ τῶι κόσμωι τῶι δι' αὐτὸν εὐαγγελίων ἡ γενέυλιος ἡμέρα τοῦ θεοῦ]." Source: "The Priene Inscription," Internet Archive: WaybackMachine, https://web.archive.org/web/20170722070724/http:/www.masseiana.org/priene.htm. The online entry also shows two photos of part of the inscription and the Greek text. In addition, the same entry quotes "Virgil's Prophecy of the Saviour's Birth: The Fourth Eclogue" (see n. 13, below). Not only is Bavinck's knowledge of this inscription noteworthy (it was first published in the *Mittheilungen des Deutschen archaeologischen Institutes in Athen*, 1899, vol. 24), but also his linkage of the religious expectations and hopes of the pagan world to the fulfillment of biblical, prophetic hope. As he does frequently in the *Reformed Dogmatics*, Bavinck ties the specifics of salvation in Christ to broader *human* needs and articulated longings in the world's religions.

of the New Testament books used it repeatedly to refer to the joyful message of salvation in Christ. Originally, however, the Greek word did not mean good or joyous tidings but was used especially in the neuter plural to refer to the payment given to the bringer of a message of good news or to the sacrifice rendered to the gods for receiving a message of good news. Nevertheless, already before the influence of Christianity, the word as used in ordinary Greek occasionally had the meaning of a message of good news. This meaning of the word seems never to have been the usual meaning; but a remarkable example of this meaning was preserved in the inscription found several years ago in Priene (an ancient Ionian city in Asia Minor, situated south of Ephesus), which states concerning the birthday of the emperor that, for the world, this was the beginning of things that were, due to him, "*evangelia*," good tidings.[12]

The mention of an emperor in this inscription, dated at 9 BC, was probably referring to Emperor Caesar Augustus; his birthday was viewed as the birthday of "a god," as a message of good news for the world, as the beginning of a new calendar. In the first century before the birth of Christ, a widespread expectation existed that a King-Savior would come forth from the East, who would bring peace and rest to the earth. Various testimonies from Plutarch, Cicero, Suetonius, and Tacitus provide us with the proof of that, and in that connection especially Virgil's Fourth Eclogue becomes relevant, in which the poet sings that now the last era has dawned of which the Cumaean Sibyl spoke and that a great cycle of periods is now inaugurated. The virgin already returns, and the golden age of Saturn returns; already a new offspring descends from heaven, through whom the iron race will cease, and a golden race will arise throughout the entire world.[13]

In 40 BC, this expectation was strengthened by the peace and settlement treaty that Gaius Julius Caesar made with Antony, which assigned the western kingdom to the former, and the eastern kingdom to the latter. And it obtained again a powerful confirmation when on September 2, 31 BC, Octavian won the victory in the sea battle at Actium against his rival and opponent, added to his territory in the west the entire eastern portion, and thus in fact became the sovereign over the entire Roman Empire. In this way, the hope most deeply needed by humanity after the terrible disasters of recent years, hope of peace, security, and rest, came more and more to be built on this Octavian.

---

12. See n. 11, above.

13. "Now is come the last age of the song of Cumae; the great line of the centuries begins anew. Now the Virgin returns, the age of Saturn returns; now a new generation descends from heaven on high. Only do thou, pure Lucinda, smile on the birth of the child, under whom the iron shall first cease, and a gold race spring up throughout the world! Thine own Apollo now is king!" (Virgil, opening of "Eclogue IV," in *Virgil in Two Volumes*, 1:29 [LCL 63]).

And Octavian did not disappoint that expectation. As a person of extraordinary talents, of deep knowledge of people, and of wise administration, of cool calculation and tough endurance, he allowed the ancient names and forms of the republic to continue and avoided every kind of pomp and splendor. He left the domestic administration for the most part to the senate, but he himself controlled the direction of foreign politics and the command of the military. He applied his power and influence on the creation of ordered circumstances everywhere and to the advancement of peace and rest, security, and welfare throughout the whole empire. He improved the administration of the cities, he honored the ancient customs, he was successful in constructing many enormous building projects, including many temples, he filled the vacant priestly positions, advanced literature and art, and inaugurated a period of universal welfare and flourishing. In 27 BC he received the title of Sebastus (*augustus*: esteemed, holy); in 7 BC his genius was taken up under the "protective gods,"[14] whose images stood at the intersections. After his death in AD 14, there followed his consecration, his canonization, and his inclusion among the gods. In reference to the first emperor, this deification was not pure flattery; it arose from the deep impression that his rule had generated the peace so intensely thirsted for by his subjects. According to the pagan perspective, Augustus was the visible god of the powerful world empire; in his manner and in his measure, he was the "savior" and "benefactor" of humanity.[15]

First-century Christians agreed with this, up to a point. Initially, they too saw in the Roman Empire a providential preparation for the peaceable kingdom of Christ; church and world kingdom in the beginning constituted absolutely no polemical opposition. From the image and the inscription of the Roman coin, with which the tax was supposed to be paid, Christ himself in Matthew 22:21–22 derived the right of the imperial government and the obligation of all subjects of the Roman Empire to give to Caesar what belonged to Caesar, not only the tax but also the respect and obedience to which he as Caesar was entitled. These are not opposed to, but can and must accompany, what is due to God, even though whenever they possibly collided, one must obey God rather than people (Acts 5:29). With this, Christ was in principle indicating the posture his disciples were to take toward the earthly government. Since there is no authority except from God, and the authorities that exist have been ordained by God, the government is God's minister, to whom subjection is due for the sake of conscience, which for evildoers is a reason for fear, but a

14. LO: *lares compitales.*
15. GrO: *sōtēr* and *euergetēs.*

source of praise for those who do good (Rom. 13). This is not an anti-Christian authority, but an authority that restrains the Antichrist (2 Thess. 2:6–7). This authority ensures that under its leadership, Christians also may lead a tranquil and quiet life in all piety and dignity (1 Tim. 2:2). And this authority lays claim upon Christians for their obedience, respect, and intercession (1 Tim. 2:2; Titus 3:1; 1 Pet. 2:13, 17). It is not unintentional that in Luke 2 a connection is made, and in a certain sense a parallel is drawn, between the government of Augustus and the birth of Christ; when the time was fulfilled, the kingdom of God drew near (Mark 1:15); when the fullness of time had arrived, God sent his Son, born of a woman, born under the law (Gal. 4:4). With both—that is, with Augustus on the throne and with Christ in the manger—a new age dawned, a time of earthly and heavenly peace. The birth of both was good news for the world, a joyful gospel. The unity and power of the world kingdom was advantageous for the coming of Christ, for the establishment and spread of his kingdom.

That this coming of Christ and his kingdom is repeatedly identified in the New Testament by the term "gospel" can be explained very well from the fact that, by way of contrast with the pagans, Christians understood [the difference between Christ and Caesar]. Even though in a certain sense the birth of Augustus was a kind of gospel for the world, the coming of Christ is nonetheless the gospel, the good and joyful message par excellence. The former brought merely an earthly and temporary peace, while the latter brought a peace that is heavenly, spiritual, and eternal. Another explanation, however, is far more obvious. In the Old Testament, the Hebrew words *basora* and *bisser* ("a message" [noun] and "to message" [verb]) were rendered in the Greek translation of the Septuagint by *to euangelion* and *euangelizomai*.[16] In addition, this distinction was employed, that when *to euangelion* referred to the reward for bringing a good message, it was used in the neuter plural, and when it referred to the good tiding itself, it was used in the feminine singular. One passage seems to be an exception to this—namely, 2 Samuel 18:25, where the word clearly refers to a good message (and not to a reward), and some nevertheless read it as a neuter singular; others, however, correctly regard it as probable that in that passage the feminine singular is preferable, since this word appears also in verses 20 and 27 of the same chapter. The Greek translation did not use the neuter word *euangelion* in the sense of "glad tiding," but used the feminine *euangelia* (2 Kings 7:9; 2 Kings 1:42; 2 Sam. 18:20, 25, 27).

---

16. Bavinck only has the Dutch *evangelium* and *evangeliseeren*.

"GOSPEL" IN THE OLD TESTAMENT

In the Old Testament, this term *euangelia* was applied especially to the joyful message that would be brought to Jerusalem after the captivity, which message consists in the news that the Lord would rescue and bless his people. "Go on up to a high mountain, O Zion, herald of good news; lift up your voice with strength, O Jerusalem, herald of good news; lift it up, fear not; say to the cities of Judah, 'Behold your God!'" (Isa. 40:9; cf. also Isa. 52:7; Ps. 40:10). Salvation, redemption, peace—these are the content of the message that God had his servant bring to his people, or, as it is described more broadly in Isaiah 61:1–3,

> The Spirit of the Lord GOD is upon me,
>> because the LORD has anointed me
> to bring good news to the poor;
>> he has sent me to bind up the brokenhearted,
> to proclaim liberty to the captives,
>> and the opening of the prison to those who are bound;
> to proclaim the year of the LORD's favor,
>> and the day of vengeance of our God;
>> to comfort all who mourn;
> to grant to those who mourn in Zion—
>> to give them a beautiful headdress instead of ashes,
> the oil of gladness instead of mourning,
>> the garment of praise instead of a faint spirit;
> that they may be called oaks of righteousness,
>> the planting of the LORD, that he may be glorified.

"GOSPEL" IN THE NEW TESTAMENT AND EARLY CHURCH

Coupled with this promise of the Old Covenant, the word "gospel" now obtains a special meaning in the New Testament. In the synagogue in Nazareth, Jesus himself explained that the prophecy cited above was now being fulfilled in his person and work (Luke 4:15–21). The content of the gospel thus consists first of all in the fulfillment of the promise of the Old Testament; what was at that time *epangelia* (promise) has now become *evangelium*, as Paul later testified in the synagogue in Antioch of Pisidia: we proclaim (evangelize) to you the promise (*epangelia*) that was made to the fathers, which "he has fulfilled to us their children by raising Jesus" [Acts 13:33].[17] That gospel, the fulfillment of the

17. The direct quote and Scripture reference were added by the editor for greater clarity.

Old Testament promise, began, according to Mark 1:1–2, with the appearance of John, surnamed the baptizer, who proclaimed the coming of the kingdom of God, who preached the baptism of conversion unto the forgiveness of sin, and who pointed to the Stronger One who would come after him. Shortly thereafter, Jesus came from Nazareth in Galilee to the Jordan, to be baptized by John. And when this baptism and then the temptation in the wilderness had occurred, Jesus began his own preaching, and this preaching had as its content the gospel of God, the good news that the time was fulfilled, and the kingdom of God had come near; repent and believe that gospel (Mark 1:15). The promise in the Old Testament and its fulfillment in the New Testament further consisted in the reality that the kingdom of God has come, the kingdom with the righteousness, the well-being, the peace, and the joy of God, unto the salvation of all who expect it and receive it along the path of repentance and faith.

But during New Testament history, this content of the gospel is unfolded still further. This development was presented by Harnack[18] in such a way that the content of the first gospel preached by Jesus—namely, the coming of the kingdom—was replaced by the apostles, especially Paul, with the second gospel, whose center was the person and work of Christ. The gospel of Jesus supposedly changed into a gospel about Christ, such that its subject was transformed into its object. But this construal definitely conflicts with the testimony of the New Testament. For, in the first place, in the first three Gospels, Christ assigns himself an entirely unique place in the kingdom of heaven, such that people's destruction or salvation depends on the relationship in which they stood to him. Second, it is completely understandable that Jesus first had to be crucified, resurrected, and glorified at the Father's right hand before the disciples could obtain full insight into the significance of his person and work. Thus, the gospel of the kingdom, which Jesus himself preached and which consisted fundamentally in his self-proclamation, proclamation by Christ of his own Sonship and Messiahship, developed gradually under the influence of the events and under the leading of the Spirit into the gospel of God about his Son, as Paul explains it in Romans 1:1–2. The preaching of Philip the evangelist constituted, as it were, the transition—or, better, the connection—between both; for he preached—or, as it actually says in Acts 8:12, he evangelized—about the

---

18. Carl Gustav Adolf von Harnack (1851–1930) was a German theologian, prominent church historian, and author of the multivolume *History of Dogma* (*Lehrbuch der Dogmengeschichte*; originally published 1886–90), which was an extended argument claiming that Christian dogma "in its conception and development is a work of the Greek spirit on the soil of the Gospel" (Harnack, *History of Dogma*, 1:17). Harnack summarized his own understanding of the gospel as a reduction to "two heads: the idea of God the Father and the infinite value of the human soul" (Harnack, *What Is Christianity?*, 68).

kingdom of God and the name of Jesus Christ. Thus, the preaching of God's kingdom became more and more clearly the preaching about Christ, who is simultaneously the king and prophet and priest of that kingdom. Thus, the gospel of the New Testament has as its center and content the person and work of Christ, Jesus Christ and him crucified; there is no other gospel. Therefore, since the second century, the meaning of the word "gospel" could change, in the sense that it came to refer to the sayings and actions of Christ, and beyond that, to the words and deeds of Christ as written down, just as today we speak of the Gospel of Matthew and Mark, Luke and John. But these four Gospels, according to the original view, were not four, but only one gospel in four forms or descriptions. And that single gospel had Christ as its content.

The origin of this gospel lies in God; it is his grace that the gospel reveals and bestows and causes to be proclaimed (Mark 1:14; Acts 20:24; 1 Pet. 4:17; Heb. 1:1). After the Old Testament prophets had passed from the scene, at the beginning of the new dispensation the gospel was first proclaimed by the angel who appeared to Zechariah (Luke 1:19) and to Mary (Luke 1:30–31), and especially by the angel of the Lord who, in connection with the birth of Jesus, spoke to the shepherds in the fields of Ephrathah: "Fear not, for behold, I bring you good news of great joy that will be for all the people. For unto you is born this day in the city of David a Savior, who is Christ the Lord" (Luke 2:10–11). This preaching of angels was, however, preparatory, having an extraordinary and temporary character. Later, John and Jesus appear as preachers of the gospel, and then the disciples and the seventy, who during Jesus's life received a particular assignment (Luke 9:2; 10:9), and then the apostles, especially after Jesus's glorification, were to serve as his witnesses and were to preach the gospel to every creature, beginning in Jerusalem and spreading it throughout Judea and Samaria to the end of the earth (Matt. 28:19; Mark 16:15; Acts 1:8).

To refer to this preaching of the gospel, the New Testament uses especially three words: first, *kerussein*, which refers to the kind of announcement a herald makes in connection with the arrival of his prince; then *katangellein*, which means "to bring a message," "give a report," "proclaim," "reveal"; and finally, *euangelizein*, which identifies that message as good news, a joyful tiding. But all these three realities lead to a fourth, which in Holy Scripture is identified by the word *didaskein*, "to teach." This was not yet the case with John the Baptist; he is and remains a herald, one who prepares the way. But Jesus appears not only as a preacher of the gospel but also as master and teacher; he instructs his disciples regarding the secrets of the kingdom of God. And when, before his ascension, he gave the assignment to his apostles to preach (*kerussein*, "proclaim and declare") the gospel to all creatures (Mark 16:15), he described this elsewhere in this way: instruct all the nations and teach them to observe everything I have commanded you (Matt. 28:19).

CHALLENGES TO GOSPEL TEACHING

In the initial period, this preaching and teaching were not tied exclusively to a leadership office. Indeed, the church was never without leadership office; one could say that in the apostolate that Christ established, leadership office in a certain sense existed prior to the church. It was specifically the twelve apostles who had received the calling to serve as ear- and eyewitnesses of Christ and to lay the foundation of the church in the Jewish and pagan world (John 17:20; Eph. 2:20; 1 John 1:3; Rev. 21:14). When these apostles had established churches in various locales, they rather quickly appointed overseers (elders) and deacons in them, who were tasked with the governing of the church and with providing for the poor (Acts 6:1–6; 11:30; 14:23; 20:28). But we must remember that during that initial period, an abundant distribution of various gifts occurred (Rom. 12:6; 1 Cor. 12:4–5) and that therefore wide latitude could and should have been provided for the exercise of those gifts. They pertained both to teaching and to serving (Rom. 12:7; 1 Cor. 12:10; 1 Pet. 4:11); and postapostolic literature teaches us more clearly than the New Testament that there were men and also women who did not serve in a leadership office and were not tied to a local church who, as Origen states, devoted everything to the spread of the faith, traveled from city to city, from village to village, to win new believers for the Lord. In a broader sense, all these itinerant preachers, whose number in the second century must have been rather large, were called evangelists or teachers. Initially they were highly respected, and many sought to become recognized in the church as teachers (cf. also James 3:1). But decay soon entered this group; stumbling in teaching occurred frequently among these teachers, and not only in the sense that they lacked the gift of speaking, which they thought they possessed, but, more seriously in this regard, that they misused their speaking, knowingly or unknowingly, to proclaim various errors.

Paving the way for this abuse was especially Gnosticism, which had spread widely in the second century and had altered the preaching of the gospel by means of the slippery words of human wisdom. Because of this, the church needed to guard against these unaccountable teachers. Although the church highly esteemed the teaching labor of men like the apologists, who had continued building on the foundation of the apostles, she nevertheless gradually bound together both leadership office and doctrine; already in the ancient catholic church, teaching was withheld from the laity and turned into a privilege of the bishop. Remarkably, so little is known about these unaccountable itinerant teachers. Although their number must have been rather large—for they appear throughout the entire second century into the beginning of the third century—only a few of their names have been preserved. Their influence appears not to have been as great as we would initially have expected. The church of Christ was established in the world during the first century by means of the missionary labor of the apostles, especially Paul, and thereafter was multiplied and expanded from within, through the confession and the life of believers themselves. These people were nurtured in the teaching of Christ and the apostles not to abandon their families and occupations immediately after conversion so they might work for the conversion of others, but, on the contrary, to remain in the calling in which they had been called (1 Cor. 7:20) and to be faithful precisely where God had placed them, as husband or wife, as master or servant, and to persevere to the end. In the initial period, believers conducted themselves accordingly. Christians themselves were the best missionaries, through their confession and life, through their courage and steadfastness, especially through their martyrdom; their blood was the seed of the church; and that church itself in its totality was the strongest instrument of missions (Harnack).[19]

Therefore, evangelization in our sense of the term[20] did not occur during the first centuries. Perhaps in a certain sense we can identify the labor of the Old Testament prophets by that term; for as the people of Israel fell more and more into idolatry and covenant breaking, God sent his prophets, who were preachers of repentance, who summoned the people to repentance and conversion, and thereafter comforted them with the promise of salvation. John and Jesus also directed their preaching to the Jews, whom they, like the prophets, continued to view as the people of God. They may have been apostate and faithless children, but they were still children, from whom salvation proceeded, to whom the words of God had been entrusted, to whom along with their seed the promise applied. But when the Jews rejected the gospel, denied the Holy and Righteous One, and killed the Prince of life, at that point they came to stand on the same line as the pagans, and together with them were the object of the same missionary activity. Even then there is a difference in priority and method, but "gospel proclamation," "evangelizing," is nevertheless the single

19. The reference to Harnack here is likely to his two-volume *The Mission and Expansion of Christianity in the First Three Centuries*.

20. "In our sense of the term" refers first to the mission outreach of the church to those who have left the church, those who have "fallen away" from the faith; what Bavinck has in mind on this point might perhaps be better termed as "reevangelization"; see propositions V and VIII at the beginning of this chapter. In addition, Bavinck's understanding of evangelization also has in view an important *consequence* of reevangelization: the broad reformation of life in society and culture; see proposition VII, above, and the next section of this chapter.

term with which the work of the apostles among both Jews and pagans was identified. In this way, there was a twofold work to which the New Testament church was called: mission work directed outward in the world of Jews and pagans (evangelism in the New Testament sense), and edifying work directed inward on the foundation of apostles and prophets, through the administration of the Word, for the perfecting of the saints and the upbuilding of the body of Christ (Eph. 2:20; 4:12).

EVANGELIZATION AS RENEWAL AND REFORM

The history of the church soon made yet another activity necessary, however, which came to stand, as it were, between the inward upbuilding of the church and its outward mission work, and in our time has come to be called evangelization.[21] As the church deteriorated in doctrine and life, attempts were made to lift it out of decay and lead it back to its original purity. That began already in the apostolic era, as shown especially in the book of Revelation in the letters to the churches of Asia Minor, which contained warnings about faithful perseverance, but also about repentance and renewal of life. From this time forward, the history of the Christian church was not only a history of inward upbuilding and outward mission work but also an interconnected narrative of reformations and separations, all of which were intended to restore the church's original purity of confession and conduct.

In connection with all these attempts at restoration, it is very remarkable that salvation[22] was sought in returning to the origin of Christianity. In this context, that original Christianity was understood quite differently; frequently what was grasped was not Christianity in its totality, but only one idea, such as, for example, chastity or poverty or nonresistance, which was then put one-sidedly in the foreground. But except for those who in our day have broken finally with Christianity and come to expect salvation from a new religion or from a new philosophy—like monism, for example—one can say that theoretically and practically, all Christians were guided by the principle that only the original gospel contains the power for renewing the fallen church.

This reality explains the meaning that people have come gradually to attach to the notion of evangelization. One can derive this new view in principle from Marcion, to the extent that he was the first to formulate a clear insight into the

---

21. See immediately preceding note.

22. DO: *heil*. The word "salvation" here is not to be taken in a full soteriological sense (i.e., salvation from sin) but as deliverance from a situation of decline and decay in the life of the church.

sharp distinction, made by Paul, between law and gospel, although Marcion exaggerated this distinction into a hostile opposition between the two and applied it very arbitrarily in evaluating the books of the Bible. But neither did the emerging Roman Catholic Church correctly understand this Pauline distinction. Rather than join forces with Marcion, it went to the other extreme and began more and more to view the law as an incomplete gospel and the gospel as an incomplete law. This drove all the Reformers involuntarily in a direction in which they felt obligated to register their protest against every kind of corruption of the church in the name of and with appeal to the original gospel.

That has happened in nearly every century. Thus, Peter Waldo in 1176 and Francis of Assisi in 1209, in obedience to the law of Christ,[23] abandoned all their possessions to imitate the impoverished life of Christ and to devote all their strength to preaching and to the works of mercy. In the twelfth century, Joachim of Fiore [ca. 1135–1202], believing church history to progress in three ages—that of the Father, that of the Son, and that of the Holy Spirit—announced the coming of the third and last period of church history, the age of the Spirit. The Father imposes the law, since he is the fearful one; the Son imposes discipline, since he is wisdom; and the Holy Spirit brings freedom, since he is love. According to Joachim, this last period would dawn in 1260 and proceed from the monks; it would be marked by the increase in the spiritual understanding of Holy Scripture and itself become spirit and life in the church. The "eternal gospel"[24] would reign. A century later, in England, John Wycliffe (1330–84) came to prominence. Of all the Reformers before Luther, Wycliffe most powerfully proclaimed and defended the principle of Scripture. For him, the Word of God was completely sufficient, the foundation and rule of doctrine and life, so that, even though there were one hundred popes and all the mendicant cardinals, one may believe them only insofar as they agree with the gospel, the "law of Christ."[25] In the line of this "evangelical teacher,"[26] Jan Hus (1369–1415) declared that only what was taught by Scripture was valid as gospel.

With this history behind them, the adherents of the Reformation in the sixteenth century preferred to call themselves "evangelicals," for they were fundamentally not followers of Luther, Zwingli, or Calvin, as the Roman Catholics liked to identify them, but followers of Christ and confessors of his gospel.[27] Although the name "evangelical" never became the common name for the adherents of the Reformation, and soon had to yield to the name "Protestant,"

---

23. LO: *lex Christi.*
24. LO: *evangelium aeternum.*
25. LO: *lex Christi.*
26. LO: *Doctor evangelicus.*
27. DO: *Evangelie.*

that name "evangelical" continued to be used repeatedly in the churches of the Reformation, especially in contrast to Roman Catholics. Just as in 1648 the *Corpus Evangelicorum* was established in opposition to the *Corpus Catholicorum*, so too in 1817, in the three-hundredth anniversary year of the Reformation, the Lutheran and Reformed churches in Prussia were united by Friedrich Wilhelm III into the Evangelische Kirche. In this way, the name "Evangelical" has become another name for "Protestant," is used widely, and is beloved in many circles. People speak of the Evangelical Alliance, the Evangelical Federation, an evangelical society, an evangelical newspaper, and so on, and these are often in contrast to Rome. Evangelization in this sense leads people to think especially of the spread of the pure gospel[28] among a Roman Catholic populace.

THE RISE OF MODERN UNBELIEF; ITS SPIRITUAL AND SOCIAL CONSEQUENCES

But since the eighteenth century, the gospel has witnessed a far sharper opposition arise against it. A general deterioration set in very quickly in the Protestant churches, proving that the Reformation had restored many groups only outwardly and superficially. For that reason, deism and rationalism found easy entrance, and in the eighteenth century they prepared the way for naturalism, which parted ways with the supernatural, thereby undermining the very foundation of Christianity, and nature took the place of God. In the nineteenth century, this naturalism was significantly strengthened by the movement in which natural and historical sciences operated. Having emancipated itself from all of Christianity and from all religion, this effort sought no other and no higher goal than to observe and determine as accurately as possible phenomena in nature and facts in history, and then to trace in a precise manner the connection that bound them together indissolubly. Thereby modern people came so deeply and so strongly under the influence of the power of nature that they lost faith in the almighty power of God. Fortunately many still do not dare to speak so boldly as professed atheists, who call God the final and greatest enemy of the human race. Furthermore, with respect to invisible realities a fearful doubt and spiritual malaise dominates, which corrodes the powers of the soul. People may concede that there is perhaps still a God who reveals himself and can perform miracles, but we cannot know this with certainty; life is a mystery, we walk about in riddles, on every side we bump our heads against the wall that divides firmly and immovably the knowable from the eternally unknowable. There have been, so people say, so many instances of what we in our immaturity have considered

28. DO: *Evangelie*.

to be indubitable truth in nature and history. Now the history of humanity makes us, especially in the arena of religion, familiar with so many errors clothed in naïveté and childlike faith that it appears presumptuous to speak of knowledge of the truth beyond the boundaries of exact science. Let us therefore abstain from making a judgment, and comfort ourselves with the notion that God, if he exists, has reserved for himself the possession of the truth and has entrusted to us merely the quest for the truth.[29]

As always, however, superstition accompanies this unbelief. Not only the superstition of the Roman Catholic Church, which appeals to many romantic-oriented natures with its symbolism and art, but especially that many-headed modern superstition which nests and spreads in our cultural centers in the forms of spiritism and theosophy, astrology and magic, spiritual and bodily quackery. Paganism lives again among us, both in its despair regarding the truth and in its belief in what is false. This century is often compared with the first century AD; and this is absolutely correct, for the more one gets to know both centuries, the more points of similarity emerge.

But there is difference in terms of one aspect. Back in the first century, early Christianity, borne by men full of faith and of the Holy Spirit, penetrated the world victoriously; in this century the church of Christ, existing in a tight spot between unbelief and superstition, is being gradually robbed of its respect and influence. Church attendance and church membership are declining everywhere.[30] According to Dr. Carroll, in the United States in 1912 the number of people joining a church did not keep pace with the increase in population, for in that year only 597,800 people joined a church, which is 15,500 fewer than in 1911. The last census of church attenders in the city of Liverpool showed their number to have decreased in the preceding decade by about 18,000, whereas the population rose during that decade by about 45,000 residents. According to some, in France the number of those belonging to no church or religious affiliation increased to approximately one-fifth of the population; even though less than absolute credibility should be given to this estimate, everyone agrees that their number increases annually. In our own country, the number of those unchurched in 1879 was merely 12,000, but it increased in 1889 to 66,000, in 1899 to 150,000, and in 1909 to about 290,000. As disconcerting as these

29. Bavinck is alluding here to a famous statement of the German philosopher Gotthold Ephraim Lessing: "If God were to hold all Truth concealed in his right hand, and in his left only the steady and diligent drive for Truth, albeit with the proviso that I would always and forever err in the process, and to offer me the choice, I would with all humility take the left hand, and say: Father, I will take this one—the pure Truth is for You alone." Taken from Gotthold Ephraim Lessing, *Anti-Goetze: Eine Duplik* (1778), in *Werke*, ed. H. Göpfert (1979), 8:32–33; translation is by Scott Horton and comes from his essay "Lessing's Search for Truth."

30. Bavinck provides no references for the statistics that follow.

numbers are, much more troubling is the additional fact that thousands upon thousands who still belong nominally to a church have in fact broken with the church and with Christianity entirely. Entire neighborhoods in cities as well as in rural areas, and large segments in our society, don't bother at all with religion, and, as Paul once wrote about Ephesian Christians of old, they live in the world without God and without hope. The religious and moral degradation of our people is becoming rampant. In many groups, Bible knowledge is becoming more and more pathetic. Ministers have abandoned their post, and many people view ministers only as obsolete. Sundays and religious holidays serve only for boredom, or for tiring and exhausting amusements.

In addition to this spiritual misery there is the physical distress. In recent centuries, science has been able to make its inventions and discoveries serviceable to everyday use and has amazed the world with the miracles of technology. By these means, human life has in many respects been enriched and made more comfortable, but the entire society has also changed in appearance. Whereas formerly, every city, village, and family, every occupation and business, every class and rank were independent, nowadays every wall of separation has been torn down and every distinction has been erased. All people, nations, and countries are now swallowed up by the single great, ever-expanding global concourse and have become dependent on each other to the strongest degree possible. Out of this new, continually morphing society, the great contrast emerges ever more strongly, identified with the terms "capitalism" and "proletariat." Socialism is guilty of an enormous exaggeration when it portrays the whole history of humanity, especially in the present time, from the viewpoint of class struggle; but nevertheless, the amassing of capital in the hands of millionaires, multimillionaires, and billionaires, of unions and banks, is also an objectionable phenomenon; it is in contrast to this reality that the lives of millions of laborers in mines and factories compare so meagerly and darkly.

In the previous month, Philip Snowden,[31] the socialist delegate to the British House of Commons, said that the returns from foreign trade in 1912 increased by 1.2 billion guilders over 1911, and nevertheless three million inhabitants had to seek refuge that same year in public welfare; that one-fourth or perhaps even one-third of the laborers live in poverty, and 33 percent of adult wage earners earn less than fifteen shillings per week, and many day laborers earn less than twelve shillings per week. Snowden added more contrasting "facts" that are troubling:[32]

31. Philip Snowden (1st Viscount Snowden; 1864–1937) was a British politician known for his criticism of capitalism and advocacy of socialism.

32. This sentence and the bullet points that follow are the editor's reconstruction, for the sake of clarity, of a series of subordinate clauses in the original.

- in 1912, members of the House of Commons spent ninety-six thousand guilders in the coffeeshop on wine, an average of six guilders per week per person;
- in 1912 wages rose by twelve million guilders, but mostly due to pressure from labor strikes;
- mine owners earned ten to twelve times more than was needed to cover the adopted minimum wage;
- the price of coal had risen 48 percent in the previous fourteen years.

All this gives the firm impression of an acute disparity that cuts deep into one's soul and cries out for reconciliation.[33]

Additionally, we bring to people's attention the terrible destruction brought about in our modern society through alcoholism, prostitution, and criminality! Recently, testimony based on expert information was given in the *Nieuwe Rotterdamsche Courant* that, in terms of its results, alcoholism is the most terrible of all dangers threatening public health. Slavery to drink produces poverty and misery, sickness, and lawbreaking. More than any other evil, it steals the fortune of families. One-sixth of those being cared for in insane asylums are victims of alcohol. Hundreds lie in our hospitals sick from the results of alcoholism. More than half of those sentenced to prison have abused alcohol. And what is most disastrous is that descendants of those afflicted with drunkenness face an abnormally difficult struggle for existence, in which they, through their lack of physical and psychological capacities for resistance, succumb so much more quickly to illness and lawbreaking.

The second national sin, prostitution, poses no less a danger. Although people do not flatter themselves with the expectation that this sin can ever be eliminated, because it has existed always and everywhere, and after Augustine the church fostered the opinion that the state must tolerate this due to human weakness—nevertheless in our society it has reached such widespread proportion that one can risk a heart attack when thinking about where all of this must lead. For in our time, it is facilitated by social evils, lack of housing, low wages, cost of living, challenging marriage opportunities, increasing numbers of young men and women who live in barely affordable circumstances, and so on. In addition, prostitution is, as it were, systematically encouraged by the scintillating literature, the immoral presentations in literature and on screen, which repeatedly tend to glorify fornication and prostitution—indeed, even by the so-called scientific defense of free love and homosexuality. This occurs most certainly in rural areas, but its breeding ground is in the large cities, of

33. DO: *verzoening*.

which there are more than thirty in Europe that each have more than five hundred thousand residents, which serves to combine the most acute contrasts. There one encounters the brightest of lights and the blackest darkness, the most opulent luxury and the most grinding poverty, the most beautiful homes and most miserable slums, the most glamorous streets and malls and the most miserable ghettos. But prostitution can find its way anywhere and everywhere; it blossoms in the palaces of the great just as easily as in the shabby hovels of the poor; it conducts business using white slaves, and does so around the entire world, undermining the life of society by destroying marriage, by dissolving households and family living, by its constant stream of venereal diseases.

In addition, in the third place, there is criminality. Just as in several other countries, in our land too the number of criminals is not disturbing, since they have been declining throughout recent years. But there are nonetheless some facts that cause concern. First, there is an increase in the number of assaults against life and dignity; one can observe a growing brutality on the part of lawbreakers, of which the auto thieves in France provide a very intense demonstration; they no longer adhere to any limits and consider human life to have no value. That comes to expression also in the increasing number of suicides, which occasionally are defended in full seriousness from a scientific perspective as a personal right to die; for example, in Vienna in the previous year the number of suicides rose 20 percent, and through all of Europe, this number is estimated to be more than forty thousand in one year. Crime statistics bring yet another fact to light—namely, that crimes are being committed at an increasingly younger age, sometimes by boys and girls of ten or twelve years old; that statistic merely increases when, after being punished for their first offense, they later return to society and fall back into the same or a similar crime. All of this indicates that the awareness of sin and crime, of guilt and punishment, has weakened to a considerable degree; and this would become much clearer if the defective crime statistics could be supplemented with reliable moral statistics.

AMELIORATION EFFORTS; THE INNER MISSION

Such circumstances of spiritual and material distress can exist for years before someone engages them intentionally and pursues improvement. But if these circumstances develop further down their frightening path, eyes will finally be open, and men and women will stand up everywhere to sound the alarm and look around for help and rescue. This is how it went with those situations that arose during the eighteenth and nineteenth centuries in religious, moral, and social arenas. Fortunately, at that time the helping hand was extended not only from religious and ecclesiastical corners. For the situations that we briefly described above affected not only Christians and the church but also the state and all of society together with every citizen; the church alone seemed unqualified and incompetent to provide improvement. With gratitude we acknowledge the assistance offered by government, associations, and individuals for relieving human suffering and lessening social distress. For example, when the government took children and women and workers under its wings, to protect them from violence and fraud, when individuals and associations were drawn toward the manifold miseries and took to heart the care of the distressed in hospitals and institutions, then all of that and much more deserves our appreciation and gratitude. Anyone working in these areas is not our enemy, but our collaborator and ally. The need is so great that the cooperation of as many as possible is required.

But we nevertheless rejoice as well that from a positive Christian motive, and in a proportionally large number, men and women have arisen who, when they have seen these situations, have felt the compassion that moved Christ when he saw the multitudes who had become weary and dispersed like sheep without a shepherd. In this context it would be impossible to mention here the names of those who have walked in Jesus's footsteps. But I must make an exception for brothers Wesley and Whitefield, the fathers of Methodism, who in the religious and moral degradation of England in the eighteenth century literally went out to the multitudes and brought them the gospel of faith and love in word and deed. In that same century, rationalism extended its dominion more and more over the human spirit across the continent—that same rationalism that originated in England but had been beaten back and had been robbed of its influence over the nation—until it was celebrated in triumph in the French Revolution and simultaneously experienced its dissolution. Only when that revolution had subsided did the spirit of compassion awaken across the continent, and in our own country, one century after Wesley, the spirit of compassion that sought in the name of Christ to reclaim the lost and to raise up the fallen. Here, too, I wish to avoid the praise of men. But I may not omit mention, in connection with our own land, of the name of Otto Gerhard Heldring,[34] and for Germany that of Johann Hinrich Wichern,[35] for it was especially they who opened our eyes to the work of domestic missions[36] and bound this labor upon our hearts. To

---

34. Otto Gerhard Heldring (1804–76) was a Dutch preacher and philanthropist known for his work in the Dutch temperance movement and for establishing homes and schools for women caught up in prostitution.

35. Johann Hinrich Wichern (1808–81) was a founder of the home mission movement in Germany; the German term is *Innere Mission* (inner mission).

36. DO: *inwendige zending*.

Wichern we owe the term "inner mission," ordinarily used to refer to this labor. For although this term was used perhaps first by Professor Lücke from Göttingen[37] in 1843, Wichern popularized it and caused it to find entrance, translated or untranslated, far beyond the boundaries of his people and his country. That resulted first from the treatise he published in 1844, titled "The Predicaments of the Protestant Church and Her Inner Mission."[38] But a far stronger impulse for this terminology emerged from the incisive speech he delivered at the first German Evangelical Church Day in Wittenberg in the revolutionary year of 1848, in which he appealed to all believing Christians with the following famous words: "One thing is necessary for the Evangelical Church to recognize: The work of inner mission is mine, love belongs to me like faith!"[39]

As far as I know, there is no overriding objection against adopting this term "inner mission." Though the term "missions"[40] was forged in connection with laboring in the gospel among pagans, when we speak of "evangelization" we are using a term that had another meaning in the New Testament and was used specifically for what we today call missions. In addition, the concept is more precisely and clearly described with the addition of the adjective "inner," and thereby we maintain the notion that the labor conducted among straying Christians does not depend on the whims of the church but belongs to its calling. Finally, we need a term that is universal and comprehends everything that belongs to the arena of inner mission, and until now a better term for that has not emerged.

For with Wesley, and also with Wichern and Heldring, this labor began everywhere very small, but meanwhile has increased so much that it extends to virtually every arena and circumstance of life, to every circle and class of society. Both church and theology had to clarify their boundaries, to make room for the practice and theory of this labor. But no matter how extensive that labor may be, it clearly falls into two groups of activities, which can be identified as evangelization and philanthropy, witness and welfare, labors of faith and love, spiritual and social work. Of course, no separation is intended here, for just as no genuine philanthropy exists apart from Christianity, so too no true faith exists without its expression in works of love. Thus, whereas the term "inner mission" refers to all these forms of labor that seek to liberate Christians who have become estranged from God's Word through unbelief and superstition,

---

37. Gottfried Christian Friedrich Lücke (1791–1855) was a German theology professor, first at the University of Bonn (1818–27) and then at the University of Göttingen (1827–55).

38. GO: *Die Nothstände der Protestantischen Kirche und die Innere Mission.*

39. GO: *Es thut Eins not, dass die Evangelische Kirche anerkenne: Die Arbeit der Inneren Mission ist mein, die Liebe gehört mir wie der Glaube!*

40. DO: *zending.*

in addition to various forms of suffering and distress, the term "evangelization" is used specifically for that extension of the gospel verbally and in writing that occurs on the part of or under the supervision and leadership of the church among those baptized Christians who have become more or less alienated from the faith.

This description diverges from others in that from the outset it connects evangelization directly or indirectly with the church. Many enthusiastic advocates of God's kingdom and many zealous laborers in that kingdom begin by positioning church and evangelism in a sharp opposition to each other and understand evangelization to mean specifically the kind of labor that is taken to heart and taken in hand not on the part of or through the church, but outside the church through individual persons or societies, according to their own goals and preferences.

The sad circumstances characterizing the church today may, to a certain extent, justify this line of action, since it is always far better that something be done incorrectly than that nothing be done at all. But proper evangelization ought nevertheless to proceed directly or indirectly from the church, and through the church's labor, evangelization ought even to be rendered unnecessary and superfluous.

If things in a church proceeded to such an extent that evangelization in the sense described above nevertheless became necessary, then that is in the first instance a proof that the church has neglected its calling, failed in its duty. Then the church itself needs to repent. Genuine repentance always consists in a heartfelt sorrow about, hatred of, and fleeing from sin, in addition to an upright desire and love for living according to the will of God in all good works. Thus, it does not consist in the kind of confession of guilt that is coupled with a passive acquiescence to the sinful situation and even suggests that this situation is a judgment imposed by God that must be borne with patience. Genuine sorrow is manifested and proven when people renounce their own will and proceed to do God's will. For a Reformed church, uncertainty can hardly exist regarding the will of God and its calling for believers; Scripture speaks about this clearly enough. When the nation of the Jews opposed Jesus, he gathered his disciples around him, spoke of them already before his resurrection and ascension as a church (*ecclesia*), and bestowed upon that church a unique existence and life, a unique government and authority, a unique ministry and discipline. Thus, the church is an institution of Christ, with which we cannot do as we please, but which is subject to him alone and which must walk according to his commandments. It is founded upon the confession of his name, built on the foundation of apostles and prophets, established in the world to be a pillar and ground of the truth. In this way it must be manifested as the body of Christ, remove from its midst the manifest unbeliever and wicked person, and preserve itself without blemish unto the future of its Lord Jesus Christ.

All these commands for the life of the church in the New Testament are so manifold and at the same time so clear that no Christian conscience can escape their grip. Nevertheless, this is frequently attempted. Up until our own day, people have attempted specially to urge departure from the path of obedience, since it leads to separation, and this separation is condemned a priori as an abandonment of national unity and of the national church. Aside from the fact that this argument entails the acknowledgment that there is no room in the national church for fidelity to the Lord's Word, if it proves anything, it proves too much; for by this argument, the leading of the New Testament church out of the national church of Israel, and the reformation of the church in the sixteenth century, would be rejected as illegitimate. Indeed, with this argument people weaken their own position, in that people persist in remaining separated from the Roman Catholic Church, which has no fewer than two million members, almost one-third of our population. Furthermore, within the ecclesiastical realm thousands upon thousands of members have in fact surrendered to various winds of doctrine, because there is no spiritual nurture. But additionally, considerations of utility and opportunity can never set aside the command of God nor rob it of its power. Blind regarding the future, the Reformers had only the commandment in view; along that route they were a blessing for our entire land and nation. After all, a kingdom that is divided against itself cannot stand; if the salt becomes flavorless, it can no longer be flavorful. By contrast, when the church, no matter how small, is a city on the mountain and a light in the candlestick, then power and blessing flow from it to distant reaches. Keeping God's commandments always yields great reward.

This kind of church, restored to the foundation of the confession, must first see to it that no need for evangelization exists within its sphere. As soon as this becomes necessary, the church has already fallen short of its duty. Thus, it must work preventively, for here too prevention is better than rehabilitation. So, according to the teaching of Scripture, its first task consists in the perfecting of the saints, in the work of ministry, in the upbuilding of the body of Christ. The church must demonstrate its loyalty to God's commandment in the faithfulness with which it administers Word and sacrament, maintains governance and discipline, instructs the immature members of the church, visits believers in their homes, cares for the sick, and provides for the needs of the saints. If the small number of office-bearers or the immense size of the church means it can no longer fulfill the requirement, it may not throw in the towel in discouragement but must either (1) divide the congregation into districts or sections or (2) increase the number of office-bearers or (3) engage assistants as catechism teachers, visitors to the sick, fundraisers, deaconesses, canvassers, and so forth. In the church there are no offices without gifts, but in the church, there are indeed many gifts without offices, gifts that may not be neglected, but must be zealously developed, belonging to the ministry of the church and able to be enlisted far more effectively than they have been until now.

Which of these three solutions deserves preference in a given instance depends on various local circumstances and cannot be discussed further here. But if a general rule may be valid, it would be that the personal contact of the minister of the Word with each member of his congregation should be maintained and should not be denigrated without notice to a mere sinecure; when the shepherd no longer knows his sheep by name, they stray and scatter. If this practice is neglected, then within a short period of time, in the face of the extraordinary expanse of territory belonging to many cities and in the face of the powerful influence of modern culture, the church fades into the background, is driven from people's consciousness, and comes to be forgotten even among its own members. Though it is difficult and burdensome, the church must nevertheless keep pace in the competition with the forces surrounding it. It must not only stay up with the times but must also lead the way and remain in front, as in the time of the Reformation. In no instance may it lag; never through its own culpability may it be the reason why, as the century unfolds and moves forward, it is viewed and treated as a "negligible entity."[41]

This kind of church, in connection with others throughout the entire country, becomes a pillar and ground of the truth, a dam against the stream of all kinds of error, and at the same time a hearth of sacred fire and a center of activity. The first centuries of our era provide us with the proof of this. For at that time, to remind us once more, after the missionary labor of the apostles, the church was multiplied and expanded especially from within, through its inner development, through the faithful confession and holy living of its members. The church itself was the first and greatest missionary force in the world. And this was how it manifested itself once again in the time of the Reformation on Reformed soil. For there is a considerable difference here between Luther and Calvin. The German Reformer gradually came to be satisfied that the pure administration of Word and sacrament had been restored in the church, and he left matters of church government, discipline, and benevolence to the state and to society. In the Reformer from Geneva, however, there lived a different spirit. He understood, and brought to bear in practice, that the kingdom of heaven was a leaven that had to permeate all the dough; it was a mustard seed that grew into a tree large enough for the birds of the sky to come and nest in its branches. Calvin saw in

41. FO: *quantité négligeable*.

Christianity not merely a principle of new spiritual life but also an element, the preeminent element, of culture; for him the gospel was a joyful message to all creatures, also to family, society, state, science, and art. His followers, viewed properly, did not at all follow principles of separation, but only reformational principles that influenced the entire country and the entire society. Separation is not a principle that they accepted; it was at most a necessity imposed on them, even as the Act of Separation in 1834 declared with no unclarity.

Thus, reformation in the church begins in its unity of organism and organization but proceeds from this base of operation outward into all of national life and extends into every sphere. When the Anti-Revolutionary Party, which counts its most numerous and faithful members among Reformed groups within and outside of the Dutch Reformed Church,[42] has from the beginning of its existence onward devoted itself to the liberating of school and church and society, it thereby demonstrates in fact that the principles guiding it are directed not toward the separation of a segment of the people, but toward the reformation of the entire nation, if possible. Thus, there is no difference about the goal, but only about the best method leading toward this goal. In that case, such reformation, which begins with the church and expands from there in continually increasing scope, is far preferable to all other attempts devoted to Christianizing national life. For it operates not only with individuals but organically with the entire nation; it does not labor merely from the outside to the inside but also from inside to the outside; it attacks the enemy not only in its strongholds but at the heart of the fortress itself. Article 36 retains its place in our confession as well, although in connection with this reformation, every use of force is to be condemned, precisely for the sake of the gospel.[43]

But people can and must do the one without neglecting the other. If people think that in the Reformed churches no need exists for evangelization because all members of these churches are cared for in adequate measure (an opinion whose evaluation we leave aside for the moment), then this would still not relieve us of this labor of internal mission, since we are surrounded on every side by an increasingly growing multitude of people who perhaps to some degree still think of the church in connection with one or another ceremony or rite, but for the rest and for the most part no longer understand practically anything of the gospel of Christ and live their lives in the deepest spiritual ignorance. When in 1848 Wichern watched the passions rage that the revolutionary spirit had aroused in every country, he wrote in connection with his return home from

---

42. DO: *Nederlands Hervormde Kerk*.

43. Bavinck refers here to article 36 of the Belgic Confession; see the section on this topic in chap. 3, "The State," pp. 131–40.

his audience with King Friedrich Wilhelm IV in Berlin: "A thousand facts and concerns dictate the necessity of Inner Mission";[44] and in saying this, he was not exaggerating. People can scarcely estimate how deeply and broadly the utter ignorance about the Bible and about Christianity, the coarsest unbelief, and the most settled indifference in reference to all spiritual things have permeated the spheres of national life. The atmosphere we are living in—especially in the cities, of course—is so unwholesome for spiritual and moral life that people can easily understand the statement once declared by a woman in a German metropolis: "Here in Berlin people have no alternative but to be ungodly!"

We may not close our eyes to these circumstances; we cannot, as we imagine washing our hands in innocence, retreat from that great multitude of people who are in danger of sinking away in spiritual and material misery; far less are we allowed to act like Pharisees and pronounce a curse upon that multitude because these people don't know the law, nor may we, like Cain, excuse ourselves from all responsibility for the brother. As citizens of the same country, as sons of the same people, as children of the same Reformation, and as those baptized in the same name, we are not free from this multitude. Jesus left us with an entirely different example. Immediately upon entering upon his labor, he declared in the synagogue in Nazareth,

> The Spirit of the Lord is upon me,
>> because he has anointed me
>> to proclaim good news to the poor.
> He has sent me to proclaim liberty to the captives
>> and recovering of sight to the blind,
>> to set at liberty those who are oppressed,
> to proclaim the year of the Lord's favor. (Luke 4:18–19)

In accordance with this goal of his mission, he went throughout the land preaching and doing good, healing every kind of sickness and disease among the people, so that he could send this proof of his messiahship when he told John's disciples to tell their master: "The blind receive their sight, the lame walk, lepers are cleansed, and the deaf hear, the dead are raised up, the poor have the good news preached to them. And blessed is the one who is not offended by me" (Luke 7:22–23). Jesus wants his disciples to labor in the world in the same way; he set before them the compassionate Samaritan, who showed mercy to the man who had fallen among murderers, whom priest and Levite

---

44. GO: *Tausende von Thatsachen und Besorgnissen diktieren die Nothwendigkeit der Inneren Mission.*

had arrogantly passed by. He commanded them, in the parable of the master who had prepared a great supper and invited many, to go out into the streets and neighborhoods of the city—indeed, out to the highways—to bring in the poor and the maimed, the crippled and the blind, so that the house might be full and no seat at the table be unoccupied. At the end of his life, he told them that the heirs of the kingdom would be recognized and judged in terms of whether they had ministered to him in the hungry whom they fed, in the thirsty whose thirst they had quenched, in the strangers whom they had housed, in the naked whom they had clothed, in the sick whom they had nursed, and in the prisoners whom they had visited.

Whether this evangelizing happens verbally or through literature, by a minister of the Word or by a member of the congregation who holds no office, in a tent or in a hall, at home or at work, it must always happen according to this rule, that we have received at no cost and thus ought also to impart at no cost. Thereby everyone who wants to devote themselves to this glorious but onerous labor will first encounter the question whether they themselves have indeed received what they wish to bring to others, for only the kind of testimony that arises from faith has any power and is able to speak from one heart to another. In addition, this labor shall not occur for the sake of applause or reward, nor to glorify one's own name or expand one's own kingdom, but purely for the Lord's sake. All ecclesiastical chauvinism is therefore alien to evangelization! The objects of its labor are generally not those who belong consciously and voluntarily to a different church and are being cared for spiritually by that church, but all of those who for several years have been neglected by the churches and left to their own fate. Among them there are significant differences in rank, status, development, refinement, and so on, and evangelization must take those into account, just as Paul became a Jew to the Jews, a Greek to the Greeks, and all things to all people, so that he might save at least some. Among these people are those who are averse and hostile, who should not be approached; others who are carefree and indifferent, among whom evangelization is plowing on rocks; but among them there are also the neglected, the abandoned, the straying, who have no peace of heart, and with whom, through a good word spoken at the right time, one can make a connection.

Finally, the rule mentioned above regarding the Christian's own free reception will protect them against exaggerated expectations as well as against bouts of discouragement. Like foreign missions, so too inner missions should count on facing strong resistance and severe disappointments. This mission must not think that it will ever close the chasm between church and world, or ever reconcile these opponents; the duality will continue until, and beyond, the end of the age. Therefore, in a certain sense, the beginning of this labor is easy, for it occurs when the passion of hearts is aroused by people like Wichern; but continuing and persevering is difficult, so that serious reflection should be done beforehand. But nonetheless, the times should not be viewed unfavorably. For despite the radiance of its discoveries and victories, science has become more aware than ever of its limitation; a need has awakened for higher things and eternal values, which people thought for a long time could be satisfied by culture, but which today seeks fulfillment in all kinds of other directions. Furthermore, in a wide circle, a sense of solidarity with and sympathy for the distressed is being manifested, which does not always function according to our method or our chosen path, but about which we may nevertheless rejoice. Jesus, too, did not condemn the casting out of demons by the sons of his accusers. Therefore, it is time to go to work, or rather, to continue the work better and more powerfully than in the past; let us perform the labor, however, no differently than in the name of him who came not to be served but to serve and to give his life as a ransom for many.

5

Humanity and the Kingdom of God

In this chapter, rather than trying to reinvent the wheel by creating a pastiche of Bavinck's writings on the kingdom of God, I chose to use an English translation of Bavinck's essay "The Kingdom of God, the Highest Good," translated for publication in *The Bavinck Review* by Bavinck editorial team member Nelson Kloosterman.[1] Notice that Bavinck introduces his subject with an extended discussion of ethics. A historical observation: This material was initially given (see note 2) as a lecture to Kampen Theological School students before Bavinck began his professorate there, and the topic of humanity, especially human individual personality, features prominently in the lecture. Twenty years later, as Bavinck completed his work in Kampen, never to return to university lecturing on ethics, would he have envisioned any significant changes to a sketch for lectures on "humanity and the kingdom of God"? For our benefit it would have been nice to have a point of comparison as we

---

The original Dutch wording of this chapter's title is *Menscheid Rijk Gods*. After the word *menscheid* Bavinck added *Wundt* with no further specification. He may have had in mind Wilhelm M. Wundt's three-volume *Ethics: An Investigation of the Facts and Laws of the Moral Life*. In the section "The Ends of Humanity" (3:84–91), Wundt concludes that humanity's perfection is the ultimate end of morality.

1. Bavinck, "The Kingdom of God, the Highest Good." The essay was originally a lecture that Bavinck delivered to the Student Corps—*Fides Quaerit Intellectum*—of the Theological School in Kampen on February 3, 1881. The lecture was first published in serialized form in *De Vrije Kerk: Vereeniging van Christelijke Gereformeerde Stemmen* 7, no. 4:185–92; no. 5:224–34; no. 6:271–77; no. 7:305–14; no. 8:353–60 (April–August 1881). These articles were republished as a single essay in the posthumous collection of Bavinck essays prepared by his brother, C. B. Bavinck, in *Kennis en Leven*, 28–56. For the benefit of scholars we include the pagination from *Kennis en Leven*, as was done in *The Bavinck Review*. Bavinck's original notes will be marked "Bav. note"; all unmarked notes are from the editor.

do, for example, with his two different essays on the "imitation of Christ."[2]
I leave teasing out possible nuances and changes to future Bavinck scholars.

The Kingdom of God, the Highest Good

Introduction

[28] Amid all the distress surrounding the discipline of theology today, it is
undoubtedly a heartening phenomenon that the science identified as Ethics
seems to be enjoying an unheralded resurgence of interest, compared to former
times. This does not mean, of course, that everything in this discipline is flourishing. Not all of the causes to which Ethics is indebted for this resurgence are
heartwarming. The way in which people try to dislodge the firm foundations of
this discipline, or seek to caricature and deny its eternal principles, is far from
encouraging. But that people are curious about the moral life and attempt to
clarify its nature, principle, and essence do provide reasons for rejoicing and
gratitude, I think.

Formerly, the discipline of Ethics received sparse attention, consisting mostly
of explaining the doctrines of virtues and duties. Simply knowing what kind of
persons we must be is inadequate, however, for realizing the moral good—the
description of which is supplied by the doctrine of the virtues. Nor is it sufficient
to know the duties or laws according to which we must pursue that moral good.
We also need to understand those moral goods themselves according to their
nature and essence, in their unity and interconnectedness, in order to realize
them within and around us.

Perhaps the most influential theologian of the nineteenth century was Friedrich Schleiermacher, who was both deeply misunderstood and too highly
esteemed.[3] Yet it was he who identified that above-mentioned flaw in the earlier
view of Ethics and ensured a fixed place in this discipline for the "doctrine of
virtues."[4] In this way he contributed a complete revision and an enduring benefit
to the discipline of Ethics.

[29] Add to this the fact that, formerly, people placed earthly and heavenly
goods alongside each other and failed adequately to plumb the depths of their
interrelationship, which is one of the most difficult problems that exists. People

---

2. See Bolt, *Imitatio Christi*, especially appendix A and appendix B.
3. Bav. note: For evaluating our perspective regarding Schleiermacher, one might find the
following article helpful: R. Nesselmann, "Schleiermachers Wertschätzung."
4. GO: *Güterlehre*.

usually hesitated to include earthly goods in the realm of the moral, thereby running the risk of viewing the moral good only spiritualistically.

Our current age represents such a sharp opposition to that direction. People had been holding out hope for a future that was gloriously portrayed and eagerly believed, one that would make up for all our suffering. Since it did not happen, they have been trying to recover their loss by bathing in the delights of the moment. The invisible, eternal goods—people had been waiting for them in vain for so long that they turned to the temporal and the visible for what they could give! The invoice for the difference, already charged to heaven's account, has remained unpaid and has in fact turned out to be worthless. For a long time already people have been believing; now they want to see—indeed, to live and to enjoy themselves. And since the future is delivering nothing, the sooner the better, the more the better.

That very challenging relationship between this life and the life to come, between earth and heaven, between the temporal and the eternal, the visible and the invisible—people have come to resolve this challenge most simply by insisting that one side of this relationship does not exist. In opposition to that materialist impulse of our age, though acknowledging the truth this monumental error contains, I shall proceed to share with you a glimpse of the glory of our catholic, Christian faith, as I speak to you about the Kingdom of God as the highest good.

The choice of this as my subject immediately offers me the significant advantage that I am standing at the heart of a concept that is genuinely biblical and specifically Christian. This notion could never have grown in pagan soil. All the elements that constitute this concept are absent in paganism. The value and significance of personality remains unknown and uncomprehended; the individual-personal has no unique purpose but appears as a mere means and instrument for the group. Thus the pagan worldview lacks the concept of humanity as a single interrelated organism and could never come up with the idea of a kingdom in which both the individual and the group would develop their full identities. Moreover, the religious moral life was tied most closely with political life and never attained independence. The ethical remained indistinguishable from and virtually bound to the physical, attaining no independent dominion and appearing as merely a particular mode of the one, grand, all-encompassing process of nature. Just as, on Mount Olympus, [30] fate exercised dominion over the gods, so too on earth the freedom of personality was bound by the chains of impersonal nature.

Consequently, the highest good was viewed variously as being either individualistic or communistic, either exclusively sensual or abstractly spiritual. The highest good was identified variously: with Aristotle, for example, as the happiness[5] of the individual, or with the Stoics, as living according to nature, or with Epicurus as happiness experienced through desire. Even for the "spiritual" Plato, who delved so deeply into the essence of the good, the highest good consisted in being released from the senses and being elevated to true, pure, ideal being, to be achieved under the reign of philosophy and realized in the State, wherein everything is common and the individual is completely subjected to the power of the group.

Basically none of the ancients got beyond a morality of utility and calculation. The notion of a Kingdom of God that fosters the development of both individual and community, that is both the content and the goal of world history, encompassing the whole earth and all nations—such an idea arose in neither head nor heart of any of the noblest of the pagans.[6]

The matter was different among Israel. Through divine revelation a "middle wall of separation"[7] was erected between that people and the pagans in almost every area of life. Israel was the people of the Sabbath, the pagans were the people of the week. In art, science, statecraft, in everything belonging to the arena of culture, Israel was far inferior to many a pagan nation. But to her the words of God were entrusted. She knew the value and significance of personality, first of all of God's personality, but then also that of his image, human beings. For that reason Israel kept in view first and foremost that dimension of a person whereby one would rest in and depend on God. By contrast, the pagans developed especially that dimension of human personality whereby one stood above and over against nature. But since true freedom lay in serving God alone, the freedom idolized by pagans had to result in bankruptcy. Israel's destiny, by contrast, lay embedded in the requirement to be holy as God is holy. Israel was called to be a Kingdom of God, to constitute a theocracy wherein God's will governed and directed everything. Amid Israel, the Kingdom of God was enclosed within the narrow boundaries of the national state. It was not a unique sphere alongside the state and alongside culture, but existed within them and included them, exercising dominion over all the rest. [31] In this way the Kingdom of God was particularistic, and it had to be in order to attain historical existence, in order not to be obscured or to hover as an abstract idea somewhere above history, in order genuinely to enter into the history of the human race.[8] Only

---

5. GrO: *eudaimonia*.

6. Bav. note: Cf. Friedrich Ueberweg, *A History of Philosophy*, 1:264–71 (§72).

7. DO: *middelmuur des afscheidsels*; Bavinck took this phrase directly from the *Statenvertaling* of τὸ μεσότοιχον τοῦ φραγμοῦ in Eph. 2:14; ESV and NIV translate this as "dividing wall of hostility."

8. Bav. note: Cf. E. Riehm, "Der Missionsgedanke im Alten Testament."

by means of that particularistic character could the Kingdom of God genuinely become, if I may put it this way, a "universal-historical power."[9]

So from the very beginning, the Kingdom of God possessed a universal scope. Israel's God was the God of all peoples. The meaning of personality was familiar, which included the idea of a single humanity. Israel herself was fully aware of that very special calling to constitute a Kingdom of God, so much so that as the luxuriously chivalrous period of the judges was drawing to a close, the very serious question arose whether earthly kingship was compatible with theocracy. Samuel resolved this by making Israel's kingship an instrument of God's rule. But soon thereafter they became separate. Often kingship in Israel became an instrument for opposing theocracy. And to the extent that the national state and the Kingdom of God became disassociated and came to stand sharply in opposition to each other, in Israel's history the Kingdom of God became disconnected from the national character and became more and more universal-human, purely ethical.

At that point, the most remarkable and heartwarming phenomenon appeared that had ever appeared in the history of the human race. In the tiny land of Palestine, closely surrounded on all sides by pagans, the gaze of Israel's faithful ones looked toward the future, the last day, encompassing all the earth and all the peoples. Israel's prophets, whose gaze looked far beyond the limits of the nation, contrary to every empirical proof and all outward evidence, strengthened by their expectation and the heroism of their faith, spoke of the ends of the earth one day being full of the knowledge of the Lord.

When after the Exile another attempt was launched to provide the Kingdom of God a visible form and a historical face, that attempt failed as well, and at that point prophecy ceased. But the Jewish people did not forget their calling, clinging anxiously to the once-spoken prophetic word, developing their expectation still further. In the apocalyptic, apocryphal literature of the Old Testament, an entire messianic dogmatics was developed. [32] Because it lacked prophetic animus and genuine understanding, its high and lofty ideal was packaged within national limitations, cast within sensate forms, and thereby defiled and materialized.[10]

Then the Elijah of the New Testament appeared proclaiming the approach of the Kingdom of Heaven. And then appeared the One in whom the Kingdom of God was fully present, who was its Founder, and from whom alone this Kingdom could expand and develop still further. In line with the prophets, Jesus removed

---

9. GO: *universal-geschichtliche Potenz.*

10. Bav. note: Cf. Carl Wittichen, *De Idee des Reiches Gottes*, 90–162; and Emil Schürer, *Lehrbuch der neutestamentlichen Zeitgeschichte*, 511–99.

the national, tight-fitting garment with which Judaism had clothed, indeed, had concealed, but—and let us not forget this—had also preserved such a glorious idea. For Jesus, the Kingdom of God was the purpose of all of his activity, the main content and central idea of his teaching, whose essence, expansion, development, and fulfillment were presented by him in the most variegated way, with and without parables. Moving outward from his own person, he established this Kingdom in the hearts of his disciples.

Initially, the Kingdom of God was realized in the church. But to the extent that this Kingdom entered into the world, the two became distinct. The contrast between church and world lost something of its sharpness. The Kingdom of God permeates the world, and the world permeates the church. Its catholicizing impulse, however, surrenders neither term and reconciles the tensions through a process of give and take and, where necessary, makes the ideal crystal clear in the face of the real.

By wedding itself to the state, the church distances itself from none of its former claims as it identifies itself with the Kingdom of God. According to the Roman Catholic perspective, the "reign of Christ" is identical to the "reign of the papacy,"[11] and the earthly Kingdom of God is completely identical to the historical organization of the established Roman Catholic Church. In this way the Jewish theocracy is imitated in the church. Christianity is judaized and ethnicized.

In opposition to that organization, the Reformation registered its sharp and well-considered protest. Cleansing Christianity of its Jewish and pagan elements, the Reformers once again viewed the Kingdom of God in its ideal, spiritual, eternal character and declared in their distinction (not separation) between the visible and invisible church that here on earth the Kingdom of God can never be perfectly realized in a visible, historically organized community. Nonetheless, it may be viewed as quite remarkable that, despite the prominent place occupied by the term *Kingdom of God* in Holy Scripture, especially in the prophetic books and in Jesus's teaching, this term nevertheless virtually disappeared from Protestant theology, [33] and gets replaced by the phrase *invisible church*. Without losing anything of the rich content contained in this idea, however, the phrase *Kingdom of God* cannot continue to be neglected. For that reason, I am going to try to present to you the *Kingdom of God as the highest good*, unfolding its content, which, on account of its richness, can be described only in its main features. To do that, I wish to give you as guideposts these four ideas:

1. The essence of the Kingdom of God
2. The Kingdom of God and the individual

11. LO: *regnum Christi, regnum pontificium.*

3. The Kingdom of God and the community (family, state, church, culture)

4. The completion of the Kingdom of God

1. The Essence of the Kingdom of God

You all know the captivating idea of Pascal: "Man is but a reed, the most feeble thing in nature; but he is a thinking reed."[12] Even, so Pascal continues, were the universe to slay man, he would be nobler than the entire cosmos, for he knows that he dies.[13] So the cosmos exists to be known, understood, and dominated by man. Were you able to conceive of a world that always proceeded in its orbit without being able to deposit its image within human consciousness, the existence of such a world would be a nonexistence like an eternal night, illuminated by no beam of light whatsoever.

But personality rises above the dark impulse of nature and dwells in the kingdom of light, of spirit, and of freedom. This is like the fanciful myth wherein Aphrodite emerges from the mist of the waves to bestow fertility and life upon the still and dead creation. Similarly, human personality rises above the world and bestows upon it the rays of enlightenment. And still, though he proceeds far beyond the world, man is not from the world. Yet he does not stand in relation to the world as a stranger, but belongs to the world, is related to the world, and is most intimately bound to the world with the strongest of bonds, by means of his own organism.

Even as the human personality, spiritual, invisible, and eternal in its essence, nevertheless requires the material body as the instrument of its activity and of its outward manifestation, so too the Kingdom of God as the highest good for humanity is indeed a kingdom that in its essence surpasses everything temporal and earthly. This in no way means, however, that the Kingdom of God therefore exists in enmity against [34] everything temporal and earthly, but much rather needs them as its instrument and is prepared to be an instrument for their sakes. At its core, in the depths of its being, the Kingdom of God is spiritual, eternal, invisible. It does not come with outward form (Luke 17:20), does not consist in food and drink (Rom. 14:17), is invisible and intangible. For it is the Kingdom of

---

12. FO: *l'homme n'est qu'un roseau, le plus faible de la nature; mais c'est un roseau pensant.* Ed. note: This is found in Pascal's *Pensées*, no. 347; translation was taken from The Project Gutenberg ebook edition of *Pascal's Pensées* (New York: E. P. Dutton, 1958), 97, at https://www .gutenberg.org/files/18269/18269-h/18269-h.htm.

13. The full statement in *Pensées*, no. 347: "The entire universe need not arm itself to crush him. A vapour, a drop of water suffices to kill him. But, if the universe were to crush him, man would still be more noble than that which killed him, because he knows that he dies and the advantage which the universe has over him; the universe knows nothing of this."

Heaven, of heavenly origin. And through heavenly, supernatural powers the Kingdom was established on earth, it is still being developed, and its future guided. But it is abstract and spiritual, though not simply a logical deduction lacking any reality. The contrast that to us is so familiar, between the sensual and the spiritual, is entirely foreign to Scripture. The Kingdom of God as the highest good consists in the unity, the inclusion, the totality of all moral goods, of earthly and heavenly, spiritual and physical, eternal and temporal goods.

The good can constitute a unity, and it does that automatically. By contrast, sin is unable to do that. Sin dissolves; sin "moves from forged unity into diversity"; sin propagates atomism and individualism to the extreme. Sin is a disorganizing power possessing no reason for existence and thus no purpose in itself. So sin can never have value as being inherently desirable, nor does it obligate anyone to follow. Sin is really unnecessary, absolute immorality, existing without a right to exist. Therefore sin can never establish an entity, a kingdom that proceeds from itself. It constitutes merely a kind of "social contract,"[14] because in no other way than as an organized power can sin attain its goal, which lies outside of it—namely, the destruction of the good—and only in this way can it break down the Kingdom of God. So when the Kingdom of God shall be perfected and no longer be exposed to the attacks of Satan, at that point the kingdom of sin will be split into pieces, all its elements destroyed, and it will turn against itself.

The good, however, constitutes a unity. Freed from the destructive power of sin, it automatically organizes. The good is at the same time the beautiful; it consists in perfect harmony. The Kingdom of God in its perfection is the unity of all moral goods.

Here on earth, however, all those goods are not yet one; here, holiness and redemption, virtue and happiness, spiritual and physical good do not yet coincide. More often here on earth the righteousness of the Kingdom of God is bound up with the cross, and through many tribulations we must enter the Kingdom of Heaven (Acts 14:22). Earthly goods, like wealth, honor, and prosperity, can even be impediments, as they were for the rich young man (Mark 10:23). For when, through sin, all these goods lose their bond of unity, each of them coming to be separated in isolation from the others, [35] they thereby all the more easily become instruments of sin.

But in itself the Kingdom of God is not hostile toward all those goods. Rather, the Kingdom of God is independent from all of those externalities; it exists above them, enlists them as its instrument, and in so doing returns to them their original purpose. For this reason Jesus came with the demand: seek first the

14. FO: *contrat social*.

Kingdom of God and its righteousness, and all the rest is then not vain, unprofitable, and sinful, but will be added to you; added, for one who possesses the righteousness of the Kingdom of God will certainly inherit the earth.

That which constitutes the bond, the unity of all those goods, is spiritual in nature—namely, righteousness. It is the righteousness that consists precisely in each thing existing according to its own nature, receiving its proper place, and being complete in its nature and essence. To that righteousness everything is subordinated, but also to that righteousness everything owes the preservation and perfection of its essence. Just as, within a human being, the personality is the highest, and the body must be its instrument, so too in the Kingdom of God everything earthly, temporal, and visible is subject to the spiritual and eternal. Since the spiritual and eternal, in order to exist in reality and not just in the mind or in the imagination, must always be personal, so too the Kingdom of God is a Kingdom of free personalities.[15] There the personality of each is fully developed and answers to its purpose.

For the righteousness of the Kingdom of God consists in this, that a person may be fully a person, such that everything within that person may be subject to the person's spiritual, eternal essence. At the moment everything within a person is torn apart, and what should be together has been torn asunder. Understanding and heart, consciousness and will, inclination and power, feeling and imagination, flesh and spirit, these are all opposed to each other at the moment, and they compete with each other for primacy.

But in the Kingdom of God all of those are once again pure instruments of the personality, arranged in perfect order around the personality as its center. There the darkened natural life no longer exists, nor any unwitting impulse. Everything moves outward from the center of the personality and returns there. All powers exist in the full light of consciousness and are fully included in the will. All compulsion is excluded since it is a kingdom of the spirit and thus of freedom. In this kingdom the natural and the visible are placed completely under the perspective of the spiritual and eternal; the physical is a pure instrument of the ethical even as everything, including our own body, which belongs to our persons and yet is not identical to our persons, [36] stands completely in the service of our personality and is glorified precisely as an instrument of the dominion of the spirit.

So the Kingdom of God is a kingdom of free personalities where each personality has reached its full development. But it is a *kingdom* of free personalities who do not live separated from each other, like individuals, but who together

---

15. Bav. note: Cf. M. des Amorie van der Hoeven, *Over het wezen der godsdienst en hare betrekking tot het Staatsregt*, 12.

constitute a kingdom and are bound to each other in the most complete and purest community. The Kingdom of God is not an aggregate of disparate components, nor even an entity bound together accidentally by a communal interest. It is not simply a "society,"[16] a club, an association like those we see established everywhere nowadays. All those contemporary associations of men and women, boys and girls, or young people, formed as they are around various interests and for various purposes, owe their existence mostly, or at least partially, to the reigning individualism of our day.

But the Kingdom of God is a *kingdom*, the social kingdom par excellence where communal life obtains its highest development and its purest manifestation. It is the most original kingdom that exists, and earthly kingdoms, including the natural kingdom, are but a faint image and a weak likeness. It is an entity where the individual parts are built for each other and fit each other, bound together by the most intimate fellowship, dwelling together under one higher authority, which forms the law of this entity. So it is an organism whose totality not only precedes and transcends the individual parts but also simultaneously forms the basis, the condition, and the constitutive power of the parts. At the same time it is no Platonic state where the rights of the individual are sacrificed to those of the group. Rather, the opposite is the case. The Kingdom of God in fact maintains everyone's personality, securing its full-orbed development.

Even individuality is not thereby destroyed because it is not an imperfection but that which supplies the essence of each person and distinguishes one from the other.[17] Without that individuality an organism would not even be able to exist. The Kingdom of God would cease being the most perfect, the most pure organism if the hand were no longer the hand, the eye no longer the eye, and each member of that organism were no longer itself. "If all were a single member, where would the body be?" (1 Cor. 12:19–26; cf. Rom. 12:4–8).

Precisely by means of the single shared life of the organism, the individual members of the organism are maintained and preserved in their differentiation and uniqueness. The Kingdom of God, therefore, is no lifeless, [37] petrified atomism, no bare uniformity, but a unity that includes and harmoniously incorporates an infinite multitude. Exactly for that reason the Kingdom of God is the highest, the most perfect community, because it guarantees to each one's personality the most completely well-rounded and richest development of its content. For the unity of an organism becomes the more harmonious, the more rich, and the more glorious to the degree that the multitude of parts increases.

16. FO: *société*.
17. Bav. note: Cf. Alexandre R. Vinet, "Sur l'individualité et l'individualisme."

For example, there is very little unity alongside very little diversity in a rock. Every rock looks like the others, and every piece of rock is just another rock.[18] But we encounter unity amid increased diversity already with a plant. Still more with an animal. We see the most rich and most glorious unity amid diversity in a human being in whom we see an incalculable diversity, an inexhaustible wealth of phenomena, an inexpressible fullness of capacities and gifts and powers. The entire world is recapitulated and represented within a human being. A human being is truly a microcosm. And yet that entire plethora of phenomena is harmoniously bound together and organically arranged in the personality, which itself is eternal and far surpasses that entire plethora, as it knows that wonderful organism by means of its consciousness and rules it by means of its will.[19]

So then, what the human being is for the world, that is what the Kingdom of God is for the human being. There the richest harmony rules together with the perfection of beauty. There the most glorious and purest unity reigns among the most inscrutable wealth and the most incalculable diversity.

Imagine it if you can: every member of that organism known as the Kingdom of God is genuinely a personality with a completeness of life developed fully in every aspect. That Kingdom itself is, in its totality, yet another personality formed along the same lines. For the personality is the most basic and original source of every system, *das Ursystem*, as Stahl calls it.[20]

The Kingdom itself is also an organic personality whose head is Christ and whose subjects constitute the body. Just as each personality has and must have an organism known as the body, so too the church is the body, the pure organism of Christ's divine-human personality, the pleroma—to use Paul's profound expression (Eph. 1:23)—of him who fills all in all. Thus, the Kingdom of God is the reconciliation of both individualism and socialism, the fulfillment of the truth of both. It could even be said that in the Kingdom of God the individual exists for the sake of the whole even as the whole exists for the sake of the individual.[21]

[38] In the community of the Kingdom of God, as we said, Christ is the head. The Kingdom of God is, then, a Kingdom of Christ. Apart from sin, the Kingdom of God would have existed among humanity from the very beginning and would have developed completely normally. Through sin, the Kingdom of God was disrupted, the various goods contained in the Kingdom were torn asunder, and

---

18. A gemologist would disagree with the literal reading of Bavinck's point here but could likely agree that inanimate objects like rocks lack the "diversity in unity" manifested in living entities like plants and animals. Bavinck is establishing a hierarchy of *being* with his comparison.

19. Bav. note: Cf. the chapter "Le principe de l'excellence" in Paul Janet, *La Morale*, 55–85.

20. Bav. note: Friedrich J. Stahl, *Die Philosophie des Rechts*⁵, 1:500.

21. Bav. note: Hans Lassen Martensen, *Christian Ethics, General Part*, 147–236.

the triad of the true, the good, and the beautiful was broken. God wanted to restore his Kingdom, for which he supplied the shadow and preparation already in Israel's theocracy, and in the fullness of time he sent his Son to establish it upon earth. On account of sin, therefore, the Kingdom of God became a Kingdom of Christ. He was anointed King in that Kingdom, and he exercises its sovereignty until he has destroyed every dominion and every authority and power and has placed all his enemies under his feet (1 Cor. 15:24–25). That is how long he must reign as King.

So the Kingdom of God is a Kingdom that does not yet exist fully but is coming into fuller existence, a Kingdom that cannot expand and develop in any other way than through fierce conflict. For the single and absolutely authoritative demand is that of righteousness, the requirement of absolute perfection. It cannot abandon this demand without destroying itself so that nothing will enter that Kingdom that defiles and does detestable things and speaks lies (Rev. 21:27). Thus it is a militant kingdom, one that cannot simply incorporate something just as it is, but must conquer and wrest from the dominion of sin everything it embraces. Since it is spiritual in nature, however, it employs only spiritual weapons. For its expansion, the Kingdom of God recognizes no other authority than the almighty power of divine grace.

In this way the Kingdom of God possesses a redemptive and sanctifying character. Just as Christ is the Founder, so too he is the moving power of the Kingdom, and he determines the nature and the manner of its development. The incarnation of the Word, the all-dominating fact and fundamental principle of all science, is also the source and continuing principle of the Kingdom of God. The incarnation indicates that the divine, the eternal, the invisible does not hover above us at an unreachable height (Rom. 10:6–8), but has entered into the human, the temporal, and the visible and now appears to our eyes in no other way than physically—in human form and in a human manner.

This is also the leading principle that now determines the nature of the expansion of the Kingdom of God. What is genuinely human may never and nowhere be snuffed out or suppressed. Always and everywhere the genuinely human must be made an organ and instrument of the form in which the divine exists. The Kingdom of God awaits that unity, which we behold in Christ in an entirely unique manner, in every domain of human living and striving, in order to make each thing real according to its nature. [39] It seeks to do this, however, not like the Greeks, for whom the divine disappeared into the human, nor like the followers of Buddha, for whom the human is swallowed up in the divine. The unity of the Kingdom of God seeks to maintain both the essentiality and independence of the divine and the human so that the human may be a pure and unblemished instrument of the divine and the divine may manifest itself bodily in a completely human manner (Col. 2:9).

The incarnation itself teaches us that this is possible. The human itself is not sinful but has become the instrument of sin. The earth lies between hell and heaven. It is the land of relativity. Just as the earth is hardly the worst evil—hell—so too the highest good—the Kingdom of God—is not completely realized. Neither absolute evil nor absolute good is to be found anywhere on earth. Both principles exist on earth together and alongside one another. The two are intertwined, wrestling and contending against each other, but, contrary to what some try to tell us nowadays, they are never swallowed up into each other. Just as Peter was at one time the prize in the conflict between the praying Jesus and Satan, who wanted to sift him as wheat (Luke 22;31), in the same way there is a contest for the whole earth and all of humanity between Satan and Christ. The contest between those two personal powers—not between merely abstract ideas or vague principles, but between both of those Kingdom heads and crown-wearers—lends to history its terribly tragic character. The question nevertheless is whether all that is human will share in Satan's disdain or in Christ's glory, whether this earth will belong to hell or to heaven, whether humanity will become demon or angel.

Viewing nothing human as foreign but as spiritual in nature, the Kingdom of God is universal, bound to no place or time, embracing the whole earth and everything human, independent of nation and country, of nationality and race, of language and culture. In Christ Jesus what is legitimate is only what has been created anew, with no exceptions. This is why the gospel of the Kingdom must be brought to all nations, to all creatures, not only to people but to the entire creation (Mark 16:15). The Kingdom of God extends as far as Christianity itself. It exists wherever Christ rules, wherever he dwells with his Spirit. Everything earthly, insofar as it is cleansed and consecrated through Christ, constitutes the Kingdom of God.[22] Having entered history, having through Christ been made into a world historical power, yes, into the driving force of all history, the Kingdom expands and develops *vel nobis dormientibus* (even while we are sleeping). It proceeds quietly [40] and unobserved, more quickly than we perhaps might imagine, like the leaven that a woman takes and hides in three measures of flour until all of it is leavened (Matt. 13:33), or like a mustard seed, which "is the smallest of all seeds, but when it has grown it is larger than all the garden plants and becomes a tree, so that the birds of the air come and make nests in its branches" (Matt. 13:32).

22. Bav. note: Cf. Kling, "Christenthum."

As the Kingdom of Christ it is thus characterized as becoming, as unfolding, awaiting its completion. Then, when it is complete, when every opposition has been vanquished and the Kingdom itself is completely sanctified, then Christ will return the sovereignty granted to him to the One who bestowed it, and will give the Kingdom without spot or wrinkle to his God and Father.

In this manner the Kingdom of God is thus, finally, a Kingdom of God. Christ does indeed remain the Head of the body through whom all the divine life is supplied from God to us in a human fashion, and in turn everything of ours, all that is human, glorifies God as a well-pleasing sacrifice consecrated to him. But the absolute sovereignty is then exercised by God himself, who is the Fountain and the Source of all sovereignty, the Lord of lords, the King of kings. The Kingdom of God is a *Kingdom*, the most noble and glorious kingdom imaginable. It is no imperium, for that makes us think of a world power and of tyrannical domination, but this is a Kingdom in which sovereignty rests upon the perfect power of the One who exercises it. In the Kingdom of God, God himself is the King-Sovereign. In this Kingdom he rules over a free people who serve him willingly and who find in that subjection precisely the source and the security of all their freedoms.

2. The Kingdom of God and the Individual

That Kingdom, whose essence we have attempted to make known to you, is, as the unity of all moral goods, the highest good for each person, for every individual no matter who and what he may be. To all without distinction, the Kingdom comes with the intensely serious demand to surrender everything else on its behalf, even father and mother, sister and brother. For it is the pearl of great price which a merchant found and went out to sell everything he possessed so that he might purchase it (Matt. 13:44).

Nor is the human person a quickly passing developmental moment in [41] the grand process of nature. A human person exists not merely for the sake of something else, but a person's existence has value in itself. The human person possesses an inherent goal or purpose. For each person that purpose is to be always fully himself—that is, to be his personality. The goal of personal existence is simply to obey that law given us by God simultaneously as the law of our own personality and as the law that continues to echo faintly in the human conscience. As we exist in the present we are bound on all sides by various attachments that are foreign to us. This law, resounding above nature, governs us more often than we think. Natural life occupies an extremely broad place within our existence. So extremely broad, in fact, that this natural life appropriates a third of our entire earthly life through our sleep, and thereby dooms our personality, our consciousness, and our will to inactivity.

Moreover—and this is the real slavery of our personal spiritual lives—in our conscious life we are also bound by that law in our members which engages in conflict against the law of our mind. Sin is the enemy of the personality, to which it nevertheless owes the possibilities of its existence. Sin desires no self-consciousness and no freedom; sin hates both of these with a perfect hatred. It moves about in the dark recesses of life. The coercion of nature is the ideal form of the power with which sin desires to rule. For that reason sin hides us from ourselves; sin pretends and dissembles with us. Knowing oneself, after all, is the first step on the road to conversion.

By contrast, we all receive the demand that we always be fully self-conscious and genuinely free in order to live that spiritual, eternal life that we lost through sin, in order that we be ruled by nothing else than the law of our own spiritual being, which makes all the rest an instrument of our personality. Our calling is to take up this dark natural principle which we now carry within us, to expose it completely to the light of our consciousness, to peer through ourselves thoroughly, leaving nothing darkened within us. Our calling is that our entire being and essence be reflected in the mirror of our consciousness and that we thus become like God, who is nothing but light and in whom is no darkness (1 John 1:5).

It comes down to this: making our personality the only cause of all our thinking and acting. We are called to embed our entire personality in every deed, in every thought, in order to do nothing unselfconsciously and arbitrarily, but to do everything with full consciousness and will, freely and morally.

This demand corresponds fully with that of the Kingdom of God and can be fulfilled only through the work of that Kingdom. Every other good that we pursue unconsciously and unintentionally [42] becomes ours only partially and can produce some benefit to us. By contrast, every labor for the Kingdom of God that is done without consciousness and will, without our entire personality, is impossible—at least vain and useless—for ourselves, and worse yet, it destroys us eternally.

In a certain sense everybody without distinction labors for the Kingdom of God, voluntarily or involuntarily, if not as an independent collaborator, then as a blind and will-less tool. For if we ourselves are unwilling to work for the Kingdom of God freely and without compulsion, then Almighty God will still use us as an unwilling instrument to do everything that his hand and his counsel had determined beforehand should happen. In this sense even Satan collaborates for the Kingdom of God. For just as the curse comes from evil,[23] going so far

---

23. Bav. note: August Tholuck, *Die Lehre von der Sünde*, 19.

as to seek the good opportunity for sin, even so it is the privilege of the good to turn evil for good. But then once God has used us, God will treat us not as persons but as blind tools and cast us away from before his face. Just as the Kingdom of God is a kingdom of free personalities, even so it can be brought into existence within us only through our full personality with consciousness and will, or, as the Scripture puts it, with all our mind and with all our soul and with all our strength. But also in return, we are called to labor for that Kingdom with consciousness and will, to advance it freely and independently within and beyond us, to consecrate our entire lives to it. We are equipped to count everything in connection with this labor to be the source for tempering our will, for strengthening our consciousness, for doubling our strength, for expanding our spirit to the full range of our personality, and for laying up a treasure that neither moth nor rust can consume.

Even as the Kingdom enlists our entire personality and all our strength, it also demands us perpetually. We are indeed still bound here on earth; we do not rule time but are often ruled by it. Nevertheless, the ideal that we must attempt to grasp is that we be free of time and that we distance ourselves from this freedom only as much as necessary in order to maintain our personality. God never grants us time off in order not to be what we are supposed to be. As someone who himself is working until now, he demands that we be like him in that respect and, like Christ, work as long as it is day. In itself, time is an empty form, without content and therefore "tedious." But time is given to be filled with eternal content, and for this reason it always flows into eternity so that thereby time itself "contains eternity in every moment." [43] After all, eternity is no intellectual deduction, no barren shape, no empty void, but precisely the opposite: eternity is time with an infinite, eternal content in every moment. God is working all the time; he fills every moment with eternal content and thus does everything in its time even as he sent his Son in the fullness of the times. Our time is genuinely full and filled only when we do not spend it on things that serve merely to pass the time but only when we fill time with laboring in work that is eternal and abiding. So we are called to work not for the food that perishes but for the food that endures unto eternal life (John 6:27). In summary, our time must be filled with work on behalf of the imperishable and immovable Kingdom of Jesus Christ, our Lord.

This is not to say, however, that we need to labor for that Kingdom of God apart from any earthly calling. To be sure, the Kingdom of God is not *of* the world, but it is nevertheless *in* the world. The Kingdom does not exist within the narrow confines of the inner closet, restricted to church and monastery. The Kingdom is not entirely "otherworldly" but has been established by Christ upon earth and stands in a most intimate—yet for us in many respects inexplicable—relationship with this earthly life and is prepared by this life. Nevertheless, it is just as true that the Kingdom is not exhaustively present in this life, it is not merely "this-worldly." The Kingdom *is* and *becomes*.

The eternal Sabbath is not yet here, and yet we have a foretaste of it already now. At this point, however, Sunday and the rest of the week exist alongside each other. Our heavenly calling is not swallowed up in our earthly calling.

We must be on guard against both errors. On the one hand, our earthly calling may not be misunderstood on account of various ascetic, pietistic, and methodistic emphases, while, on the other hand, our heavenly calling may not be denied on account of theoretical or practical materialism. Our ideal continues to be that we exalt the other days of the week to the loftiness of the Sabbath and that we continually exercise our heavenly calling more and more in and amid our earthly calling.[24]

Our earthly calling is, after all, the temporal form of our heavenly calling. It is marked somewhat by the sentiment that "in order to be an angel, you must first be a fit human being."[25] Our earthly calling has been given to us, says Calvin,[26] so that we may have a firm foundation and not be cast about hither and thither for our entire lives. By means of our earthly calling we form ourselves, therefore, with a view to developing our personality and preparing a pure instrument for it in our body and in all things earthly. [44]

It is a distinguishing feature of Christianity that it does not condemn any earthly calling in itself nor does it consider any earthly calling in itself to be in conflict with our heavenly calling. The Greeks viewed manual labor as something embarrassing and assigned it to their slaves. But Christianity recognizes no dualism of spirit and matter and views nothing as unclean in itself. A person who does not labor, who has no occupation, also has no calling, becomes deadweight for society and thereby disgraces his human nature. For only in an occupation can we demonstrate and develop what lives within us. Only in an occupation can we manifest ourselves, not only to others but also to ourselves. Only in this way do we learn to know ourselves, our strengths, our capacities, and thus obtain awareness of the content of our own personality. Only in this way can we become a full personality, fully human. Otherwise not only our physical powers but also our spiritual and moral powers suffocate and corrode within us.

However, we must devote every effort to choosing that earthly occupation in which the exercise of our heavenly calling is not hindered for us, for our

24. Bav. note: Martensen, *Christian Ethics, Special Part*, 2.2:306–14; cf. also Luther's reflections regarding our earthy vocation in Christoph Ernst Luthardt, *Die Ethik Luthers*, 71–72.

25. Bav. note: Johann Julius Baumann, *Handbuch der Moral*, 238.

26. Bav. note: Calvin, *Institutes*, III.x.6.

individuality, and for our powers. For this demand abides—namely, to bring this life, its calling and its labor, into relationship with the eternal, to view all that is temporal and earthly *sub specie aeternitatis*.[27] Otherwise, to echo Calvin once more, the components of our living will always lack symmetry.

Everything earthly must thus remain subservient to the Kingdom of Heaven. We must possess everything as though not possessing (1 Cor. 7:30), such that we are willing to surrender anything if it comes into conflict with the demand of the Kingdom of God. In other words, everything may be our domain such that we possess it and rule over it so that it functions as the instrument of our personality. Every pursuit of more than we can rule over, more than we can actually make our domain, is immoral and conflicts with the Kingdom of God and its righteousness. As soon as what is earthly possesses us and rules over us, whether goods or kindred, art or science, the demand must be repeated that Jesus gave to the rich young man: go, sell everything you own and give to the poor, and you will have treasure in heaven (Matt. 19:21). For everything earthly has been given to us in order with it to cultivate our personality, in order to make it an instrument of God's Kingdom. Indeed, everything comes down finally not to what we accomplish through our earthly work, for often the work we accomplish is broken to pieces before our eyes by God himself. But the essential feature of all our labor that we perform under the sun is what we become through our work, what our personality acquires by way of the consciousness, spirit, power, richness, and fullness of living. [45] That is what abides. That is never lost. That does not disappear like so many insignificant works of our hands. That is what we carry with us out of this world into the future world. That constitutes the works that follow us. We are, finally, the totality of what we have ever willed, thought, felt, and done. The profit that we yield for ourselves in this way is profit for the Kingdom of God. Even a cup of cold water given to a disciple of Jesus receives a reward.[28] God calls us to work in such a way that, amid all that we do, we should envision the eternal work that God desires to bring about through people, knowing that we cannot be lord and master of ourselves and of the earth in any other way than in subjection to him. And in that consciousness, working with all our powers as long as it is day, God calls us to subject all that is visible and temporal to ourselves in order then to consecrate it along with ourselves as a perfect sacrifice to God—even if our work space be ever so small and our

---

27. Literally, "under the aspect of eternity"; the term comes from Baruch Spinoza and denotes that which is universally and eternally true.

28. Bavinck's correct reading of Matt. 10:42 is noteworthy because many contemporary versions of social Christianity reverse the order and take Jesus's words here and similar ones in Matt. 25 as calls for Jesus's followers to give cups of cold water to the thirsty outside of the church.

occupation ever so nondescript. This is truly and essentially working for the Kingdom of God.

3. The Kingdom of God and the Community (Family, State, Church, Culture)

The Kingdom of God is the highest good not only for the individual but also for the whole of humanity. It is a communal project that can be realized only through united powers. It is the most universal good imaginable, and therefore also the destiny and goal of all those life spheres that exist in a society. There are especially three of them: state, church, and culture. Each of these three develops the human personality in terms of a particular aspect. The state regulates mutual human relationships; the church norms their relationship to God; and culture governs relationships with the cosmos or the world. Rather than being an additional fourth life sphere alongside these, the household or family is the foundation and the model of these other three life spheres. The family possesses a religious moral element in its piety, a juridical element in its parental authority and sibling affection, and an element of culture in family nurture. All three life spheres lie embedded within the family in a complex way, and each is connected to the family. Since the Kingdom of God consists of the totality of all goods, here on earth one finds its purest image and most faithful representation in the household family. The Kingdom of God is the Father's house. Family relationships are applicable there as well. God places us in relationship to himself as children. [46] We are born of him and thus resemble him; only a child resembles the father. God is King, but at the same time Father of his people. Jesus called the subjects of this King the children of the Kingdom (Matt. 8:12 and 13:38). Christ is the oldest, the firstborn, among many brothers, and everyone who does the Father's will is Jesus's brother and sister and mother (Rom. 8:29; Matt. 12:50). For this reason the family will correspond to its design to the extent that it constitutes a Kingdom of God in miniature. For the Kingdom of God does not exist for the sake of the family, but, as is true of everything else, the family exists for the sake of the Kingdom of God. The husband is the image and the glory of God, head and priest of the family, as Christ is the head of the church (1 Cor. 11:7; Eph. 5:23). God gives us children so that we may form them into children of God. The relationships of family life have their reflection and standard in that communal life of a much higher order, found in the Kingdom of God. Should the demand of the Kingdom of God occasionally conflict with the duties of the family, such that the latter must yield (Matt. 10:37), anyone who leaves house or parents or brothers or wife or children for the sake of the Kingdom of God will receive back many times in this age and in the age to come eternal life (Luke 18:29–30).

In the family everything is yet undifferentiated. There we find a natural life that has not yet entirely transitioned into the free, ethical, personal life, but nonetheless is destined from that unconscious and involuntary identity to develop into complete independence and freedom.

State, church, and culture constitute those life spheres that have achieved independence in terms of those elements already present to a smaller or larger degree in the family. Let us consider for a moment the relationship of each of these three to the Kingdom of God. First, something about the relationship of the church and the Kingdom of God.[29]

Religious life developed into its true essence and full independence for the first time within Christianity, becoming independent of civil and political life, to which religion had always been closely associated among the Greeks and the Romans. Christ rendered religious life—faith in him—independent of changing earthly circumstances. Thus we see that Christianity established but one church as a single, unique sphere alongside the state and culture. This occurred because faith in Christ is completely independent and develops a unique life that differs in specific ways from every other kind of life.

[47] Certainly Christianity is in the first place a religion, but not merely a religion. It is an entirely new life that can penetrate and enliven every life sphere and life form. Thus Christianity is not coextensive with the church. It is far too rich to allow itself to be pressed within its walls. Indeed, it would not be the true religion if it had no influence on the richly fulsome human life. Christianity cannot be restricted to the church as a historical organization viewed as a visible community. For that reason we speak of a Christian society, of a Christian school. There is nothing human that cannot be called Christian. Everything within and outside the church that is enlivened and governed by Christ, who exercises sovereignty over all things, constitutes and belongs to the Kingdom of God. For Rome, the church and the Kingdom of God are one. Thus, Rome's church views everything that does not flow from it and is not consecrated by it to be unholy and profane. But the Reformation recognized the life spheres outside the church in their independence. No Protestant church may denigrate the territory of human living outside the church as unclean or profane. Rather, we must accept the distinction between the church and the Kingdom of God. The church *already exists*; the Kingdom of God is *becoming*. The church is a historical, visible organization; the Kingdom of God is invisible and spiritual. The church was established for the first time by Christ to be a unique sphere for the

29. Bav. note: Cf. J. H. A. Ebrard, *Christliche Dogmatik*², 2:388; Scheutel, "Kirche," 561; Carl Immanuel Nitzsch, *System of Christian Doctrine*, 361–65 (§198); Richard Adelbert Lipsius, *Lehrbuch der evangelisch-protestantischen Dogmatik*, 763–75; and Albrecht Ritschl, *Die christliche Lehre von der Rechtfertigung und Versohnung*, 3:270–75.

cultivation of the Christian-religious life. The Kingdom of God has existed since the beginning of the world. The Kingdom of God was present already among Israel. It progresses secretly like leaven and does not—unlike the church—constitute a separate community over against the state and culture.

Far from losing anything of its significance by accepting this distinction, the church instead rises in value and fulfills its calling all the more when it understands that the church itself is not the Kingdom of God and cannot be the Kingdom of God, but is the means of preparing for the Kingdom of God and ensuring its arrival.

For apart from the historical organization, the power, and the activity of the church, Christianity would be unable to maintain itself, to find entrance, to be a power in history, and would dissolve into a collection of vague and rarefied notions.

That is the significance of the church, but its goal lies in part beyond itself, in the Kingdom of God. The church is not itself the Kingdom of God in its entirety, but the indispensable foundation of the Kingdom of God, the preeminent and best instrument of the Kingdom of God, the earthly institution, the heart, the core, the living center of the Kingdom of God.

With that self-understanding the church aims to consecrate people to God, not only in their religious life but also, proceeding from that source, in their natural life, moral life, civic life, and political life. Sunday may not stand alongside the other days of the week but must sanctify them [48] and seek to lift them up to their highest purpose. The church is what she is supposed to be when she labors beyond herself and is not satisfied when people are pious on Sundays in church. Only then will the church, as the preserver and bearer of the noblest good of humanity—namely, the truth that is according to godliness—strive to bring that good into contact with all other moral goods and in this way advance the coming of that Kingdom of God, which, as the unity of all goods, does not destroy the good of the church but incorporates it within itself in its purified form. Just as remarkable, in the second place, is the connection that exists between the state and the Kingdom of God. No matter how often the state misunderstands that connection or even denies it altogether, that may not induce us to muffle the protest that the state, which has been instituted by God, is not a necessary evil but a very real good. After the church, the state is indeed the greatest and richest good on earth. Only through the state is that community life required of human beings made possible wherein a person, for the first time, can develop his full personality.

Family, church, culture, all the various spheres of rich human living do not owe their origin and existence to the state—they possess a "sphere sovereignty"—but they do nonetheless owe to the state the possibility of their development.

The state secures the full unfolding of human personality. The state, however, is not the highest good but finds its purpose and goal in the Kingdom of Heaven. Anyone who misunderstands this will eventually end up denying the church her noblest calling and instead value the state itself, viewed as the creator of culture and caretaker of freedom and equality, as the initial realization of the Kingdom of God. And denying every connection of the state to the eternal, people will view the state as the highest good and the highest purpose of humanity, as that which alone is worth living for.

Such a glorification of the state destroys the freedom and independence of human personality. The state develops only one dimension of human personality— namely, justice. The state is not, contrary to Rothe,[30] the moral community, but merely one particular form of moral community. It consists of morality merely in the form of justice. The purely ethical lies beyond its domain. Therefore it must recognize and maintain the various life spheres of family, church, and culture, and so forth, in their independence.

Moreover, the state is always national and particular, an individuated state.[31] So it cannot be the highest—which is to say, universal—good. [49] But the Kingdom of God is one and the same over all the earth. It knows no boundaries of land or nationality. Each state and each nation has its purpose and reason for existence in terms of that Kingdom. The Kingdom does not call the state to surrender its special, national calling. On the contrary, just as the individual person must not seek the Kingdom of God outside of but in his earthly vocation, so too the Kingdom of God does not demand that the state surrender its earthly calling, its own nationality, but demands precisely that the state permit the Kingdom of God to affect and to penetrate its people and its nation. Only in this way can the Kingdom of God come into existence. For this Kingdom is not a labor of these or those people, not even of one nation and of one state, but of all peoples and all states. It is the total task[32] of the human race.

As we saw with the individual, so also each nation and every state makes its own contribution to that task and adds its own value, willingly or unwillingly, consciously or unconsciously. Thus the Kingdom of God does not vitiate the individuated state,[33] the nationality and particular calling of a people, but purifies them and incorporates each individual state and nation as a particular instrument in the cooperation of the whole.

When it understands its purpose in this way, the state maintains its true nature and labors for its own perfection. To be sure, the state cannot establish

---

30. Bav. note: Richard Rothe, *Theologische Ethik*, 2:418–75 (§§422–48).
31. GO: *Einzelstaat*.
32. GO: *Gesammtaufgabe*.
33. GO: *Einzelstaat*.

the Kingdom of God. The state is not redemptive. Nor may the state attempt to foster the free, moral, spiritual life. The state functions in terms of the law. But by holding that law in high esteem, by cultivating respect and reverence for the law, by upholding its majesty, by inculcating respect for the moral world order as the unconditionally valid moral order, the state can become a tutor unto Christ. In this sense the state can and indeed does have the calling to labor for the Kingdom of God. By providing space for the various life spheres to do their work, and by guaranteeing for each of its subjects the development of this full and variegated life of the personality, the state fulfills its own nature and works for that Kingdom, which itself is also a state wherein God himself is the Lord and absolute King-Sovereign.

Thirdly, it remains for us yet to discuss the connection between culture and the Kingdom of God. As with the state, so also with culture: before the Reformation they both existed in service to the church. The Reformation restored to culture its freedom and independence. The right of culture is expressed in the mandate: "Be fruitful and multiply and fill the earth and subdue it and have dominion over the fish of the sea and over the birds of the heavens and over every living thing that moves on the earth" (Gen. 1:28; cf. Gen. 9:1–3). Culture exists because God bestowed on us the power to exercise rule over the earth. It is the communal calling of [50] the human race to make the world its own and to shape it as the property and instrument of personality. Humanity was given power to transform the entire treasury of created life forms—whether spiritual, moral, or natural—into a pure organism and to rule over it. That occurs in two ways: science and art. In order to rule over nature in the broadest sense, its essence, operation, pathways, and laws must be known. Here as well the saying is valid that only the truth makes one free. In ruling over nature, every form of arbitrariness is immoral and irrational. As Francis Bacon wrote, "We cannot command nature except by obeying her."[34] Science incorporates nature in the understanding, casts its image in our soul, and reproduces it through ourselves in thought and in word.

But knowledge is power. To know is to be able. In the most universal sense, art renders nature, as an instrument of our will, serviceable to a higher purpose and transforms it through us into a work of art, into a complete artistic organism.

For the third time in the history of the world, culture has become a power. First came the Hamite culture of Assyria, Babylon, and Phoenicia. Then followed the Japhethite culture of Greece and Rome, whose culture remains the foundation of our own and in philosophy, art, and jurisprudence still sets the standard for our own. Today, modern culture emancipates itself more and more

---

34. LO: *Naturae non imperatur, nisi parendo.*

from Christianity, denigrating the church to the status of maidservant and slave girl. To that extent modern culture also faces the judgment that came upon the Hamite and Japhethite cultures: destruction through debauchery and sensuality, worshiping genius and deifying the material, of which Babylon and Rome are the abiding symbols in Scripture.

From these considerations we see that culture can find its purpose and reason for existence only in the Kingdom of God. The lord of the earth is but the child of God. Idolizing the material and serving the flesh is the destination of all who acknowledge no master above themselves. For then nature is too powerful for us and compels us to bow before its tremendous forces. But when by God's hand we are elevated above the material, then we are more powerful than the material, then we develop the material with our own hand and form it into an instrument of personality. Then culture is a deeply essential good, worthy not of our denigration but of our amazement.

Cult and culture ought then to be sisters, independent to be sure, but still sisters, bound to each other through love. And even though Martha, who represents the culture that is occupied with many things, may differ from Mary, who represents the cultus that has chosen the best portion, nevertheless the truth remains that Jesus loved them both.

The ideal is that the oppositions appearing everywhere—with the individual, the family, the state, the church, culture, and so forth, and whereby [51] each of these repeatedly interferes with the others—that all those oppositions gradually disappear and find their resolution in the unity of the Kingdom of God.

To the extent that each of these various life spheres answers more and more to its essential idea, it loses its sharpness and isolation from the others and prepares the way all the more for the coming of the Kingdom of God. For that kingdom, since it is the highest good, destroys nothing but consecrates everything. It includes every good, a kingdom wherein all the moral good that is now spread throughout various spheres and comes into being in each sphere according to its nature and in its appropriate manner is incorporated as purified and perfected. It is a kingdom wherein the human personality obtains its richest and most multiform manifestation, a community life of the highest order wherein all oppositions are reconciled and individual and community, state and church, cultus and culture are integrated in perfect harmony. It is a kingdom wherein the true, the good, and the beautiful are perfectly realized and have become one. In this Kingdom of God, full sovereignty is handed over to the Messiah, a sovereignty that had descended from him in the various life spheres and returns completely once more to God, who will be all in all.

So in spite of so much that seems to contradict it, do not deprive me of the idea that this Kingdom of God is the essential content, the core, and the purpose of all of world history. Let not my faith and my hope seep away whereby I acknowledge that the historical description initially summarized by Israel's prophets and set forth so profoundly and gloriously by Paul in his letter to the Romans will finally appear to be the true portrait—namely, that the history of the nations and of their states finds its principal idea and explanation to be the Kingdom of Heaven.

4. The Completion of the Kingdom of God

It might appear that up to this point I have lost sight of the tremendous opposition between the Kingdom of God and that of the world. It might seem as though I harbored the naïve notion that by means of mission and evangelism, by means of Christian philanthropy and antirevolutionary politics, that opposition would gradually disappear and the world would slowly be won for the Kingdom of God. But that notion has no appeal to me. Even if the prophetic word of Scripture were not enough, then a glance around would be able to disabuse me of such illusions. Although God desires to expand his Kingdom on earth [52] through people, although our working for that kingdom remains our treasured calling and duty, although between our activity and the coming of the Kingdom of God there certainly and undeniably lies a close connection, the Kingdom of God is not purely a product of our moral activity. Even as it was established from beyond the world, and develops and expands by means of supernatural powers, so too the completion of the Kingdom of God is a supernatural act that occurs by means of divine cataclysmic intervention.[35]

Earthly history is not finished with the coming of the Kingdom of God, but it is interrupted by its completion. If history is not a process of nature, but genuine history and real action, a connected series of acts, then the wrestling such history displays to us must also reach a climax wherein the kingdom of Christ and that of Satan are arrayed so sharply against each other, as Christ and Antichrist fight for the final, decisive victory. The good ones become increasingly better, but the evil ones become increasingly worse. The completion of the Kingdom of God cannot occur any other way than after the absolute manifestation of the evil one—that is, the Antichrist. Nevertheless, that divine cataclysmic intervention will not occur without preparation and mediation.[36] Just as with everything God does, this occupies the primary focus when the time is "full." The Kingdom of God cannot be completed before all the material is present from which the

---

35. Bav. note: Cf. Kling, "Eschatologie"; M. Ebrard, "Offenbarung Johannes"; and Lange, "Wiederkunft Christi."

36. GO: *Vermittelung.*

Kingdom of God will be constructed. All of the moral goods must first come into existence, all of the elect must be gathered together.[37]

The completion of the Kingdom of God or of the kingdom of Satan partially occurs for each individual immediately after death. This life is, by virtue of an indestructible connection, decisive for the life to come. Nevertheless, the situation that arises for each person at death is not only immutably decisive but preliminary as well. The lot of the individual is determined definitively only in connection with the lot of the whole, only at the end of history in the universal judgment. Before then, here on earth and beyond this arena the contest continues between the Kingdom of God and the kingdom of Satan, between life and death, light and darkness, spirit and flesh, Christ and Antichrist.

That conflict continues throughout all of history, from the moment when enmity was established between the two. The Kingdom of God and the kingdom of the world develop alongside and over against each other—the latter, however, in order time and again to be destroyed, but also time and again to be restored. History is a sequence of failed world kingdoms, [53] of kingdoms erected apart from God and in opposition to him, supported and built by human power. The tower of Babel was the first failed attempt at constructing such a world kingdom. But time and again it was attempted, in the kingdoms of Pharaoh and Nebuchadnezzar, of Xerxes and Alexander, of the Roman emperors, all the way to the kingdom of Napoleon himself. Babel and Rome brought such a world kingdom to the pinnacle of development and therefore also to its deepest fall, and both have remained fixed symbols and types in the Christian church of the kingdom of the world.[38]

Israelite prophets, seers, and watchmen on Zion's walls saw the signs of the times and explained them in the light of the Kingdom of God. Their nation was small, their national influence was little, but the light of that kingdom supplied them with a world-encompassing and centuries-embracing view that extended further than any view ever obtained by the greatest wise men. In that same light of the Kingdom of Heaven—that is, in the light of their prophecy—history must still be viewed, its riddles solved, its signs understood and explicated.

Scripture is the book of the Kingdom of God, not a book for this or that people, for the individual only, but for all nations, for all of humanity. It is not a book for one age, but for all times. It is a Kingdom book. Just as the Kingdom of God develops not alongside and above history, but in and through world

---

37. Bav. note: Rothe, *Theologische Ethik*, 2:559–601 (§§449–58).

38. Bav. note: Chantepie de la Saussaye, *De Toekomst: Vier eschatologische voorlezingen*. Ed. note: The four chapters are "I. Israel's Calling" ("Israëls Roeping"); "II. The Messiah" ("De Messias"); "III. The Kingdom of the World and the Antichrist" ("Het Wereldrijk en de Antichrist"); "IV. The Millennium" ("Het Duizendjarig Rijk").

history, so too Scripture must not be abstracted, nor viewed by itself, nor isolated from everything. Rather, Scripture must be brought into relationship with all our living, with the living of the entire human race. And Scripture must be employed to explain all of human living.

The portrait and explanation of these world kingdoms in the light of the Kingdom of God reaches its climax, in the Old Testament, in Daniel's prophecy. There the world kingdom is portrayed with the image of a metal statue standing on feet of clay that was ground to dust by a hewn stone, symbolizing the Kingdom of God, which will exist into eternity (Dan. 2). Elsewhere, in the seventh chapter, that world kingdom is portrayed for us as a beast from the depths that was slain and destroyed and given over to be burned with fire. By contrast, power and dominion and honor and the kingdom were given unto all eternity to the Son of Man, who appeared on the clouds of heaven. This prophecy continued into the New Testament and is closely connected to the picture in John's book of Revelation.

In the New Testament the universal expectation is that the princes and nations of the earth will once more array themselves against the Lord [54] and against his Anointed. Frightening times precede the coming of God's kingdom. Everything human—the state, the church, and culture—will once more offer themselves as instruments of Satan.

On such a basis this prince of the world will, as it were, constitute a surrogate of the three offices of Christ. He fashions for himself an instrument—namely, the state, the world kingdom presented by John—with the image of the beast that rises from the sea, the vibrant world of nations—that is Satan's kingly office (Rev. 13:1–10). He fashions for himself an instrument in the church, the apostate church, portrayed as Babylon, the great harlot sitting upon the scarlet beast that rises from the bottomless pit (Rev. 17)—that is Satan's priestly office. Finally, he fashions false culture into an instrument of his activity, the beast that rises from the earth and the power of the world kingdom established by means of false arguments and great signs (Rev. 13:11–18) and leading the spirits astray—that is Satan's prophetic office.

The world kingdom comes to be concentrated, and finds its highest manifestation, in the Antichrist, the man of sin, in whom humanness has become diabolical, who sinks down into bestiality and, supported by the false church and the false culture, places himself in the temple of God, presenting himself as though he were God (2 Thess. 2).

But at the apex of its power, the world kingdom will also have reached the end point of its development. First, Babylon, the great city, falls (Rev. 14:8; 17:18). Deprived of the support of the false church, the world kingdom and the false prophet can no longer survive. Both are seized and thrown alive into the lake of fire (Rev. 19:20). Deprived of its human instruments and no longer able to work through people upon people, Satan himself is seized and bound for a thousand years. At that point the time has arrived of the so-called thousand-year kingdom.

In the period of the early Christians chiliast belief was universal, or at least widespread. Still more than with the opposition of Origen in the East, however, the opposition of Augustine in the West occasioned the fall of chiliasm when the place that the church occupied in the world changed. Instead of being persecuted, the church came to dominate society. Once Christians became contented with themselves and satisfied with the age in which they lived, they thought that the Kingdom of God had been virtually realized among them. Chiliasm retreated to the sects that, because they came under persecution, continued fixing their hope on the future.

The Reformers and later Reformed were particularly less inclined toward this chiliast error.[39] But this could reverse. Belief in a thousand-year kingdom is held today by not a few as proof of incontestable orthodoxy. In any case, of all the loci in Christian dogmatics, eschatology is one that has received the least consideration and development. [55] Frequently in this area, instead of a decisive answer, we must respond: "Scripture does not give a clear answer."[40]

Regardless of what one believes about the nature, duration, and timing of such a kingdom, chiliasm does contain a profoundly true element.[41] For with chiliasm, the Christian faith expresses the certainty and indubitable knowledge of its truthfulness and its ultimate triumph. Therein the Christian faith celebrates its apotheosis and develops its own philosophy of history. In the first century and still today, chiliasm was and is the first concession that the Kingdom of God would come not abruptly, not simply accompanied by a divine cataclysmic intervention, but also in part through and after an earthly preparation. It constitutes a transition between the "here" and the "hereafter."[42] Irenaeus expressed the attractive idea that in the thousand-year kingdom believers would, by means of personal concourse with Christ, be prepared for beholding God. Chiliasm expresses the healthy expectation that Christianity will once again manifest its full blessing and bounty of its life, in spiritual, moral, and natural arenas. The social power and significance of Christianity must appear once more to the eyes of all the nations. After the preliminary victory of the anti-Christian powers within church, state, and culture, there will come a time of righteousness and peace. Nature is initially glorified, understood,

39. LO: *error Chiliastarum.*

40. LO: *non liquet*; lit., "it is not clear."

41. Bav. note: Isaak August Dorner, *History of the Development of the Doctrine of the Person of Christ*, 1.1:150–60.

42. GO: *Diessets, Jenseits.*

and ruled. Peace will dwell even in the animal world (Isa. 11:6–9). On earth it will be a paradisal situation, the last preparation, the richest harvest for the Kingdom of God, the great harvest from among Jews and pagans. Then Christianity will understand its world mission and fulfill its calling to purify the state from all ungodly and antigodly power, to cleanse the church of all harlotry with the world, to purify culture from all vanity and false prophecy. But this is not yet the end. One final critical contest must be waged. The anti-Christian powers are certainly bridled but not subdued. Satan will be unleashed. And at that time the question will be able to be put clearly: Will this earth belong to God or to Satan? For or against the Kingdom of God will then be the war cry accepted and acclaimed with consciousness and will by everyone. While at the present time the Kingdom of God and the kingdom of Satan still dwell alongside each other, the boundaries of both cannot be accurately distinguished by our eyes. But at that time, both will manifest themselves in their true form before the eyes of all. Every pretense will then fall away, every excuse will then be in vain. And when the Kingdom of God makes itself known in its full glory, in its genuine essence, as the highest good, [56] then the kingdom of Satan will also display its true and naked form as the highest evil. At that point it will commence battle in conscious revolution, in public enmity against the Kingdom of God. That final wrestling will be fierce but brief, unspeakably intense and decisive for eternity.

"Then I saw," writes John, "a new heaven and a new earth. And I heard a loud voice from heaven saying: behold, the tabernacle of God is with people, and he will dwell with them and they will be his people." Then the kingdom of God will be complete, the destination of history will have been reached. All things will be renewed, all oppositions reconciled. A new development will begin, no longer restrained by sin but progressing from virtue to virtue and from strength to strength. A new and eternal work awaits us there with which we will fill eternity but which we will perform without disturbance and without exhaustion; for each one's organism will stand completely in service to each one's personality. There will be no night, there will be no time. Even distances will disappear there before the dominion of spirits. The Kingdom of God will be exalted above the limitations of time and space and will completely fulfill both time and space. The Kingdom of God will include everything in heaven and on earth. By the blood of the cross, Christ has reconciled all things to himself and thus to each other (Col. 1:20). Under him as the Head, everything will be gathered into one and recapitulated in him (Eph. 1:10). God himself will delight in the work accomplished by his hands, and when we behold it, the song will flow from our lips: every house is built by someone, but the builder of all things is God. God himself is its Designer and Builder (Heb. 3:4; 11:30).

Bibliography

Books

Acta der Generale Synode van De Gereformeerde Kerken in Nederland, Middelburg, August 11–September 4, 1896. Leiden: D. Donner, 1897. https://kerkrecht.nl/sites/default/files/ActaGKN1896.pdf.

Athanasius. *Against the Arians.* NPNF² 4:303–37.

———. *Against the Heathen.* NPNF² 4:1–30.

Baumann, Johann Julius. *Handbuch der Moral, nebst Abriss der Rechtsphilosophie.* Leipzig: Hirzel, 1879.

Bavinck, C. B. *Kennis en Leven.* Kampen: Kok, 1922.

Bavinck, Herman. *The Certainty of Faith.* St. Catharines, ON: Paideia, 1980.

———. *Christelijke en Neutrale Staatkunde.* Hilversum: Witzel & Klemkerk, 1905.

———. *Christelijke Wetenschap.* Kampen: Kok, 1904.

———. *The Christian Family.* Translated by Nelson D. Kloosterman. Grand Rapids: Christian's Library Press, 2012.

———. *Christian Worldview.* Translated and edited by Nathaniel Gray Sutanto, James Eglinton, and Cory C. Brock. Wheaton: Crossway, 2019.

———. *De Taak van het Gereformeerd Schoolverband.* Hilversum: G. M. Klemkerk, 1906.

———. *Essays on Religion, Science, and Society.* Edited by John Bolt. Translated by Harry Boonstra and Gerrit Sheeres. Grand Rapids: Baker Academic, 2008.

———. *Evangelisatie.* In *Christendom en Maatschappij,* series 5, no. 9, edited by P. A. Diepenhorst. Utrecht: G. J. A. Ruys, 1913.

———. *Foundations of Psychology.* Translated by Jack Vanden Born, Nelson D. Kloosterman, and John Bolt. Edited by John Bolt. *TBR* 9 (2018): 1–252.

————. *Our Reasonable Faith*. Translated by Henry Zylstra. Grand Rapids: Eerdmans, 1956.

————. *Paedagogische Beginselen*. Kampen: Kok, 1904.

————. *The Philosophy of Revelation: A New Annotated Edition*. Edited by Cory Brock and Nathan Gray Sutanto. Peabody, MA: Hendrickson, 2018.

————. *Reformed Dogmatics*. Edited by John Bolt. Translated by John Vriend. 4 vols. Grand Rapids: Baker Academic, 2003–8.

Bavinck, Herman, et al. *Advies in zake het gravamen tegen artikel xxxvi der belijdenis*. Amsterdam: Höveker & Wormser, 1905.

Bilderdijk, Willem. *De Dichtwerken van Mr. Willem Bilderdijk*. Edited by Johannes van Vloten. 4 vols. Arnhem-Nijmegen: E. & M. Cohen, 1884.

Bolt, John. *A Theological Analysis of Herman Bavinck's Two Essays on the* Imitatio Christi. Lewiston, NY: Mellen, 2013.

Bosch, David J. *Transforming Mission: Paradigm Shifts in Theology of Mission*. Maryknoll, NY: Orbis Books, 1991.

Brederveld, J. *Christian Education: A Summary and Critical Discussion of Bavinck's Pedagogical Principles*. Translated by two members of the faculty of Calvin College. Grand Rapids: Smitter, 1928.

————. *Hoofdlijnen der Paedagogiek van Dr. Herman Bavinck, met Critische Beschouwing*. Amsterdam: De Standaard, 1927.

Bremmer, R. H. *Herman Bavinck en zijn Tijdgenoten*. Kampen: Kok, 1966.

Calvin, John. *Commentaries on the First Book of Moses, Called Genesis*. 2 vols. Grand Rapids: Eerdmans, 1948.

————. *A Commentary on the Psalms*. 5 vols. Grand Rapids: Eerdmans, 1949.

————. *Institutes of the Christian Religion*. Edited by John T. McNeill. Translated by Ford Lewis Battles. 2 vols. Philadelphia: Westminster, 1960.

Cathrein, Victor. *Glauben und Wissen*. 4th and 5th eds. Freiburg im Breisgau: Herder, 1911.

Dorner, Isaak August. *History of the Development of the Doctrine of the Person of Christ*. Translated by William Lindsay Alexander and David Worthington Simon. 5 vols. Edinburgh: T&T Clark, 1876–82.

Druskowitz, H. *Eugen Dühring: Eine Studie zu seiner Würdiging*. Heidelberg: Georg Weiss, 1889.

Ebrard, Johannes Heinrich August. *Christliche Dogmatik*. 2nd ed. 2 vols. Königsberg: A. W. Unser, 1862–63.

Geesink, Willem. *Van 's Heeren Ordinantiën*. 3 vols. in 4. Amsterdam: W. Kirchener, 1907–8.

Harnack, Adolf von. *History of Dogma*. Edited by A. B. Bruce. Translated by Neil Buchanan, James Millar, E. B. Speirs, and William M'Gilchrist. 7 vols. London: Williams & Norgate, 1896–99.

————. *Lehrbuch der Dogmengeschichte*. 3 vols. in 2. Freiburg im Breisgau: J. C. B. Mohr, 1886–90.

————. *The Mission and Expansion of Christianity in the First Three Centuries*. Translated and edited by James Moffatt. 2nd rev. ed. London: Williams & Norgate, 1908.

————. *What Is Christianity?* Translated by Thomas Bailey Saunders. 2nd rev. ed. New York: Putnam's Sons, 1903.

Harnack, Adolf von, and Wilhelm Herrmann, eds. *Essays on the Social Gospel*. Edited by Maurice A. Canney. Translated by G. M. Craik. London: Williams & Norgate; New York: Putnam's Sons, 1907.

Heymans, Gerard. *Einfüring in die Metaphysik auf Grundlage der Erfarung*. Leipzig: Johann Ambrosius Barth, 1905.

Hoekema, Anthony A. *The Centrality of the Heart in Herman Bavinck's Anthropology*. TBR 11 (2020): 1–263.

Hoeven, M. des Amorie van der. *Over het wezen der godsdienst en hare betrekking tot het Staatsregt*. Amsterdam: P. N. van Kampen, 1854.

Hooker, Mark. *Freedom of Education: The Dutch Political Battle for State Funding of All Schools Both Public and Private (1801–1920)*. N.p.: Llyfrawr, 2009.

Horace. *Satires, Epistles, and Ars Poetica*. Translated by H. Rushton Fairclough. LCL 194. Cambridge, MA: Harvard University Press, 1926.

Huet, Conrad Busken. *Het land van Rembrandt: Studiën over de Noordnederlandsche beschaving in de zeventiende eeuw*. 2 vols. Haarlem: H. D. Tjeenk Willink, 1882–84.

Jaarsma, Cornelius. *The Educational Philosophy of Herman Bavinck*. Grand Rapids: Eerdmans, 1936.

Janet, Paul. *La Morale*. Paris: Ch. Delagrave, 1880.

Jhering, Rudolph von. *Der Zweck im Recht*. 3rd ed. 2 vols. Leipzig: Breitkopf & Härtel, 1877–83.

Kant, Immanuel. *The Conflict of the Faculties*. Translated by Mary J. Gregor. New York: Abaris Books, 1979. Originally published as *Der Streit der Facultäten*. Königsberg: Friedrich Nicolovius, 1798.

Klinken, L. van. *Bavincks Paedagogische Beginselen*. Meppel: Boom, 1937.

Kruithof, Bastian. "The Relation of Christianity and Culture in the Teaching of Herman Bavinck." PhD diss., University of Edinburgh, 1955.

Kuyper, Abraham. *Christianity and the Class Struggle*. Translated by Dirk Jellema. Grand Rapids: Piet Hein, 1950.

————. *Het Calvinisme oorsprong en waarborg onzer Constitutioneele Vrijheden*. Amsterdam: B. van der Land, 1874. ET: See Kuyper, "Calvinism: Source and Stronghold," in the articles section below.

————. *Het sociale vraagstuk en de christelijke religie: Rede ter opening van het Sociaal Congres op 9 November 1891*. Amsterdam: J. A. Wormser, 1891.

————. *Lectures on Calvinism*. Grand Rapids: Eerdmans, 1931.

————. *On Education*. Edited by Wendy Naylor and Harry Van Dyke. Collected Works in Public Theology. Bellingham, WA: Lexham, 2019.

————. *Ons Program*. Amsterdam: J. H. Kruyt, 1879.

————. *Our Program: A Christian Political Manifesto*. Translated and edited by Harry Van Dyke. Bellingham, WA: Lexham, 2015.

————. *The Problem of Poverty: A Translation of the Opening Address at the First Christian Social Congress in the Netherlands, November 9, 1891*. Edited, translated, and introduced by James W. Skillen. Grand Rapids: Baker, 1991.

————. *Scholarship: Two Convocation Addresses on University Life*. Translated by Harry Van Dyke. Grand Rapids: Christian's Library Press, 2014.

————. *Scolastica, of 't geheim van echte studie*. Amsterdam: J. A. Wormser, 1889.

————. *Scolastica, II. Om het zoeken of om het vinden? Of het doel van echte studie*. Amsterdam: Höveker & Wormser, 1900.

Lessing, Gotthold Ephraim. *Werke*, vol. 8. Edited by Herbert George Göpfert. Munich: C. Hanser, 1979.

Liebersohn, Harry. *Religion and Industrial Society: The Protestant Social Congress in Wilhelmine Germany*. Philadelphia: American Philosophical Society, 1986.

Liebmann, Otto. *Gedanken und Thatsachen*. 2 vols. Strasbourg: K. J. Trübner, 1899–1901.

Lipsius, Richard Adelbert. *Lehrbuch der evangelisch-protestantischen Dogmatik*. 2nd ed. Braunschweig: Schwetschke, 1879.

Luthardt, Christoph Ernst. *Die Ethik Luthers*. 2nd ed. Leipzig: Dörffling & Franke, 1875.

Maresius, Samuel. *Foederatum Belgium orthodoxum; sive Confessionis ecclesiarum Belgicarum exegesis*. Groningen: Johannes Nicolai, 1662.

Martensen, Hans Lassen. *Christian Ethics*. Translated by C. Spence. 2 vols. in 3. Edinburgh: T&T Clark, 1885.

————. *Christian Ethics, General Part*. Translated by C. Spence. Edinburgh: T&T Clark, 1878.

————. *Christian Ethics, Special Part*. Translated by C. Spence. 2 vols. in 3. Edinburgh: T&T Clark, 1885.

Nitzsch, Carl Immanuel. *System of Christian Doctrine*. Translated by Robert Montgomery and John Hennen. Edinburgh: T&T Clark, 1849.

Pascal, Blaise. *Pascal's Pensées*. New York: Dutton, 1958. Available at Project Gutenberg, https://www.gutenberg.org/files/18269/18269-h/18269-h.htm.

Paulsen, Friedrich. *System der Ethik mit einem Umriss der Staats- und Gesellschaftslehre*. 5th rev. ed. 2 vols. Berlin: W. Hertz, 1900.

Peet, Jan, Bert Altena, and C. H. Wiedijk. *Honderd Jaar Sociaal, 1891–1991: Teksten uit Honderd Jaar Sociale Beweging en Sociaal Denken in Nederland.* Amsterdam: SDU Uitgevers, 1998.

Portig, Gustav Wilhelm. *Das Weltgesetz des kleinsten Kraftaufwandes in den Reichen der Natur.* 2 vols. Stuttgart: Kielemann, 1903–4. Vol. 1: *In der Mathematik, Physik, und Chemi;* vol. 2: *In der Astronomie und Biologie.*

Price, Timothy Sahun. *Pedagogy as Theological Praxis: Martin Luther and Herman Bavinck as Sources for Engagement with Classical Education.* Bletchley, Milton Keynes, UK: Paternoster, 2018.

Ritschl, Albrecht. *Die christliche Lehre von der Rechtfertigung und Versohnung.* 4th ed. 3 vols. Bonn: A. Marcus, 1895–1903.

Rombouts, Fr. S. *Prof. Dr. H. Bavinck, Gids Bij de Studie van Zijn Paedagogische Werken.* 's-Hertogenbosch-Antwerpen: Malmberg, 1922.

Rothe, Richard. *Theologische Ethik.* 2nd ed. 5 vols. Wittenburk: Zimmerman, 1867–71.

Rousseau, Jean-Jacques. *The Social Contract and Discourses.* Translated by George Douglas Howard Cole. New York: Dutton, 1950.

Saussaye, Daniel Chantepie de la. *De Toekomst: Vier eschatologische voorlezingen.* Rotterdam: Wyt, 1868.

Schleiermacher, Friedrich. *Die christliche Sitte nach den Grundsätzen der evangelischen Kirche im Zusammenhange dargestellt.* Edited by Ludwig Jonas. 2nd ed. Berlin: G. Reimer, 1884.

Schürer, Emil. *Lehrbuch der neutestamentlichen Zeitgeschichte.* Leipzig: J. C. Hinrichs, 1874.

Stahl, Friedrich Julius. *Die Philosophie des Rechts.* 5th ed. 2 vols. in 3. Heidelberg: J. C. B. Mohr, 1878.

Stein, Ludwig. *Der Sinn des Daseins: Streifzüge eines Optimisten durch die Philosophie der Gegenwart.* Tübingen: Mohr, 1904.

Tews, Johannes. *Sozialdemokratische Pädagogik.* 3rd ed. Langensalza: Beyer, 1904.

Tholuck, August. *Die Lehre von der Sünde und vom Versöhner.* 8th ed. Gotha: Perthes, 1862.

Ueberweg, Friedrich. *History of Philosophy.* Translated by George S. Morris and Noah Porter. 2 vols. New York: Scribner's Sons, 1887.

Virgil. *Virgil in Two Volumes.* Translated by H. Rushton Fairclough. Vol. 1. LCL 63. London: Heinemann; New York: Putnam's Sons, 1906.

Willmann, Otto. *Didaktik als Bildungslehre nach ihren Beziehungen zur Socialforschung und zur Geschichte der Bildung.* 3rd ed. 2 vols. Brauschweig: F. Vieweg, 1903.

Wittichen, Carl. *De Idee des Reiches Gottes.* Göttingen: Dietrichsche Buchhandlung, 1872.

Wundt, Wilhelm M. *Ethics: An Investigation of the Facts and Laws of the Moral Life.* Translated by Edward Bradford Tichener, Julia Henrietta-Gulliver, and Margaret Floy Washburn. 3 vols. London: S. Sonneschein & Co., 1897–1907.

Wuttke, Adolf. *Christian Ethics.* Translated by John P. Lacroix. 2 vols. New York: Nelson & Phillips, 1876.

———. *Handbuch der christlichen Sittenlehre.* 3rd rev. ed. 2 vols. Leipzig: Hinrichs, 1874–75.

Zanchi, Jerome. *Omnium Operum Theologicorum.* 8 vols. Geneva: Ioannis Tornae-sij, 1649.

Zweep, L. van der. *De Paedagogiek van Bavinck.* Kampen: Kok, 1935.

ARTICLES

Bavinck, Herman. "Calvin and Common Grace." In *Calvin and the Reformation: Four Studies*, by Émile Doumergue, August Lang, Herman Bavinck, and Benjamin B. Warfield, 99–130. New York: Revell, 1909.

———. "Christendom, Oorlog, Volkenbond." *Stemmen des Tijds* 9 (1919): 1–26, 105–33. Republished as *Christendom, Oorlog, Volkenbond.* Utrecht: Ruys, 1920.

———. "Christian Principles and Social Relationships." In *ERSS*, 119–44.

———. "Classical Education." In *ERSS*, 209–43.

———. "Conscience." Translated by Nelson D. Kloosterman. *TBR* 6 (2015): 113–26.

———. "Contemporary Morality." In *Reformed Ethics*, vol. 3, *Christian Life in Society*, edited and translated by John Bolt with Jessica Joustra, Nelson D. Kloosterman, Antoine Theron, and Dirk van Keulen, 327–73. Grand Rapids: Baker Academic, 2025.

———. "Ethics and Politics." In *ERSS*, 261–78.

———. "General Biblical Principles and the Relevance of Concrete Mosaic Law for the Social Question Today (1891)." Translated by John Bolt. *Journal of Markets and Morality* 13, no. 2 (Fall 2010): 437–46. Original title: "Welke Algemeene . . ." (see below).

———. "Heeren en knechten." *De Bazuin* 50, no. 19 (May 9, 1902).

———. "Herman Bavinck's *Modernisme en Orthodoxie*: A Translation." Translated by Bruce Pass. *TBR* 7 (2016): 63–114, https://bavinckinstitute.org/wp-content/uploads/2017/02/TBR7Pass.pdf.

———. "Het begrip en de noodzakelijkheid der evangelisatie." In *Congres voor gereformeerde evangelisatie op dinsdag 8 en woensdag 9 april 1913 te Amsterdam*, 8–9. Amsterdam: Kirchner, ca. 1913; available online at https://sources.neocalvinism.org/.full_pdfs/bavinck_1913_congres.pdf.

———. "Het levensrecht der ongeboren vrucht." *Orgaan van de Christelijke Vereeniging van Natuur- en Geneeskundigen in Nederland* 3, no. 1 (1904): 1–3.

————. "Het Probleem van den Oorlog." *Stemmen des Tijds* 4 (1914): 1–31. Republished as *Het Probleem van den Oorlog*. Kampen: Kok, 1914.

————. "The Imitation of Christ and Life in the Modern World." Appendix B in *A Theological Analysis of Herman Bavinck's Two Essays on the* Imitatio Christi, by John Bolt, 402–40. Lewiston, NY: Mellen, 2013.

————. "John Calvin: A Lecture on the Occasion of His 400th Birthday, July 10, 1509–1909." Translated by John Bolt. *TBR* 1 (2010): 57–85, https://bavinck institute.org/wp-content/uploads/2010/04/Translation-Bavinck-on-Calvin.pdf.

————. "Kerk en Politiek." *De Bazuin* 49, no. 33 (August 16, 1901); available online at https://sources.neocalvinism.org/.full_pdfs/bazuin_1901_33.pdf.

————. "The Kingdom of God, the Highest Good." Translated by Nelson D. Kloosterman. *TBR* 2 (2011): 133–270.

————. "Kort verslag van een rede, gehouden op maandag 25 Sept. in de openbare samenkomst ter opening van de conferentie in de kerk der Hersteld Evangelisch Lutherse gemeente." In *Vijf-en-twintigste algemeene Nederlandsche Zendingsconferentie gehouden te Amsterdam 25, 26, 27 Sept. 1911*. Available online at https:// sources.neocalvinism.org/.full_pdfs/bavinck_1911_verslag.pdf.

————. "Minutes of a Short Introduction Inspired by Proverbs 4:1–13, Delivered to the General Assembly of the 'Association of Reformed Schools in the Netherlands' Held on Wednesday, May 12, 1915" ["Verslag van een korte inleiding naar aanleiding van Spreuken 4:1–13, uitgesproken op de Algemene Vergadering van het 'Verband tussen Gereformeerde Scholen in Nederland,' gehouden op Woendsdag 12 Mei 1915"]. Published as an insert, *Orgaan van het Gereformeerde Schoolverband*, in *De School met den Bijbel: Weekblad voor het Christelijke Onderwijs* 13, no. 6 (August 5, 1915): 29. Available online at https://sources.neocalvinism.org /.full_pdfs/bavinck_1915_spreuken.pdf.

————. "Of Beauty and Aesthetics." In *ERSS*, 245–60.

————. "On Inequality." In *ERSS*, 145–63.

————. "Over de Ongelijkheid." *Stemmen des Tijds* 2 (1913): 17–43. Reprinted in Herman Bavinck, *Verzamelde Opstellen*, 151–71. Kampen: Kok, 1921.

————. "The Problem of War." Translated by Stephen Voorwinde. *The Banner of Truth*, July–August 1977, 49–53. Available online at https://sources.neocalvinism .org/799-Herman+Bavinck.+The+Problem+of+War.

————. "Trends in Pedagogy." *ESSR*, 205–8.

————. "Welke algemeene beginselen beheerschen, volgens de H. Schrift, de oplossing der sociale quaestie, en welke vingerwijzing voor die·oplossing ligt in de concrete toepassing, welke deze beginselen voor Israël in Mosaïsch recht gevonden hebben?" In *Proces-Verbaal van het Sociaal Congres gehouden te Amsterdam, den 9, 10, 11, 12 November 1891*, 149–57. Amsterdam: Höveker & Zoon, 1892. ET: "General Biblical Principles . . ." (above).

Blake, William. "Preface to Milton: Book the First." In *The Prophetic Books of William Blake: Milton*, edited by E. R. D. Maclagan and A. G. B. Russell, xix. London: A. H. Bullen, 1907.

Bolt, John. "Herman Bavinck's Contribution to Christian Social Consciousness." *Journal of Markets and Morality* 13, no. 2 (Fall 2010): 413–36.

Bruining, A. "Het aggressief karakter van het vrijzinnig godsdienstig geloof." In *Religion and Liberty: Addresses and Papers at the Second International Council of Unitarian and Other Liberal Religious Thinkers and Workers, Held in Amsterdam, September 1903*, edited by P. H. Hugenholtz Jr., 165–78. Leiden: Brill, 1904.

Cramer, S. "Does Liberal Christianity Want Organizing in Special Churches and Congregations?" In *Religion and Liberty: Addresses and Papers at the Second International Council of Unitarian and Other Liberal Religious Thinkers and Workers, Held in Amsterdam, September 1903*, edited by P. H. Hugenholtz Jr., 227–37. Leiden: Brill, 1904.

David, Eduard. "Die Eroberung der politischen Macht." *Socialistisch Monatshefte* 8, no. 3 (March 1904): 199–207. Available online at http://library.fes.de/cgi-bin/digisomo.pl?id=03738&dok=1904/1904_03&f=1904_0199&l=1904_0207.

De Jong, Marinus. "The Heart of the Academy: Herman Bavinck in Debate with Modernity on the Academy, Theology, and the Church." *The Kuyper Center Review* 5 (2015): 62–75.

Doumergue, Paul. "Jean-Jacques Rousseau: Ce qu'était sa religion; ce que fut son christianisme." *Foi et Vie* 15, no. 14 (July 16, 1912): 411–19.

Ebrard, M. "Offenbarung Johannes." *PRE¹* 10:574–90.

Feuerbach, Ludwig. "Das Geheimniss des Opfers, oder Der Mensch ist, was er isst (1862)." In *Gesammelte Werke*, vol. 11, edited by C. H. Beck, 26–52. Berlin: Akademie-Verlag, 1972.

Glenn, Charles L. "Look to the Dutch for True Educational Pluralism." *Acton Commentary*, September 12, 2018. https://www.acton.org/pub/commentary/2018/09/12/look-dutch-true-educational-pluralism.

Green, Harold M. "Adolf Stoecker: Portrait of a Demagogue." *Politics and Policy* 31, no. 2 (2003): 106–29.

Groenewegen, Herman IJsbrand Y. "Wetenschap of Dogmatisme." *Theologisch Tijdschrift* 37, no. 5 (1903): 393.

Harnack, Adolf von. "The Evangelical Social Mission in the Light of the History of the Church." In *The Social Gospel*, edited by Maurice A. Canney, translated by G. M. Craik, 3–91. London: Williams & Norgate; New York: Putnam's Sons, 1907.

———. "The Moral and Social Significance of Modern Education." In *The Social Gospel*, edited by Maurice A. Canney, translated by G. M. Craik, 95–141. London: Williams & Norgate; New York: Putnam's Sons, 1907.

Herrmann, Wilhelm. "The Moral Teachings of Jesus." In *The Social Gospel*, edited by Maurice A. Canney, translated by G. M. Craik, 145–225. London: Williams & Norgate; New York: Putnam's Sons, 1907.

Horton, Scott. "Lessing's Search for Truth." *Harper's Magazine*, November 1, 2007. Available online at https://harpers.org/2007/11/lessings-search-for-truth/.

Kling, Christian Friedrich. "Christenthum." *PRE¹* 2:674–81.

———. "Eschatologie." *PRE¹* 4:154–57.

Kristensen, Willem Brede. "Over den wetenschappelijken arbeid van Herman Bavinck." "Levensberichten" in *Jaarboek der Koninklijke Akademie van Wetenschappen te Amsterdam, 1921–1922*, 1–12. Amsterdam: Koninklijke Academie van Wetenschappen, 1923. Available online at https://babel.hathitrust.org/cgi/pt?id=osu.3243506 5042756&seq=248&q1=Bavinck. ET: See next entry.

———. "W. B. Kristensen's 'On Herman Bavinck's Scientific Work.'" Translated by Laurence O'Donnell. *TBR* 10 (2019): 85–99.

Kuyper, Abraham. "Calvinism: Source and Stronghold of Our Constitutional Liberties." In *Abraham Kuyper: A Centennial Reader*, edited by J. Bratt, 279–322. Grand Rapids: Eerdmans, 1998.

———. "Indien het mijn broeder ergert." *De Heraut*, no. 620 (November 10, 1889), 2.

Lange, Johann Peter. "Wiederkunft Christi." *PRE¹* 18:126–32.

Maurenbrecher, Max. "The Evangelical Social Congress in Germany." *American Journal of Sociology* 9, no. 1 (1903): 24–36.

Mayer, E. W. "Über den gegenwärtigen Stand der Religionsphilosophie und deren Bedeutung für die Theologie." *Zeitschrift für Theologie und Kirche* 22, no. 1 (1912): 41–71.

Naylor, Wendy. "Editor's Introduction." In Kuyper, *On Education*, xi–xli.

Nesselman, R. "Schleiermachers Wertschätzung." *Der Beweis des Glaubens* 5 (1869): 103–15.

Paret, Heinrich. "Adiaphora." *PRE¹* 1:124–26.

Pentz, Wolfhart. "The Meaning of Religion in the Politics of Friedrich Naumann." *Zeitschrift für Neuere Theologiegeschichte* 9, no. 1 (2002): 70–97.

Riehm, E. "Der Missionsgedanke im Alten Testament." *Allgemeine Missions-Zeitschrift* 7 (October 1880): 453–65.

Riou, Gaston. "Un sermon sur Jean-Jacques [Rousseau]." *Foi et Vie* 15, no. 13 (July 1, 1912): 398–99.

Scheutel, [?]. "Kirche." *PRE¹* 7:560–99.

Telman, D. A. Jeremy. "Adolf Stoecker: Anti-Semite with a Christian Mission." *Jewish History* 9, no. 2 (1995): 93–112.

Vinet, Alexandre. "Sur l'individualité et l'individualisme." In *Mélanges*, 83–101. Paris: Chez les éditeurs, 1869.

Wijck, B. H. C. K. van der. "De wereldbeschouwing van een Nederlands wijsgeer." *Onze Eeuw* 5, no. 4 (October 1905): 129–57.

Scripture Index

Old Testament

Genesis
1:3 59
1:6 61n9
1:28 195
2:12 52
2:16 45n79
3:15 145
9:1–3 195
9:6 52, 120
12:2 17
13:16 17
38:9–10 52

Exodus
19:5 16
19:6 16
20:10 18
20:13 52
21:20 17
21:21 52
21:22–23 52
21:22–25 52n111
21:23 52
22:20 18
22:21 18
22:22 18
22:26 18
23:9 18

Leviticus
19:9–10 18
19:14 18
19:32 18
25 17
25:5 18
25:23 17
25:29–30 17
25:36 18
25:39 17
25:40 17
25:47 17
27:16–21 17

Numbers
27:8 17
36:1–13 17

Deuteronomy
14:7 18
14:28–29 18
15 18
15:7 18
15:11 17
15:12 17
16:10–15 18
22:6 18
22:28 18
24:6 18
24:10–12 18
24:15 18
24:19–21 18

25:4 18
25:5–10 17
25:19 18
26:12–13 18
27:18 18
28:4 17, 52

Joshua
13–19 17

2 Samuel
18:20 150
18:25 150
18:27 150

1 Kings
15:12 134n39

2 Kings
1:42 150
7:9 150
23:1 134n39

Psalms
33:6 59
40:10 151
104:24 59
113:9 17, 52
127:3 52
127:3–5 17

213

Name Index

Subject Index

219